The Cambridge Companion to Philip Roth

From the moment that his debut book, *Goodbye, Columbus* (1959), won him the National Book Award and earned him attacks from the Jewish community, Philip Roth has been among the most influential and consistently controversial writers of our age. Now the author of more than twenty novels, numerous stories, two memoirs, and two books of literary criticism, Roth has used his writing to continually reinvent himself – and in doing so remake the American literary landscape. This *Companion* provides the most comprehensive introduction to the works and thought of this major American author in a collection of newly commissioned essays from distinguished scholars. Beginning with the urgency of Roth's early fiction and extending to the vitality of his most recent novels, these essays trace Roth's artistic engagement with questions about ethnic identity, postmodernism, Israel, the Holocaust, sexuality, and the human psyche itself. They recognize that Roth's work resonates through American culture because he demands that his readers pursue the kinds of self-invention, the endless remakings, that define both Roth's characters and his own identity as an author. New and returning Roth readers, students and scholars, will find this Companion authoritative and accessible.

THE CAMBRIDGE
COMPANION TO
PHILIP ROTH

EDITED BY
TIMOTHY PARRISH
Texas Christian University

CAMBRIDGE
UNIVERSITY PRESS

CAMBRIDGE UNIVERSITY PRESS
Cambridge, New York, Melbourne, Madrid, Cape Town, Singapore, São Paulo

Cambridge University Press
The Edinburgh Building, Cambridge CB2 2RU, UK

Published in the United States of America by Cambridge University Press, New York

www.cambridge.org
Information on this title: www.cambridge.org/9780521682930

© Cambridge University Press 2007

First published 2007

Printed in the United Kingdom at the University Press, Cambridge

A catalogue record for this publication is available from the British Library

Library of Congress Cataloguing in Publication data
The Cambridge companion to Philip Roth / edited by Timothy Parrish.
p.   cm. – (Cambridge companions to literature)
Includes bibliographical references (p.) and index.
ISBN-13: 978-0-521-86430-5
ISBN-10: 0-521-86430-5
ISBN-13: 978-0-521-68293-0
ISBN-10: 0-521-68293-2
1. Roth, Philip – Criticism and interpretation.   I. Parrish, Timothy, 1964–   II. Title.
PS3568.O855Z617   2006
813'.54 – dc22
2006023588

ISBN-13 978-0-521-86430-5 hardback
ISBN-10 0-521-86430-5 hardback
ISBN-13 978-0-521-68293-0 paperback
ISBN-10 0-521-68293-2 paperback

Cambridge University Press has no responsibility for the persistence or accuracy of URLs for
external or third-party internet websites referred to in this publication, and does not
guarantee that any content on such websites is, or will remain, accurate or appropriate.

CONTENTS

CONTENTS

CONTRIBUTORS

VICTORIA AARONS, Professor and Chair of the English Department at Trinity University, Texas, is the author, most recently, of *What Happened to Abraham: Reinventing the Covenant in American Jewish Fiction* (2005).

JEFFREY BERMAN is Professor of English at SUNY-Albany, New York. His most recent book is *Empathic Teaching: Education for Life* (2004).

EMILY MILLER BUDICK holds the Ann and Joseph Edelman Chair in American Literature at Hebrew University, Jerusalem, where she is also chair of the American Studies Department. Her most recent publication is *Aharon Appelfeld's Fiction: Acknowledging The Holocaust* (2005).

JOSH COHEN is Senior Lecturer in English and Comparative Literature at Goldsmiths College, University of London and the author, most recently, of *How to Read Freud* (2005).

DONALD M. KARTIGANER holds the Howry Chair in Faulkner Studies at the University of Mississippi, and has recently completed a book-length study, *Repetition Forward: The Way of Modernist Meaning*.

TIMOTHY PARRISH, Associate Professor of English, Texas Christian University, is the author of *Walking Blues: Making Americans from Emerson to Elvis* (2001).

MICHAEL ROTHBERG, Associate Professor of English and Director of the Unit for Criticism and Interpretive Theory at the University of Illinois, Urbana-Champaign, is the author of *Traumatic Realism: The Demands of Holocaust Representation* (2000).

DEREK PARKER ROYAL, Assistant Professor of English at Texas A&M University-Commerce, is the editor of the journal *Philip Roth Studies* and *Philip Roth: New Perspectives on an American Author* (2005).

MARK SHECHNER, Professor of English, SUNY-Buffalo, New York, is the author, most recently, of *Up Society's Ass, Copper; Rereading Philip Roth* (2003).

DEBRA SHOSTAK, Professor of English, The College of Wooster, Ohio, is the author of *Philip Roth – Countertexts, Counterlives* (2004).

HANA WIRTH-NESHER, Professor of English Literature and the Samuel L. and Perry Haber Chair on the Study of the Jewish Experience in the United States at Tel Aviv University, is the author of *Call It English: The Languages of Jewish American Literature* (2006).

CHRONOLOGY

1933   Philip Roth is born on March 19 in Newark to Hermann Roth
(b. 1901), an agent with the Metropolitan Life Insurance Company,
and Bess Finkel Roth (b. 1904). The Roths live in the Weequahic, a
lower-middle-class neighborhood.

1942   Roth family moves to 385 Leslie Street.

1946   Graduates elementary school in January.

1950   Graduates high school.

1951   Enrolls at Bucknell University.

1952   Founds Bucknell literary journal, *Et Cetera*.

1954   Elected to Phi Beta Kappa and graduates magna cum laude in
English. Accepts scholarship from The University of Chicago to
study English.

1955   Receives MA. Enlists in US Army. "The Contest for Aaron Gold"
reprinted in Martha Foley's *Best American Short Stories 1956*.

1956   Hospitalized for two months due to spinal injury. Receives
honorable discharge. Returns to University of Chicago to enroll in
Ph.D. program but quits after one semester. Continues as an
instructor teaching freshman composition.

1957   Meets Saul Bellow. Writes novella, "Goodbye, Columbus."

1958   Publishes "The Conversion of the Jews" and "Epstein" in *The Paris
Review*. Houghton Mifflin agrees to publish novella and five
stories. Resigns teaching position.

1959   Marries Margaret Martinson Williams. Publishes "Defender of the
Faith" in *The New Yorker*. Story provokes charges of anti-Semitism
from Jewish organizations. Wins Guggenheim award from
American Academy of Arts and Letters. Spends seven months in
Italy writing *Letting Go*.

1960   *Goodbye, Columbus* wins National Book Award. Teaches writing
at the University of Iowa. Meets Bernard Malamud.

1962   Accepts position as writer-in-residence at Princeton University. Separates from wife. Publishes *Letting Go*. Participates with Ralph Ellison in Yeshiva University symposium that would influence self-perception as a Jewish-American writer.

1963   Visits Israel.

1965   Teaches comparative literature at University of Pennsylvania. Does this intermittently for ten years.

1966   Protests Vietnam War.

1967   *When She Was Good.*

1968   Margaret Roth dies in auto accident.

1969   *Portnoy's Complaint.* Novel causes a sensation and becomes bestseller.

1970   Elected to National Institute of Arts and Letters. Begins *My Life as a Man*.

1971   *Our Gang.* Writes *The Breast* and *The Great American Novel*.

1972   *The Breast.* Buys an eighteenth-century farmhouse in northwest Connecticut. Irving Howe publishes attack on *Portnoy's Complaint*.

1973   Publishes *The Great American Novel*. Meets Milan Kundera and becomes interested in blacklisted writers from behind the Soviet-dominated Iron Curtain. Becomes General Editor of Penguin's "Writers from the Other Europe" series. Introduces, among others, Jerzy Andrzejewski, Tadeusz Borowski, Bohumil Hrabal, Danilo Kis, Tadeusz Konwicki, Ivan Klíma, Kundera, Witold Gombrowicz, and Bruno Schulz to American readers.

1974   *My Life as a Man.* Meets Vaclav Havel. Becomes friends with Vera Saudkova, a niece of Franz Kafka.

1975   Publishes *Reading Myself and Others*.

1976   Moves to London with Claire Bloom. They will alternate between living in London and Connecticut. Visits Israel for the first time since 1963 and frequently visits thereafter.

1977   *The Professor of Desire.*

1979   Publishes first Nathan Zuckerman novel, *The Ghost Writer*.

1980   *A Philip Roth Reader.*

1981   *Zuckerman Unbound.* Mother dies unexpectedly of a heart attack in Elizabethtown, NJ.

1984   *The Anatomy Lesson.*

1985   Publishes *The Prague Orgy* in one volume with *The Ghost Writer*, *Zuckerman Unbound*, and *The Anatomy Lesson* as *Zuckerman Bound*.

1987   *The Counterlife.* Wins National Book Critics' Circle Award for Fiction.

1988   *The Facts*. In Jerusalem attends trial of Ivan Demjanjuk, accused of being Treblinka guard "Ivan the Terrible." Begins teaching at Hunter College for the next three years.

1989   Father dies of brain tumor. Roth's care for father during the year-long illness will become the basis for *Patrimony*.

1990   *Deception*. Marries Claire Bloom in New York.

1991   *Patrimony*. Wins National Book Critics' Circle Award for biography.

1993   *Operation Shylock*. Wins PEN/Faulkner Award for fiction. Separates from Claire Bloom.

1995   *Sabbath's Theater*. Wins National Book Award for fiction.

1997   *American Pastoral*. Wins Pulitzer Prize for fiction.

1998   *I Married a Communist*. Wins Ambassador Book Award of the English-Speaking Union. Receives National Medal of Arts at the White House.

2000   *The Human Stain* completes the trilogy begun with *American Pastoral*. Wins second PEN/Faulkner award. In the UK wins the W. H. Smith Award for best book of the year. In France wins the Prix Medici for the best foreign book of the year.

2001   *The Dying Animal* and *Shop Talk*. Receives the Gold Medal in fiction from the American Academy of Arts and Letters.

2002   Awarded the National Book Foundation's Medal for Distinguished Contribution to American Letters.

2004   *The Plot Against America*. Wins W. H. Smith Award.

2005   Third living American author to be included in the Library of America.

2006   *Everyman*.

Introduction: Roth at mid-career

The author of more than twenty novels, numerous stories, two memoirs, and two works of literary criticism, Philip Roth has been perhaps the most critically significant and consistently controversial American writer of the past fifty years. Twice Roth has been awarded the National Book Award (1960, 1995), the National Book Critics' Circle Award (1987, 1991), and the PEN/Faulkner Award (1993, 2000). He is a recipient of the National Medal of Arts (1970), the Pulitzer Prize (1997), and France's Medici Foreign Book Prize (2000), among other recognitions. In 2001, *Time* Magazine named Roth "America's Best Novelist." Perhaps more telling, the distinguished literary critic Harold Bloom has included more of Roth's novels (six) in his *Western Canon* than of any other living American author; beginning in 2005, Roth became the third living American author to have his works collected by the Library of America. When Roth was honored with the National Book Foundation Medal for Distinguished Contribution to American Letters in 2002, his place as a major American author was one that no serious critic would be willing to dispute.

That Roth could become so widely revered by the end of his long and fruitful career seems unlikely when one recalls the controversy with which his career began. His early fiction excited the anger of many Jewish readers who accused him of exploiting Jewish-American culture in order to gain acceptance as an "American" author. Roth's notoriety reached its apex in 1969 with the publication of *Portnoy's Complaint* (1969). The book was a *New York Times* bestseller for 1969 and it helped to usher in a new era in American writing devoted to issues of ethnicity and cultural authenticity. So pervasive was the cultural influence of *Portnoy* that the prominent critic Irving Howe, who had helped to establish Roth as an important author ten years earlier, famously dismissed the novel as a betrayal of Roth's early promise. Howe reinforced the point of view of Roth's early critics by complaining that Roth had compromised the "authenticity" of Jewish American experience. Howe's dismissal of Roth, while unsuccessful in its aim to diminish Roth's career, implicitly recognized how Roth's work portrayed American-Jewish experience being transformed into something no longer connected to its nineteenth-century European origins.

The tension between holding to a historically grounded identity yet suspecting that identity is something that can only be known through its reinvention has animated Roth's best work. Most Roth critics (including Roth himself) have emphasized that his career has largely been constructed out of his creative and cultural conflict with his Jewish audience. Yet, his wide audience does not consist only of Jewish readers. His characters have risked their selves in diverse locations such as Newark, New Jersey, Chicago, New York, London, Prague, Jerusalem, and Palestine. His narrative strategies and literary models have been similarly varied: Henry James, Marcel Proust, James Joyce, and Franz Kafka are clear influences on his work and his novels have employed the many different literary strategies implied by the work of these great predecessors. It is important to recognize, though, that Roth understands himself as more than just the representative writer of a particular ethnic group. Along with faithfully recounting the range of intellectual positions implicit within American identity politics, Roth explores their practical consequences by rendering them in fictional form. For Roth, the self takes its form through experimentation and should be perceived as a type of fiction. Asserting one's identity is, as Roth understands it, always a transgressive act. This means that for Roth no form of identity – ethnic or otherwise – can ever be fixed. To paraphrase what he once told Mary McCarthy, Roth is far more a novelist than he is a Jew.[1] By 2001 when Roth published *The Human Stain*, the story of a black man who passes for a white Jew, it was clear that much of the appeal of Roth's work has been its ability to portray not just American-Jewish experience in all of its historical variety but to challenge in ways that are distinctively postmodern the meaning of identity altogether.

This *Companion* attempts to do justice to Roth's multifacetedness, the constant reinvention, that is at the heart of his extraordinary career, and attempts to do so in essays that will appeal both to the new reader of Roth and to those who keep coming back to Roth to be renewed by that seemingly endless capacity for reinvention. Roth's remarkable creativity since 1986 has in many ways outstripped the attempts of critics to keep up with him. Many fine anthologies of Roth criticism and appreciation have appeared in the last several years, yet Roth himself has perhaps been his own best critic. The remarkable recent American Trilogy (*American Pastoral* [1997], *I Married a Communist* [1998], and *The Human Stain*) provides an instance of Roth's own critical rereading of his previous literary achievements: in these volumes, he returns to Nathan Zuckerman, who was so central to his work of the 1950s, 1960s, and 1970s, but does so with a new understanding of his and our pasts.

Rather than attempting to exert a critical control over Roth (to collect, finish off, and assert meaning over), this *Companion* is instead designed to encourage students to recognize and participate in the central demand that Roth makes of his readers and critics: to pursue the kinds of self-invention that define both Roth's characters and his own changing authorial identity. In understanding the trajectory of Roth's later work as a rethinking of Roth's familiar early fiction, readers of this *Companion* will see the path not just of Roth's career but also of the key themes and problems of contemporary American literature as a whole. At the heart of both Roth's fictions and the realities of American culture are such subjects as intertwining personal and communal identities, sexual politics and practice, the postmodern world and the place of America in that world, self-invention in the context of human annihilation and acts of terror, and racial and cultural pluralism. It is because he speaks to these central issues that Roth is widely taught as a central figure in American literature classes, Jewish and ethnic studies classes, and fiction-writing courses.

This *Companion* approaches Roth's work as a whole made of diverse and recurring parts, with any given part providing a perspective from which the whole can be challenged, or reconceived. Consequently, the essays in this volume reflect the basic tendency of Roth's work to reinterpret what has gone before in light of what has been discovered, or essayed, later. What connects these essays is that each one performs an intense interaction between author and reader that is, if anything is, the essence of Roth's writing. Whether it is Alvin Pepler confronting Nathan Zuckerman in *Zuckerman Unbound* (1981) or Pipik usurping Philip Roth's identity in *Operation Shylock* (1993), the reader in Roth's work is framed as the author's intended, his antagonist, and his collaborator.

To read Roth is to be challenged to risk that which Roth and his characters always risk: the premises that seem to define one's very self. Each of the distinguished Roth critics in this volume is true to this premise. Although they reveal multiple and often contradictory Philip Roths, their versions of Roth make good companions for readers pursuing their own adventures with one of the best writers American literature has yet produced.

As a way of introducing Roth to students who may be encountering his work for the first time and reintroducing Roth to his longtime readers, it may be appropriate to begin by looking at a critical moment in Roth's career from 1986 when his eminent future standing was not yet so evident. By this time Roth's early promise had been more than fulfilled and his *Zuckerman Bound* (1985) had answered his fiercest critics. Had he never written another word no one would have questioned that he was a significant post-World War American writer. He was fifty-three years old. Yet, arguably, Roth's career since 1986 has been more extraordinary than his career prior to that point. It is difficult to think of another American writer, with the exception of Henry James, who has been as successfully productive as Roth has been in the mature phase of his life. *The Counterlife* (1986), *The Facts* (1988), *Patrimony* (1991), *Operation Shylock* (1993), *Sabbath's Theater* (1995), *American Pastoral*, *I Married a Communist* (1998) *The Human Stain*, *The Dying Animal* (2001), *Shop Talk* (2001), and *The Plot Against America* (2004) represent an extraordinary run of novels that any writer would envy.

Yet, in 1986 such a future could have been barely imaginable even to Philip Roth. Indeed, as Roth acknowledged in *The Facts* and *Operation Shylock*, he suffered in the late 1980s and early 1990s a mental breakdown that took years to diagnose and remedy. In retrospect, 1986 can be seen as a kind of turning point for Roth because he was on the cusp of what would become in effect his mature phase. Roth's sense of himself as a writer whose career was noteworthy but not yet fulfilled is revealed in his powerful response to Bernard Malamud's death that year. Malamud was for Roth a friend, a rival, and, as an older Jewish writer whose critical fame coincided with Roth's own fame, a kind of uneasy father figure against whom Roth measured his own achievement. Roth's tribute to Malamud, published as "Pictures of Malamud," hints at the mental turbulence Roth was suffering then. In the essay, Roth dispassionately portrays Malamud as a dying artist who is too weak to summon the will required to complete his last work. Beneath Roth's account of Malamud's death, though, one perceives Roth's own fear.

Intended to commemorate the passing of Malamud, Roth's essay is also a powerful account of the mortality of his own literary achievements and ambitions. In Roth's response to Malamud's death, which is not entirely generous but always impassioned, we see an encounter that foreshadows the second and almost entirely unexpected half of Roth's career. It anticipates *Patrimony*, Roth's memoir about his father, in that its subject is the writer's necessary battle to make over the forces that have made the writer's identity prior to writing. Roth's portrait of the dying Malamud is tender and merciless. The essay is merciless because it makes Malamud the sacrificial victim of Philip Roth's insatiable will to aesthetic truth; the essay is tender because Roth knows that Malamud's death is a portent of his own. Roth speaks to the dying writer and himself to say that a writer's work at its best is sacred; thus, facing the inevitability of one's death the only moral choice is *to write* – to write as well and as truly as one can. From Malamud's death will come Roth's second life – one that he will make out of books.

In "Pictures of Malamud" Roth tacitly acknowledges that his own conception of himself as a writer is crucially linked to his perception of Malamud's example. Roth first associated himself with Malamud in his 1960 essay, "Writing American Fiction." There Roth had noted that Malamud had "not shown specific interest in the anxieties and dilemmas and corruptions of the modern American Jews" but instead wrote about timeless Jews who happened to live on the Lower East Side.[2] In contrast to Malamud's Jews with their archetypal moral dilemmas that are only incidental to their stories' settings, Roth's Jews experience their selves as transitive entities always being transformed by the flux of American experience. Nearly twenty years after Roth's first published critical encounter with Malamud, he evoked him again through Nathan Zuckerman's portrayal of E. I. Lonoff in *The Ghost Writer*. In that novel, Zuckerman, Roth's fictional alter ego, goes as a pilgrim to sit at the feet of the master, Lonoff. In "Pictures of Malamud" Roth recalls how he first met Malamud in the early sixties but he also seems to be rewriting Zuckerman's pilgrimage to Lonoff as well.

In "Pictures" Roth recalls how he read the stories that Malamud was publishing in the early fifties "the day they appeared." In *The Ghost Writer* Zuckerman thinks of Lonoff as "the chief rabbi, the archdeacon, the perpetual high priest of perpetual sorrows."[3] Young Nathan sees himself as Lonoff's adopted "twenty-three year old son" and seeks affirmation. Zuckerman's visit with Lonoff will help Zuckerman find his voice as a writer – one very different from Lonoff's. The crucial transformation occurs when Zuckerman, giddy from having been toasted at dinner by Lonoff, spends the night in Lonoff's study. Taking a break from contemplating the moral austerity implied by Lonoff's example as an artist, Zuckerman stands on a volume of Henry James stories that is placed on Lonoff's desk and then cups his ear toward the ceiling so he can eavesdrop on an intimate conversation between Lonoff and his student, Amy. Zuckerman transforms what he hears above into a fantasy about Anne Frank having survived the Holocaust and come to Lonoff as Amy Bellette, his love-struck writing student. Zuckerman stops short of portraying Lonoff as Frank's illicit lover but he does transform Lonoff's moral austerity into something comic and impossible to sustain. Moreover, Zuckerman's impiety toward Lonoff is the narrative mechanism by which he is able to renew Anne Frank's story as being one more complicated than that of an unlucky martyr murdered by historical necessity. Then, by novel's end, Roth has Lonoff point toward Zuckerman's gift: the ruthless will to transform anything, even the Holocaust, into art and, if necessary, outrageous comedy. Having been thanked by Zuckerman for his hospitality, Lonoff says, "You're not so nice and polite in your fiction" (*The Ghost Writer*, 180).

Neither is Roth so nice in "Pictures of Malamud," but his respect for Malamud is as deep as Zuckerman's for Lonoff. Roth acknowledges that Malamud wrote "four or five of the best American short stories I'd ever read (or I ever will)" and characterizes *The Assistant* as "his masterpiece" ("Pictures," 121). Roth speaks of Malamud's English as "a heap of broken verbal bones that looked, until he came along and made them dance to his sad tune, to be of use no longer to anyone other than a Borscht Belt comic or a professional nostaligist" (121). Identifying Malamud's artistic penchant for portraying lonely, suffering Jews, Roth suggests that Malamud did for his characters what Samuel Beckett did for his misery-ridden Molloy and Malone.

Despite the general note of appreciation that hovers over the essay, though, Roth writes less to praise "Bern," as he calls him, than to put him and the counterexample he represented to rest. "I wonder," Roth speculates, "if early in adult life Bern didn't have an insight about himself still more terrifying: that he was a man of stern morality who could act only like he was" (124). Roth, the flamboyant performer whose ideal artist impersonates someone impersonating, has always been attracted to characters that challenge the aura of a legitimately stern moralist. He suggests that Malamud suffered from "a need so harsh that it makes one ache to imagine it. It was the need to consider long and seriously every last demand of a conscience torturously exacerbated by the pathos of a need unabated" (124). Although Roth's characterization seems meant to distinguish Malamud's character from his own, it makes one wonder if Roth is not also describing the author of *Portnoy's Complaint* and *The Plot Against America* too. Roth's fiction usually questions the purity of any one character's motives but it may be such questioning only belies Roth's hope that a purely moral stance is actually possible. Perhaps Malamud continued to attract Roth's critical gaze over twenty-five years because he, more than Saul Bellow or Ralph Ellison, represented in his work the ethical stance Roth most wanted to emulate but instead pretended to destroy through the acts of his *shiksa*-crazed, sex-crazed, family-betraying, Jewish-son-protagonists.

Roth concludes his essay with an account of his last meeting with Malamud in July 1985. Malamud is feeble, sick from bypass surgery, a stroke, and heavy medication. He is easy prey for a grown-up Nathan Zuckerman. Roth contrasts the vibrant forty-six-year-old Malamud he'd met twenty-four years before with this "frail and very sick old man, his tenacity about used up" (127). Roth sums up his vision of Malamud with Malamud's own words. In

Malamud's story "Take Pity" an impoverished Jewish refugee dies because, as Roth puts it, quoting Malamud, he "Broke in him something." This is how Roth's Malamud dies too. Roth turns the helpless, dying Malamud into a version of one his own stories. This "heap of broken bones" asks a favor of his death's witness. Malamud wants Roth to assess his recent writing. Roth wonders how appealing the writing could possibly be given that Malamud's "memory of the multiplication tables had been clouded for several years now" ("Pictures," 128). Cruelly, Roth tells him the truth – it is unfinished and needs further development. Trying to move past this painful moment, Roth asks what comes next. "What's next isn't the point," Malamud retorts (130).

Roth's harrowing portrait captures the abject helplessness Malamud must have felt while dying before he had sufficient opportunity to rework his sentences into something memorable. Roth in effect writes "Bern's" obituary for literary history. Yet, his account also freezes Malamud as if he were a character in a Malamud story being written by Philip Roth. This Malamud dies not as the author of "four or five of the best American short stories I'd ever read" but as a version of the poor Jewish refugee – Rosen from Malamud's "Take Pity" or any other of Malamud's broken immigrant Jews – but now told by the writer who rejected such stories in his work. In Roth's "Pictures of Malamud," the typical Malamud hero seeking moral calm is cast as a writer who has failed to make the crossing to where his imagination would carry him. In the dying writer's place stands the still quick and inventive Roth whose will to rewrite sentences thrives and finds expression in – and over – the dying writer's immutable end.

This final picture of Malamud is a confession of fear on Roth's part that is also yet another of his peculiar self-portraits, or self-impersonations. Writing on the verge of his own mental breakdown and what will become a long and extraordinary period of creativity, Roth confronts the dying Malamud and sees something Nathan Zuckerman could not see when he confronted Lonoff: his own end. In *The Ghost Writer*, before his reverie about Anne Frank, Zuckerman notices that Lonoff has been reading Henry James's "The Middle Years," a story about a writer who dies before his great work is done. "A second chance," James's artist says, "*that's* the delusion. There was never to be but one."[4] Midway through his own first, last chance, Roth projects his own "Middle Years" nightmare on to Malamud. What if I were to die a writer's death, at his desk, mid-sentence, and far from the vigor of his earlier work, Roth asks.

"He died on March 18, 1986, three days before spring," Roth writes in the essay's final sentence ("Pictures," 130). Roth's spring goes on, as does the critical conversation about Roth's work.

NOTES

I am grateful to Charlotte Willis and John Wood for their help preparing the typescript.

1 Philip Roth, *Shop Talk* (Boston: Houghton, 2001), p. 118.
2 Philip Roth, *Reading Myself and Others* (New York: Penguin, 1985), p. 183.
3 Philip Roth, "Pictures of Malamud," in *Shop Talk*, p. 121; *The Ghost Writer*, in *Zuckerman Bound: A Trilogy and Epilogue* (New York: Farrar, Straus and Giroux, 1985), p. 180.
4 Henry James, *Complete Stories 1892–1898* (New York: The Library of America, 1996), p. 354.

I

VICTORIA AARONS

American-Jewish identity in Roth's short fiction

Eli Peck, Philip Roth's characteristically neurotic protagonist in the short story "Eli, the Fanatic," ardently maintains of the Jewish refugees who, emerging from the devastation of the Holocaust, settle in the suburban town of Woodenton, "I am me. They are them." In this way, he defiantly dissociates himself from the defining and, to him, static markers of Jewish identity and history, both past and immediate.[1] Eli Peck, a product of the secularization of American Jewry in the mid-twentieth century, believes himself freed from the restricting weight of a legacy linked to him only by an imposed inheritance, the remnants of history and blood. For Eli, the weight of such identification is as heavy as the stone tablets and a liability in America. In his insistent separation from his identity as a Jew, represented by his uneasy fear of the Jewish refugees, whose yeshiva is a constant reminder to Eli and the other Jews of Woodenton of the dangers of seeming "too Jewish," Roth's apprehensively charged protagonist unconsciously exposes his fears of marginalization, shared by the other "assimilated" Jews of suburban Woodenton, of forever being considered outsiders and interlopers among the rightful inheritors of American culture.

Eli Peck's disavowal of the European refugees, the displaced men and "the little kids with little *yamalkahs* chanting their Hebrew lessons," who have come to infiltrate the suburban haven of Woodenton, is motivated by the sure conviction that their very presence will threaten the "good healthy relationship in this town [among] modern Jews and Protestants" ("Eli, the Fanatic," 277–78). What Eli Peck fears is the eruption of their carefully and precariously constructed place among the gentiles, whose ownership defines and executes the parameters of possibility for the Jews of Woodenton, who, in their paranoid and reactive suspicions, consider themselves in jeopardy, at risk of being seen as Jews. But what Eli Peck should fear most is his own stealthy attempts to redefine himself in opposition to Judaism and to lead, as a later Roth character would call it, a "counterlife,"[2] a life anxiously figured by bumbling attempts to escape oneself by manufacturing and trying on different selves. What Eli and the entourage of other Roth characters try and inevitably fail to create is an alternate identity, an impossible exchange that will protect them from themselves, that is, from themselves as Jews.

Eli Peck, so recognizably characteristic of Roth's fiction, comes to discover what it does and does not mean to be a Jew. And what it does not mean, as Eli all too readily realizes, is the pretense that he can successfully walk away from his identity as a Jew. Roth has Eli realize that to disavow his past, however obtusely understood, can only lead to a life of obsessive self-absorption, because obsessive self-absorption, the constructed self-narrative of denial, ironically blinds one to an identity rooted in an undeniable past. And so, when Eli Peck is asked "you know you're still Eli, don't you?" he's not so certain that he is; nor is he sure what it means to be Eli (297). It is exactly this obsession with identity, with trying on and discarding selves, that is the source of Roth's ironic commentary, a satirical burlesque on postwar American-Jewish identity. For despite Eli Peck's desperate entreaty that those who choose to be crazy must not be, this obsession with identity, with what it means to be a Jew, and the deluded belief that identity is extrinsic create the kinds of compulsive interpersonal rearrangements, anxiously disfigured entanglements, self-absorbed circumlocutions, parodic attempts at self-censure, and general comic disarray that make of a character definably and definitively an invention of Philip Roth.

In fact, all of the stories in Roth's debut collection, *Goodbye, Columbus and Five Short Stories* (1959), are preoccupied with Jewish identity in America when passage into socio-economic and cultural legitimacy would seem to be, if not granted, then at least increasingly available. Roth's characters seize upon Jewish identity with an insistent and obsessive fervor. In the early stories of *Goodbye, Columbus*, Jewishness seems to impede the possibility of self-invention promised by the apparent cultural mobility of postwar America. In Roth's later works, such a fixation with what it means to be a Jew becomes more a matter of how one negotiates the persistent anxieties of being a Jew. In works such as *The Counterlife, Operation Shylock*, and the Zuckerman novels, the focus would seem to be directed less toward the convolutions in agonizing about being a Jew and more on how one *manages* being a Jew. The characters in the stories in *Goodbye, Columbus*, however, are at the initial stages of attempting to define themselves as Jews or not as Jews. And this tension, this push and pull between "Jew or not" makes projected Jewish identity the single most uncompromising antagonist against which Roth's characters must contend. Their psychic machinations, endlessly replayed, make Roth's characters no longer certain what the question of Jewish identity really means. Is it that the ambivalence about being a Jew stems from being considered "other" by the gentiles? Or is it – and this is a certainly more complicated quagmire – the persistence of the conviction that being a Jew is a sure and possibly violent ticket back to whence one came. Roth's early fiction poses over and over this question: have the Jews themselves gained entrance into the dubious achievement of becoming Americans? And if they have, indeed, moved into the suburbs to stay, if they "belong" there, then what is the motivation for such constant anxiety? As one of Roth's characters in the short story "Goodbye, Columbus" puts it, "Since when do Jewish people live in [the suburbs]? They couldn't be real Jews, believe me."[3]

All the stories in *Goodbye, Columbus* pose these questions of Jewish identity. They collectively reveal a deeply felt ambivalence toward what it means to be Jewish in post-World War II America. Roth's characters vigorously try to defend themselves against these uncertainties. The very settings and locales of *Goodbye, Columbus* emphasize the displacement, vulnerability, and sense of culpability that create such unease in Roth's early characters. They are brought, however unwillingly, to acknowledge, with the same disorientation expressed by Eli Peck's confused identity, their anxiety about "belonging." These settings and locales become the stage upon which the dislocation and the sense of separation and alienation are played out.

In "Defender of the Faith," for example, Nathan Marx, a sergeant in the army, finds himself exiled, "swallowed into the alien Missouri dusk," on the army base where he is stationed.[4] Only one of very few Jews assigned to Camp Crowder, the military veteran Marx, long since inured to the vestiges of his Jewish past, discovers through his reluctant association with new Jewish recruits a felt connection to them. But as with other characters in *Goodbye, Columbus*, Marx fights against this recognized consanguinity, seeing it initially as a connection long since abandoned. The conditions of his life in the army, the equality and impartiality assumed within the ranks, make it possible for Nathan Marx to dismiss any ties to the other Jewish personnel. In the midst of war, fighting the Germans, not as a Jew, for which he might have taken some measure of private triumph, but as a soldier "so far from home," he left behind the memory of "the sounds of a Bronx playground where, years ago . . . I had played" ("Defender of the Faith," 170). But, once back home, the war ended but still on unfamiliar terrain with the Jewish soldiers under his command, it only takes the sounds of the prewar years, of "Good *shabbus* . . . One rumor of home and time past," to return Marx to "what I suddenly remembered was myself" (170). And, reluctantly, like other characters in *Goodbye, Columbus*, he finds himself, in spite of his better judgment, following Sheldon Grossbart, his antagonist and conscience, to Shabbat services held at the army base for Jewish personnel, "in search

of more of me" (170). Ironically, it is through the opportunistic, disingenuous, and manipulative Sheldon Grossbart, who, in his presumption of tribal
familiarity, breaks ranks and assumes special privileges with an officer, that
Nathan Marx, in out-maneuvering him, recognizes his obligations as a Jew.
Uttered with weary resignation but also with Roth's typical comic absurdity,
Nathan Marx comes to admit that "like Karl and Harpo, I was one of them"
(165).

It is significant that three of the central stories in *Goodbye, Columbus*
are situated at a physical remove from the familiarity of city life, from the
urban environment that defined Jewish immigrant life for the first half of the
twentieth century. In the title story, "Goodbye, Columbus," Neil Klugman
finds himself an outsider among those Jews who have fled the city for the
luxury and privilege of suburban life, here depicted by Roth as a measure of
success, of breaking into that from which Jews were historically excluded.
The space between the city – the Bronx of Nathan Marx's past, the clamor
of Neil Klugman's Newark – and suburban America becomes, especially in
a story such as "Goodbye, Columbus," the dividing line between those who
have made it economically and those who have not. As one of the assimilated
Jews of Woodenton nervously exclaims, in "Eli, the Fanatic," "If I want to
live in Brownsville, Eli, I'll live in Brownsville . . . when I left the city, Eli, I
didn't plan the city should come to me" (255). But this imaginary dividing
line between urban and suburban also, and perhaps more significantly, marks
the difference between attitudes toward Jewish assimilation into mainstream
American culture.

Neil Klugman's flight from Newark into the suburbs of Short Hills and the
allure of Brenda Patimkin is a passage into the promised land: "past Irvington
and the packed-in tangle of railroad crossings, switchmen shacks, lumber-
yards, Dairy Queens, and used-car lots . . . long lawns which seemed to be
twirling water on themselves, and past houses where no one sat on stoops,
where lights were on but no windows open" ("Goodbye, Columbus," 8).
The juxtaposition of struggling, working-class Newark with the cheerfully
luxurious abandon and ostentatious display of the Patimkins' country club
life represents an obvious, defining class distinction between those on the
inside and those who are kept out. Those on the inside, "refusing to share
the very texture of life with those of us outside," are motivated by the fear
of slipping back, a fear of the shackles of a Jewish past (8). For the class
tension between those on the inside of prosperity and those without is not
here defined by Roth in terms of Jew and gentile. The complexity in "Goodbye, Columbus" is located in terms of those Jews who, like the Patimkins,
made it out of marginalized conditions and now live like gentiles, or like a
Jewish fantasy of privileged gentile life, and those, like Neil Klugman, who

cannot "break in" and for whom the gates to suburban havens (and fantasies thereof) remain closed. As Neil Klugman uneasily discovers, it is not the gentiles who prevent entrance, but the Patimkins, who have reinvented their cultural lives as crypto Jews, and for whom Neil Klugman represents everything they have abandoned and everything that they fear. This overstated anxiety about socio-economic backsliding is comically and satirically represented by Roth in the Patimkins' excessive purchase and hording of lurid food, the forbidden fruit now garnered with seeming impunity, which they unconsciously fear will be taken away from them. In believing an excess of food to be the ultimate measure of success, the Patimkins, for all their fifties suburban trappings, become no less than caricatures of Jews:

> No longer did [the refrigerator] hold butter, eggs, herring in cream sauce, ginger ale, tuna fish salad . . . rather it was heaped with fruit . . . There were greengage plums, black plums, red plums, apricots, nectarines, peaches, long horns of grapes, black, yellow, red, and cherries, cherries flowing out of boxes . . . And there were melons – cantaloupes and honeydews – and on the top shelf, half of a huge watermelon . . . Oh Patimkin!   (43)

For Roth, an obsessive belief in the idea of what is "no-good-for-the-Jews," to borrow a phrase from the short story "The Conversion of the Jews," is the source of the ironic complexity that shapes these early stories in *Goodbye, Columbus*. It is not the gentiles who, in their seemingly dismissive, indifferent attitudes, pose the greatest threat to Jewish socio-economic and cultural acceptance. Rather, Roth's satiric commentary is framed in terms of those Jews who want to redefine themselves as imagined gentiles, those, in other words, who want to pretend that they are not Jews, or rather, not the kind of Jew who stands out as Jew, such as the Jewish refugee from Europe, in "Eli, the Fanatic," who appears in the town attired in the "black coat that fell down below [his] knees . . . the round-topped, wide-brimmed Talmudic hat . . . sidelocks curled loose on his cheeks" (253). The question in stories such as "Goodbye, Columbus" and "Eli, the Fanatic" is not simply "what it means to be a Jew," but rather, "how Jewish is *too* Jewish?"

In "Goodbye, Columbus," "too Jewish," as determined by the implied gaze of the Patimkins, is the unrefined lack of ambition and insufficient wherewithal of Neil Klugman, who will never unshackle himself from the defining conditions of Newark, which he wears like a rumpled, faintly odiferous, unfashionable suit of clothes. Despite his self-parodic leap of faith that, through his association with the Patimkins, he "the outsider . . . might one day be an insider," Neil Klugman recognizes that he will always be a reminder of what they left behind, "the Patimkin roots in Newark" (43). For the Patimkins, the new world is "theirs for the asking . . . I somehow felt I couldn't" (94, 29). Similarly, in "Eli, the Fanatic," "too Jewish" is defined by the visible presence of the yeshiva and the eighteen children who study the Talmud there. But it is finally the man in the black hat, who speaks a dead language, the man who has lost everything, from whom the Jews of Woodenton want to dissociate themselves. Their response is more extreme than Neil Klugman's, who apprehensively but gamely responds with discomfort and ambivalence toward Jews "not my own," Jews like the Patimkins, who, hyperbolically but enticingly embrace the totems of upper-middle-class ascendance ("Goodbye, Columbus," 41). For Eli Peck and the community of Jews who react in outrage over the presence of the yeshiva in their neighborhood, their fears of expulsion and persecution, which they inadvertently and ignorantly display, are displaced onto those Jews who remind them all too acutely of their past and what they fear themselves to be. Finally, Eli Peck and Neil Klugman come to discover, as does Nathan Marx, that "It's a hard thing to be a Jew . . . [but] it's a harder thing to stay one" ("Defender of the Faith," 189).

Thus, when Eli Peck, defensively insisting to the yeshiva's equally insistent headmaster, that he has no connection to the Jewish refugees – "I am me. They are them" – the ambiguous language with which Eli attempts to free himself only makes his uncertainty increasingly clear. The comically confused, shifting pronominal bantering between Eli and his antagonist – "You are us, we are you . . . They are you . . . No . . . You are you" – sets the conditions for the kind of doubling and redoubling that will haunt Roth's characters throughout his fiction ("Eli, the Fanatic," 265, 267). We hear, in Eli Peck's uncontrolled anxiety and in his phobic responses to conditions that he unwittingly creates, the prototype for Roth's later protagonists. Such characters may become more urbane, more sophisticated, and more self-ironic as his fiction develops, but they are no less comically and indelibly preoccupied and apprehensive as they attempt to negotiate the uncertain terrain of their American-Jewish lives. In "Eli, the Fanatic," Roth foundationally explores the self-inflicted dilemma of the "assimilated" Jew in the second half of the American twentieth century, an impasse that has gained continual momentum through his maturing fiction. And Eli Peck, in rudimentary and as yet undeveloped fashion, indeed comes to represent the ambivalence toward Jewish identity that sees Roth through his fiction into the twenty-first century.[5]

When appointed by the Jews in suburban Woodenton, New York to disband the offending presence of the yeshiva – "what a nerve . . . this is the twentieth century" – Eli Peck, attorney, pillar of the community, and spokesperson for the Woodenton Jews, reluctantly complies ("Eli, the Fanatic," 253, 276). He does so because he for so long has repressed his feelings for and consanguinity with a Jewish past from which he has falsely believed himself to be liberated. Eli, along with his wife and the suburban Jews of Woodenton, have willfully remade themselves as middle-class Jews, so much so that they exchange their Judaism, their connection to a war-torn, shattered, and not-so-remote past, for a wished-for gentile (and genteel) respectability.

It is important that this story takes place in suburban America not long after the end of the war, the liberation of the concentration camps, and the influx of European Jewish refugees. This is a critical period in both Jewish and American history and identity, for Roth the locus for moral reckoning and an occasion for self-assessment and identity-formation. If repression involves the deflection of instinctual drives and impulses from their original aims to more socially valuable ones, then Eli gets it wrong: he confuses what is valuable with what is socially acceptable, acceptable, that is, to the "new" Woodenton, where Jews and gentiles "live in amity . . . no pogroms" (262, 277). But the intruding presence of the yeshiva, its eighteen children and two men, threatens this precarious coalescence, maintained only by benign neglect on the one hand and cautious acquiescence on the other.

Roth stages the conflict of past and present by making Leo Tzuref, head-master of the yeshiva and visibly old-world protector of his vulnerable group of displaced persons, the main obstacle standing in the way of such a mea-sured peace. When Eli Peck hesitantly emerges from behind the supporting pillar of Woodenton's yeshiva, however, it is not his antagonist Leo Tzuref whom he encounters, but rather Eli himself, a far more ominous adversary. And it's a contest that Eli will ultimately lose, for Eli has both mistaken and underestimated the relentless tenacity of his opponent. What weighs on Eli so heavily is not only the weight of the present, but also the pull of the past, and so he defends himself, however ineffectually, against both.

So, when the well-defended Eli, armed with briefcase and sanctioned by zoning ordinances, invades the precarious sanctuary of the yeshiva's grounds, he mistakenly believes that it is Leo Tzuref with whom he must contend. The law that Eli encounters in the yeshiva is not the law of the "new" Woodenton, but rather the "old law" enshrouded in mysterious and troubling allegorical disguise in the figure of Leo Tzuref, a refugee from the past, who speaks in Talmudic riddles – "When is the law that is the law not the law?" – and who "cloud[s] the issue with issues" (251). Tzuref is here for Roth the embod-iment of ancient Hebraic law, the injunction to recognize shared history. Eli's disavowal of his obligations to the yeshiva Jews and his attendant guilt manifests itself in a tension between his inability to extricate himself from Leo Tzuref and the summons of the yeshiva and his defensive resistance in the name of progress to a law that would so uncomfortably take him back.

Tzuref thus becomes the authorizing father, in psychoanalytic terms, from whose will Eli retreats, and in this retreat his rejection of Judaism and the self-punishment that accompanies this rejection are the poles of his undoing as a suburban Jewish success story.

When Eli climbs the mount from the safety of Woodenton's "progressive suburban community," to the menacing darkness of the yeshiva's grounds, where children "in their mysterious babble . . . run at the sight of him" (250, 253), he finds there not the source of the legal dispute, "a boarding school in a residential area" (251), but rather that from which he, himself, has been running. Tzuref's response to Eli's legal mandate to disband the yeshiva is as cryptic as the language of the children who play on the grounds and whose "babble – not mysterious to Tzuref, who smiled – entered the room like a third person," making Eli "shudder" and triangulating his wish for a simply oppositional encounter (250). The children's unintelligible language, Yiddish, for centuries the language of Eastern European Jews, is foreign to Eli and thus is an object of fear. And so, for Eli, the children's speech takes human form, is anthropomorphized into the outsider, a symbol of difference, a secret unbreakable code by which Eli feels himself threatened, persecuted, ironically, by a group of vulnerable children.

This is an uneasy position in which Eli finds himself, but not without its unconscious gratification. Eli, legal spokesperson for the Jews of Woodenton, finds himself aligned, not against the Protestants, whose long-standing place in the community is never forgotten, but instead against the yeshiva Jews, "religious fanatics" who threaten the middle-class social values and comfort of the Jews who guardedly live there (278). In a parody of identity politics, the Jews of Woodenton are to the yeshiva Jews what the gentiles are to the Jews of Woodenton. Indeed, the Woodenton yeshiva calls to attention that there are Jews, calls attention to the Jews as a flagrant symbol of difference. But it's Eli's own passive acquiescence to the will of the local assimilated community that brings him, donned in the accouterments of his professional disguise, the suit and the briefcase, to the yeshiva. Once there, however, Eli, the secular laws of the community buffeting his trespass upon the grounds of the yeshiva, encounters, much to his dismay, a far more imperious authority than the law with which he believes himself to be empowered. Once on the grounds of the yeshiva, the very foundation of Eli's world shifts. And as it does so, Roth stages a return to a distant Jewish past, the ground itself for the moral authority Eli must so uncomfortably confront.

The physical setting in which Roth places Eli is a measure of his psychic landscape. In approaching the yeshiva, Eli is taken back, against his will, to a kind of eerie, prelapsarian landscape, where the "jungle of hedges . . . the dark, untrampled horse path" both obscure his course and lure him (249).

From the beginning, Eli is anxious, burdened, fearful in advance of what he will find. And he is right to be so apprehensive, for once there he is unconsoled, clearly imperiled. For Roth, Eli is the perfect candidate to come apart on the grounds of the yeshiva, an agitated, immoderate man, who, previously in the midst of a nervous breakdown "sat in the bottom of the closet and chewed on [his] bedroom slippers" (271). Once at the yeshiva, disoriented, defensive, transgressive, Eli is pulled under by the tyrannous demands of the past and the present. And the ground he loses, the loose bearings that so tenuously tethered him to himself, cause him to take flight; he literally runs from the grounds of the yeshiva. So characteristic of Roth's reluctant Jews, when their defenses no longer protect them from themselves, their response is to retreat. As Nathan Marx, in "Defender of the Faith," so wearily acknowledges, there are "strategies of aggression, but there are strategies of retreat as well" (194). Ironically, Roth's characters typically engage in strategic forms of aggressive retreat. They retreat, more often than not, through disingenuous claims to autonomy; they run from themselves. But the "trope of flight," as Harold Bloom puts it, "is hardly literal language."[6] Eli runs from himself, far less frightened by the figure of Tzuref than he is of his own repressed relations to his Jewish identity.

Yet it is Tzuref who initially threatens Eli's professional demeanor, who strips him of his guise and who demands in no uncertain terms that Eli recognize himself in Tzuref and the other Jewish refugees. Tzuref's mandate that Eli not only admit to the historical, contemporary, and habitual suffering of the Jews, but "try it. It's a little thing," unnerves Eli (265). It does so because Tzuref's nagging reminder of Eli's connections and obligations prevents the safety of his repression and denial. It sets the stage for his "conversion." The yeshiva is, for Eli, a dangerous place, exactly because being Eli, that is, being in an antagonistic relation to one's past, is, indeed, perilous. But he can't quite face his own fear; his defenses fail in the face of the imperious Tzuref. But, of course, as he comes to realize, one cannot run from oneself. When he stops resisting that which he fears and himself moves "in the shadows" of the yeshiva, rather than running from its occupants and their past, it is not to the "lights" of Woodenton that he is drawn, but rather back to his own deeply defended sense of a Jewish self. For Eli, the apostate, will become the "fanatic," like Roth's Nathan Marx, the "defender" of a faith from which he has turned.

It is typical of Roth's fiction that Eli's own dissembling, the sublimation of his own desires, ironically, brings about their expression, forces Eli to come into the open, to expose himself, to realize and fix upon his identity as a Jew, as "the fanatic." Eli, an all too willing disinheritor of that which will ultimately claim him, finds himself ambushed, both to his surprise and to his relief, by no less than his own feared denial of his belief in his Jewishness. He comes to feel, to borrow a phrase that Alan Berger uses in a related context, "the presence of an absence,"[7] the very real presence of the missing because repressed part of himself, a Jewish past. This haunting sense of a Jewish past is enshrouded in mysterious and foreboding configurations and thus is as flatly illusory as it is compelling.

In order to recreate the presence of the absent or obliterated self, Eli must reinvent himself in the object, paradoxically, of that which he believes himself to fear most. This is what Sergeant Nathan Marx, in "Defender of the Faith," finds in the duplicitous Sheldon Grossbart, who represents the worst in Jewish stereotypes: that only through stepping into the frame of one's fears can one hope to engage them and thus, ironically, reshape them, accepting, as Nathan Marx at the close of "Defender of the Faith," so generously does, "my own" (200). Eli, too, face-to-face with his own partially eclipsed character, looks to complete himself in that which he has phobically avoided. He thus finds himself, not surprisingly, in this radically depicted other, in the Hasidic Jew, whose clothes Eli literally will wear.

It is not surprising that it is the Hasidic Jew, without compromise dressed in the black garb of his European ancestors, who is the source of the town's fixation and the focus of Eli's fear. He is viewed by the suburban Jews of Woodenton as the epitome of their seized-upon difference and consequent exclusion. His very presence in the town is a measure and felt reminder of what the suburban Jews have feared all along: that they will never be accepted. The refugee's presence in the town is a warning and transgression, an uninvited and unwelcome phantom from the past, "a regular greenhorn . . . like in the Bronx the old guys who used to come around selling Hebrew trinkets . . . talking a dead language . . . making a big thing out of suffering . . . going oy-oy-oy all your life" ("Eli, the Fanatic," 255, 278). But for Eli, the man in the Talmudic hat becomes the locus of his thwarted desires and repressed impulses, which, once recognized, cannot be eradicated.

Eli's initial response to the displaced person is to flee at the sight of him. In Eli's apprehensive and agitated state, the yeshiva Jew seems disembodied, "only a deep hollow of blackness." As he begins to take shape, however, his appearance is even more frightening for Eli, because in him, Eli sees the possibilities for his own long-hidden countenance, "his face . . . no older than Eli's" (253). When Eli, characteristically, misunderstands the Jew's gesture of lamentation, throwing open his arms in despair and supplication, for an embrace, an invitation to join him, to be him, Eli runs. Running from the sight of him, fleeing "toward the lights of Woodenton," false beacons of safety and providence, Eli attempts to run from himself, from an "absence," which becomes increasingly and unbearably palpable. The symptomatic retreat and avoidance predictably become unfeasible, impossible to maintain. And so, ultimately, to combat his fear Eli faces it, becomes it, gives into it completely by "becoming" the Jew, "wearing" it, impersonating it until it becomes him, until, in fact, he mimics the man's cry of mourning, whose moan "stung and stung inside him . . . became a scream" (281). For Eli, mourning and lamentation are the signs of being a Jew and thus provide him with an invitation to shared suffering.

And so, while Leo Tzuref may be Eli's conscience, it is, rather, the man in the hat, "that hat which was the very cause of Eli's mission, the source of Woodenton's upset" (253), who comes to be Eli's alter ego and unwitting double, and whose cry evokes in Eli "a feeling . . . for whose deepness he could find no word" (281). What Eli hears in the man's cry, "some feeling [that] crept into him" (280), is not unlike the call of "good shabbus" made to Nathan Marx in "Defender of the Faith." So well defended for so long, so inured against all emotion, it only takes, for Nathan Marx, one seemingly insignificant word to evoke in him the memory of himself. It is only through recreating the Jew as "other," envisioned first as some inanimate "other," that Roth's characters can step into their identity and find themselves, again, as Jews. Eli dons the garb of the Hasidic Jew and so, in becoming him, becomes himself.[8]

Eli, pushed to the limits by his guilt, in the form of Leo Tzuref on the one side and the Woodenton Jews on the other, finds himself eclipsed by the Jew whom Roth intentionally refuses to name, his anonymity subsumed in his replacement of Eli. When Eli packs his best green suit and delivers the box of clothes to the orthodox Jew in the yeshiva, defining events are set in motion that cannot be arrested, and the one man will become the other. Not only does the Hasidic Jew attire himself in Eli's clothes, but the gift of clothes is reciprocated. Eli's actions are mirrored by the man who now looks like him, the Jew's actions mirrored by Eli. In this exchange and imper- sonation, each man sees a partially eclipsed version of himself in the other: "The recognition took some time. He looked at what Eli wore. Up close, Eli looked at what he wore. And then Eli had the strange notion that he was two people. Or that he was one person wearing two suits" (289). For one brief but cataclysmic moment, when Eli suits himself in the clothes of the orthodox Jew and parades through the town, the townspeople, Eli, and even the yeshiva Jew himself believe Eli to be other than what he is. And Eli must perform this exchange of identities in public and must expose himself to public scrutiny because in doing so he both makes claims to a historical identity and performs its exaggerated impossibility. His identity is forever linked to the identity of another, the "other," the Jew, who, ironically, indeli- bly, is, indeed, none other than Eli himself. The clothes he wears and accepts are a replacement for his own "as if they were the skin of his skin" (293), a language of kinship.

But, for Eli, the replacement of identities is, of course, here far more complicated than is the replacement of clothes. While the "greenie" can, obligingly, attire himself in Eli's suit, the replacement can never make up for the loss of his own clothes, the suit that, after everything else has been taken away, "is all he's got": "'A mother and a father?' Tzuref said. 'No. A wife? No. A baby? A little ten-month-old baby? No! A village full of friends? A synagogue where you knew the feel of every seat under your pants? Where with your eyes closed you could smell the cloth of the Torah? . . . That leaves nothing, Mr. Peck. Absolutely nothing!'" (264). Eli's faltering acknowledgment, "I misunderstood," his belated recognition of the Jew's history, a set of circumstances that only willful evasion could ignore – "No news reached Woodenton?" (264) – underscores the extent to which Eli has denied his Judaism, his connection and obligation to those whose identity he belatedly shares.

Donning the clothes becomes an allegory for the impossibility of embracing the past in any simple or single way. Eli's attempts to step into a "new" identity are not as easily made as his stepping into the clothes left on his doorstep. Just as Eli's clothes cannot replace the losses suffered by the man who resides at the yeshiva, the Jew's suit of clothes cannot finally be a replacement for Eli's loss of identity and absence of history. And the shame that Eli experiences comes in large part from the recognition that, while the displaced person's history was purloined, Eli has given up his willingly; he has no one to blame but himself.

And so Eli punishes himself. His masquerade throughout the town in the guise of the Hasidic Jew is, for Eli, self-inflicted punishment. For there is a point where Eli realizes that his actions are not irrevocable, that, in fact, he can "go inside and put on his clothes" and return to himself. And it is at this juncture that he makes a choice, perhaps for the first time, a defining, deafening moment in which he makes claims to himself. But Roth doesn't let us off so easily. When, at the story's close, in full orthodox dress, Eli arrives at the hospital where his wife has just given birth to his first child, a son, he is dragged away and administered a drug intended to calm his nervous state. The drug, however, cannot quite "touch . . . down where the blackness had reached," to the fragmentation of self that Eli can no longer control (298). As revealed in Eli's comically pathetic end, the determined attempts of Roth's characters to redefine and recreate themselves ultimately fail because their anxious unease is all too transparent.

In Eli's flailing attempts to reconstruct himself, we find the making of many of Roth's later protagonists. Eli, for better or worse, is the nervous, anxiety-ridden, conflicted Jew who comes unglued forever after in Roth's fiction. Indeed, the ironic self-mockery, self-parody, self-indictment, and chastisement that continue to plague Roth's characters begin with Eli. Eli's precarious relation to Jewish history and identity is the motivational locus that Roth's protagonists inevitably revisit. His juggling of identities makes clear, as Debra Shostak suggests, "Roth's evident pleasure in the potentialities of self-invention."[9] Eli Peck may well be an amateur, but in his "doubling," in his attempts to become the other and so create a self he can live with, Eli is the nucleus of Roth's evolving characters living out "counterlives."

NOTES

1 Philip Roth, "Eli, the Fanatic," in *Goodbye, Columbus and Five Short Stories* (rpt. 1959; New York: Modern Library, 1966), p. 267.
2 Philip Roth, *The Counterlife* (New York: Farrar, Straus and Giroux, 1986).
3 Philip Roth, "Goodbye, Columbus," in *Goodbye, Columbus and Five Short Stories*, p. 58.
4 Philip Roth, "Defender of the Faith," in *Goodbye, Columbus and Five Short Stories*, p. 170.
5 Parts of the analysis that follow are published in whole in Victoria Aarons, *What Happened to Abraham?: Reinventing the Covenant in American Jewish Fiction* (Newark: University of Delaware Press, 2005), pp. 64–81.
6 Harold Bloom, "Freud's Concepts of Defense and the Poetic Will," in *The Literary Freud: Mechanisms of Defense and the Poetic Will*, vol. IV of *Psychiatry and the Humanities*, ed. Joseph H. Smith, M.D. (New Haven: Yale University Press, 1980), p. 5.
7 Alan L. Berger, *Children of Job: American Second-Generation Witnesses to the Holocaust* (Albany: SUNY Press, 1997), p. 2.
8 This logic of becoming the "other" is expressed by Roth in the unusual essay "Juice or Gravy?: How I Met My Fate in a Cafeteria," *New York Times Book Review* (September 18, 1994).
9 Debra Shostak, "Philip Roth's Fictions of Self-Exposure," *Shofar*, 19.1 (Fall 2000): 19–39.

2

DEREK PARKER ROYAL

Roth, literary influence, and postmodernism

In Philip Roth's ninth book of fiction, *The Professor of Desire*, young David Kepesh, attending college at Syracuse University, places on the bulletin board in his room two quotes that justly capture the budding scholar's dual nature: Lord Byron's dictum, "Studious by day, dissolute by night," and Thomas B. Macaulay's remarks on Sir Richard Steele, "He was a rake among scholars, and a scholar among rakes." He places these quotes, as he discloses to the reader, "directly above the names of the girls whom I have set my mind to *seduce*, a word whose deepest resonances come to me, neither from pornography nor pulp magazines, but from my agonized reading in Kierkegaard's *Either/Or*."[1] This is just one of a many passages in the novel where Kepesh taps into the wisdom of his literary heroes, those who are presumed to have influence over his life, to justify both his intellectual and lustful passions.

In fact, if one were to look for the one novel that stands as the best indicator of Roth's forebears, at least ostensibly so, it would probably be *The Professor of Desire*. The pages of the book are swarming with direct and subtle references to a variety of literary touchstones, including Sophocles, Dostoevsky, Shakespeare, Strindberg, O'Neill, the Bloomsbury group, Joyce, Maupassant, Twain, Flaubert, Tolstoy, Henry James, Hemingway, Chekhov, Freud, Kafka, Yeats, Faulkner, Genet, Synge, Céline, Hardy, Mann, Brönte (both Emily and Charlotte), Bellow, Kundera, Melville, Colette, Updike, Henry Miller, Hawthorne, and Gogol. Of course, almost all of these references can be explained by the fact that David Kepesh is a professor of literature, and as such, citations of this magnitude are understandable given his profession, as well as his inflated sense of self. Nonetheless, most of these names are the same ones that come up in almost any discussion of those that Roth admires. Just toss in a few more names, such as Malamud, Beckett, and perhaps a touch of Dos Passos, and the list would be complete. In other words, Kepesh's influences appear to be Roth's influences. But herein lies the problem. Given the fact that Kepesh is obviously a fictional character, and one that Roth has often used as either an agent or subject of satire, might then the very concept of literary influence – at least in terms of trying to delineate an original point of tribute or departure – be "fictional" as well? Assigning literary influences can be a tricky business, and it may not be too much of a stretch to suggest that by portraying Kepesh's textual indulgences and extensive namedropping as he does, Roth may be suggesting that such efforts to forge links of legacy are inherently problematic.

This is not to suggest that Roth's fiction does not bear the imprint of authors that he admittedly admires. One does not have to look very far to see the Jamesian stamp on *Letting Go* and *The Ghost Writer*, Flaubert's mark on *When She Was Good*, the shadow of Yeats across the pages of *Sabbath's Theater* and *The Dying Animal*, the reflection of Joyce's Stephen Dedalus in the figure of Nathan Zuckerman, or the bearings of Kafka and Roth's Czech experiences in such works as *The Breast*, *The Professor of Desire*, *The Prague Orgy*, and "'I Always Wanted You to Admire My Fasting'; or, Looking at Kafka."[2] However, approaching Roth's fiction through more traditional accounts of literary influence – such as T. S. Eliot's Modernist (and even neoclassical) emphasis on the beneficial necessity of traditional models and Harold Bloom's more Romantic notions of influence as *clinamen*, a misprision or misreading of previous writers[3] – can be rather limiting. Readings that highlight the cataloging of sources, usually intentional in nature, see influence as an author-to-author phenomenon and tend to accept uncritically suppositions of authenticity and originality. What is more, they may not actually tell us anything particularly meaningful about the work under discussion, at least nothing beyond a simple assumption of linear progeny.

Indeed, Roth himself complicates any traditional readings of influence in the very novel that seems to endorse most of his idols. *The Professor of Desire* opens, not with some pedantic reference to literary greatness, but with a nine-page tribute to Herbie Bratasky, the social director, bandleader, crooner, and M.C. at Kepesh's Hungarian Royale, the mountainside resort hotel that David's family owns. As a young boy, Kepesh was fascinated with Herbie's comic antics, especially his repertoire of fart sounds. He waxes nostalgically that

> not only can [Herbie] simulate the panoply of sounds – ranging from the faintest springtime sough to the twenty-one-gun salute – with which mankind emits its gases, but he can also "do diarrhea." Not, he is quick to inform me, some poor schlimazel in its throes – that he had already mastered back in high school – but the full Wagnerian strains of fecal *Strum and Drang*. (6–7)

The unforgettable Herbie Bratasky goes on to hold at least as much influence over the development of Kepesh as do Chekhov and Flaubert, if not more.

In fact, in a profoundly disturbing dream that Kepesh experiences while on a trip to Prague, Bratasky becomes the professor's guide – the Virgil to Kepesh's Dante, if you will – into the very depths of Kafkadom, at the very center of which sits Kafka's aged prostitute. Bratasky's usurpation of influence can even be read as synonymous with the role that such figures as Lenny Bruce (another Jewish bad boy) played in determining the course of Roth's career from *Portnoy's Complaint* onward – a shift from his earlier forays into Jamesian/Flaubertian realism and, with his increased emphasis on comedy, a literary transgression which didn't rest easy with more Modernist-minded critics such as Irving Howe and Norman Podhoretz.

Perhaps a more useful way of approaching Roth's work, at least in terms of the author's stance vis-à-vis influence, is through a more postmodern lens, one that problematizes more traditional (two-dimensional and linear) notions of literary influence and instead reconceptualizes the argument in terms of two different narrative strategies: intertextuality and metafiction.[4] Regarding the former, the work of Julia Kristeva, inspired by M. M. Bakhtin, should stand as a critical starting point. She envisions a three-dimensional textual space whose three "coordinates of dialogue" are the writing subject (or author), the addressee (or ideal reader), and texts exterior to the work in question. This textual space is comprised of intersecting planes that have horizontal and vertical axes. As she describes it,

> The word's status is thus defined horizontally (the word in the text belongs to both writing subject and addressee) as well as vertically (the word in the text is oriented towards an anterior or synchronic literary corpus) . . . each word (text) is an intersection of words (texts) where at least one other word (text) can be read . . . any text is constructed as a mosaic of quotations; any text is the absorption and transformation of another.[5]

Elsewhere Kristeva defines the "'literary word' as an intersection of textual surfaces rather than a point (a fixed meaning), as a dialogue among several writings."[6] Hers is a very postmodern understanding of "influence" since the meaning of a text – or the relationship of the text to its author as well as to other texts, anterior or contemporaneous – is both contingent (in its dependence upon other texts) and local (in that its specific context, as opposed to any universal referent, determines its significance). As such, intertextuality emphasizes the relationship between one text and any knowledge of other text(s) that the writer or the reader brings to the narrative in question. In other words, an understanding of any one text is necessarily informed by a reader's encounter with previous texts. However, it is not necessary for the reader to be able to accurately pinpoint a specific exterior text, or *intertext*. According to Michael Riffaterre, all one needs to do to sufficiently interpret a text is to assume that some intertext is being transformed by the text in question. As he states, "Intertextual reading is the perception of similar comparabilities from text to text; or it is the assumption that such comparing must be done if there is no intertext at hand wherein to find comparabilities. In the latter case, the text holds clues (such as formal and semantic gaps) to a complementary intertext lying in wait somewhere."[7] As Riffaterre puts it, intertextuality "is the web of functions that constitutes and regulates the relationship between text and intertext."[8] The interconnectedness of Roth's texts – one to the other or one to those of other writers – forms a solid narrative network. As with a spider's web, you touch one part of it and other spaces reverberate.

Such instances of intertextuality occur throughout Roth's fiction. In fact, one cannot thoroughly read Roth without taking issues of intertextuality into account. There are, for instance, the references to *Portrait of a Lady* that set up the opening pages of *Letting Go*, the undercurrent of Lewis's *Main Street* that can be found in *When She Was Good*, the Freudian intertexts sprinkled throughout *Portnoy's Complaint*, the allusions to 1930s radio programming that frame the plot of "On the Air," the brief echo of Salinger's *Franny and Zooey* in *My Life as a Man*,[9] the presence of *Portrait of the Artist as a Young Man* in *The Ghost Writer*, the confessional narratives (e.g., those of St. Augustine and Rousseau) that underlie *Operation Shylock*, and the great nineteenth-century European novellas – Kafka's *The Metamorphosis*, Gogol's *The Nose*, and Tolstoy's *The Death of Ivan Ilych* – that serve as intertexts of *The Breast*. And of course, there is Roth's intertextual tour de force, *The Great American Novel*, which incorporates into its narrative fabric, among other texts, Melville's *Moby-Dick* (as well as *Typee* and *Omoo*); Hawthorne's *The Scarlet Letter*; Twain's *Adventures of Huckleberry Finn*; Conrad's *Heart of Darkness*; Anderson's *Winesburg, Ohio*; the book of Exodus; Homer's *The Odyssey*; the Epic of Gilgamesh; *The Song of Roland*; Egyptian, Hindu, Norse, and Greek mythologies; diverse pop cultural texts such as the headline format from *The Sporting News*, the slogan of Wheaties breakfast cereal, the label of Aunt Jemima syrup, the Warren Report, and the film *The Pride of the Yankees*; and, introducing each of the nine primary chapters of the novel, the narrative précis reminiscent of the nineteenth-century Victorian novel form.

What is more, there are the innumerable examples of intertextuality within Roth's corpus, where characters and events in earlier Roth texts are cited in later volumes. The various series of the Zuckerman works (those constituting *Zuckerman Bound* as well as in the American Trilogy), the "Philip Roth" books (the autobiographical tetralogy of *The Facts*, *Deception*, *Patrimony*, and *Operation Shylock*), and the Kepesh novels (*The Breast*, *The Professor of Desire*, and *The Dying Animal*) are perhaps the most obvious examples of this strategy. It is worth noting that such intertextual self-referentiality can be both narratively consistent (as in the case of most of the Zuckerman books) and historically inconsistent (as in the case of the Kepesh works, where the facts surrounding David Kepesh change depending on the text). What distinguishes this intertextual play from more conventional notions of literary inheritance, though, is that Roth integrates both "high" and "low" textual references that not only decenter any notions of authority (as it refers to both political power structures and the writing subject), but draw our attention to the ways in which texts are constructed. So by readjusting our critical lens from a focus on influence to one on intertextuality, we make possible a more expansive reading of Roth's fiction.

Complementing these readings of intertextuality are the many examples of metafiction found throughout Roth's oeuvre. While not solely a postmodern phenomenon, metafiction is a narrative form that is highly self-reflective – or put another way, a mode of writing wherein texts are aware of and refer to themselves as constructed narratives – and as such, are usually considered an expression of postmodern writing. Although there are several definitions of metafiction, perhaps one of the most general, and useful, understandings of this concept is that of Patricia Waugh, who defines metafiction as

> fictional writing which self-consciously and systematically draws attention to its status as an artifact in order to pose questions about the relationship between fiction and reality. In providing a critique of their own methods of construction, such writings not only examine the fundamental structures of narrative fiction, they also explore the possible fictionality of the world outside the literary fictional text.[10]

The postmodern implications of metafiction are quite significant and indeed underscore the "fictionality of the world": reader expectations are shattered, traditional narrative modes of understanding (as in genre distinctions) are ruptured, boundaries between reader and text become more fluid, totality and unity (of the text as well as of the narrating subject) are thrown into question, and linguistic contingency displaces metaphysical determinacy as an arbiter of meaning. All of these effects, in one form or another, can be felt throughout most of Roth's writing.

One of Roth's first, and most notable, exercises in metafictional play is *My Life as a Man*, a novel that introduces for the first time the perennial Nathan Zuckerman. However, Zuckerman isn't the protagonist of this novel. That distinction goes to Peter Tarnopol, a talented young novelist who creates the character of Nathan Zuckerman and uses him in his fiction in order to better understand the responsibilities of manhood. The novel is divided into two sections, "Useful Fictions," comprised of two Zuckerman short stories written by Tarnopol, and "My True Story," the longer memoir-like portion concerning the painful – and highly comic – links between Tarnopol's relationships with women and his writing. The two stories that make up the "Useful Fictions" section, "Salad Days" and "Courting Disaster (or, Serious in the Fifties)," are further distinguished by the fact that each presents a slightly different version of Zuckerman's relationship with his family and with women. Not long after the reader gets to "My True Story" – a tellingly ironic title, given the fictional shifts experienced up to this point – he or she begins to understand that the first two narratives are in fact Tarnopol's attempts to represent, and thus make sense of, his life in fictional form. In this way, the very structure of the novel underscores its metafictional themes: it is a fiction about the creation of fiction, and how that fiction becomes a way of constructing meaning.

The metafictional nature of the novel is made apparent even before the narrative properly begins. In "A Note to the Reader" that immediately follows the dedication page, Roth asserts that "Useful Fictions" and "My True Story" are taken from the writings of Peter Tarnopol. The effect of this non-diagetic qualifier is indeed disruptive, for not only does it plunge us directly into Roth's fictional labyrinth – who is writing about whom? – it also forces us to consider the generic make-up of the book we are about to read. Is it both a work of fiction *and* an autobiography, and if so, whose authorial presence – the fictionist's or the autobiographer's – should be privileged here? Yet at the same time, we know that what we hold in our hand is none other than a work of fiction, despite the apparently misleading "Note to the Reader." These narrative contortions are given an added twist when we turn the page and see the novel's epigraph, "I could be his Muse, if only he'd let me," a quote from Maureen Tarnopol, Peter's wife, a character in the very fiction we are about to read. One cannot help here but to think of John Barth's "funhouse" metaphor from his *Lost in the Funhouse*, where what we see in the mirror depends not only upon our angle of vision, but the degree of reflexivity as well. In true metafictional form, Roth holds a mirror up to himself as the author of *My Life as a Man* by showing us a man (Tarnopol) who is attempting to represent himself through his fiction, and whose fictional creation (Zuckerman) will also go on to represent himself through his fictions.

If *My Life as a Man* is a novel concerned with the constructedness of narrative, then *The Counterlife* is a work that foregrounds the constructedness of subjects who create those narratives. Much like the earlier novel, *The*

Counterlife is a fragmented narrative whose "facts" are in the process of being rewritten, but even more so than its predecessor, it is populated by figures who negotiate their subjectivity through their language. As Nathan Zuckerman, the book's protagonist, says at one point, "we are all the inventions of each other, everybody a conjuration conjuring up everyone else." [11] There are, for instance, Nathan's brother, Henry, who visits Israel and commits to the Zionist cause after renaming himself Hanoch; his Zionist leader, Mordecai Lippman, who employs aggressive polemics, as well as the threat of physical violence, as a means to establish his Jewish Kibbutz; left-wing journalist Suki Elchanan, whose rhetoric of liberalism functions as a counterbalance to Lippman's diatribes; Maria, Zuckerman's gentile wife (at least in certain sections of the text) who, after being represented in different guises by different characters, takes control of her narrative by writing herself out of the novel; Jimmy Ben-Joseph, an American middle-class Jew who redefines himself as a "prophet" of Israeli salvation through his advocacy of baseball and his authoring of the anti-Holocaust remembrance manifesto, "Forget Remembering"; and standing behind this entire cast of self-constructed subjects is Nathan Zuckerman, the ur-manipulator who uses the pages of *The Counterlife* to reinvent himself as a writer, an American, and as a Jew. No longer the subject of Peter Tarnopol's fictional machinations, Zuckerman becomes his own author through a realization of the fragmented and contingent nature of subjectivity. As he tells Maria toward the end of the novel,

> It's *all* impersonation – in the absence of a self, one impersonates selves, and after a while impersonates best the self that best gets one through . . . What I have instead is a variety of impersonations I can do, and not only of myself – a troupe of players that I have internalized, a permanent company of actors that I can call upon when a self is required, an ever-evolving stock of pieces and parts that forms my repertoire . . . I am a theater, nothing more than a theater.
> (*The Counterlife*, 320–21)

Such an awareness is unquestionably postmodern, and it stands in direct opposition – or as a countertext – to an understanding of identity, individual and well as textual, as a unified agent of influence. This is quite a departure from a reading of Roth that privileges traditional models of literary inheritance. Here the textual self does not so much build upon previous influences as it does imitate, or even parody, them through performance. *The Counterlife* is not only a space of subjective reinvention. Perhaps more importantly, it is a novel that is highly aware of itself as such a textual space. In fact, *The Counterlife* stands as Roth's most outstanding example of metafiction writing. It is comprised of five sections – "Basel," "Judea," "Aloft,"

"Gloucestershire," and "Christendom" – each of which revises, however slightly, the events in the chapter that precedes it. Episodes concerning a character in one chapter, such as the bypass surgery that Henry undergoes in "Basel," are rewritten to involve someone else in a later chapter (in this case, it is Nathan who undergoes the surgery in "Gloucestershire"). Events that occur in one part, such as the hijacking of the El Al flight in the "Aloft" section, seem later never to have happened once we get to the final section, "Christendom." And perhaps more significantly, there are even places in the novel where passages from certain parts of the text are referenced – in a highly metafictional manner – in other sections, and sometimes with exact page numbers. For instance, Nathan's imagined comments on the El Al flight in "Aloft" (155–56) are read in manuscript form by Henry in "Gloucestershire" (230). Words from Nathan's first-person account of his troubled relationship with Maria are repeated verbatim in the opening sentences of her letter to him (312). Passages from Nathan's eulogy in the first part of "Gloucestershire" (208–11) are repeated word for word in one of the documents that Henry finds while rummaging through Nathan's brownstone later in the chapter (231). Henry also discovers among Nathan's papers three of the chapters – "Basel," "Judea," and "Christendom" – that make up the actual text of *The Counterlife*, and even refers to the exact page number on which the last section begins (229). What is more, Maria's letter in "Christendom" (314) refers to an event that takes place earlier in "Judea," again, down to the exact page number (73).

In the final pages of *The Counterlife*, Roth, through the voice of Nathan Zuckerman, foregrounds his metafictional agenda, drawing attention to the artifice of his project, and he does so in the very text that the reader holds in his or her hands:

> The burden [of subjectivity] isn't either/or, consciously choosing from possibilities equally difficult and regrettable – it's and/and/and/and/and as well. Life *is* and: the accidental and the immutable, the elusive and the graspable, the bizarre and the predictable, the actual and the potential, all the multiplying realities, entangled, overlapping, colliding, conjoined – plus the multiplying illusions! This times this times this times this . . .   (306)

Each of the five "ands" in this passage correspond to one of the five sections of the novel, suggesting that any attempts to wrap up the text's many unanswered questions – Did Henry really survive his heart operation? Was Maria the English wife of Nathan or the Swiss mistress of Henry? Did Jimmy Ben-Joseph really attempt to hijack the El Al flight? Was Nathan really the one who suffered from impotence, and not Henry? – are ultimately futile. What is important in this novel isn't so much the believability of the events themselves as it is *how* those events are represented within the text. As the concluding ellipsis in the above passage suggests, constructing the self is an open-ended and always ongoing process.

Similar postmodern modes of narration are also apparent in Roth's autobiographical tetralogy, *The Facts*, *Deception*, *Patrimony*, and *Operation Shylock*. If, as Waugh argues, one of the functions of metafiction is to draw "attention to its status as an artefact in order to pose questions about the relationship between fiction and reality" (*Metafiction*, 2), then one will not find clearer examples of this strategy than in these four texts. In contrast to all of Roth's other works, each text within the autobiographical tetralogy possesses a subtitle that should ideally serve as a directive for interpretation. This being the case, *The Facts* should be read as "A Novelist's Autobiography," *Deception* was written as "A Novel," *Patrimony* is unquestionably "A True Story," and *Operation Shylock* is nothing more than "A Confession." Taken at face value, then, only *Deception* should be read as fiction while the others stand apart as nonfictional forms of "life writing." However, this distinction among genres – and more importantly, the differentiation between "fiction" and "reality" – is undermined in the very book where Roth supposedly sheds his fictionalizing masks. The "novelist's autobiography" is framed by two letters, one from Philip to Zuckerman and the other from Zuckerman to Philip, and together these "fictions" make up approximately a quarter of *The Facts*. It is amazing how so few pages in this book are devoted to the "facts" of the novelist's life, an irony that Roth – who has done more than his share of deconstructing the notion of "author" – must surely savor. Traditional conceptions of the totalized self, as well as the unified text, are ruptured from the very beginning. In his letter, Philip (the narrating subject, as opposed to "Roth," the living author) confides to Zuckerman that he has recently suffered a Halcion-induced depression and as a result feels himself "coming undone." In order to put himself back together, he feels that he must "go back to the moment of origins," the facts prior to fiction, despite the naiveté of such a movement.[12] In his reply to Philip, Zuckerman, demonstrating a narrative savvy apparently lacking in his creator, resists such facile measures. He clearly sees the futility of trying to recover any factual origins for the purposes of understanding himself (or at least in helping Philip's readership understand him). Zuckerman claims that what Philip has been engaged in all along, from the creation of Neil Klugman in "Goodbye, Columbus" to that of Nathan Zuckerman, is nothing more than the reinvention of the self: "You've written metamorphoses of yourself so many times, you no longer have any idea what *you* are or ever were. By now what you are is a walking text" (*The Facts*, 162). And we may rightly assume, in light of the ironic distance set up between Roth

(the living author) and Philip, that such an allegation can certainly be lev-
eled again Roth himself, although with this caveat: in contrast with Philip's
narrative innocence, Roth is fully conscious of the "walking text" he is creating. In this manner, Roth throws down the textual gauntlet and more or less
dares us to establish any incontrovertible distinctions between "fiction" and
"reality."

The remainder of the autobiographical tetralogy similarly challenges our
understanding of genre distinctions. *Deception*, which is purportedly a novel,
is structured more like a series of dramatic dialogues. The book possesses
almost no exposition – to call it "minimalist" would be to stretch its bulk.
Patrimony, although the most personal of the four texts, nonetheless betrays
much of the novelist's imaginary flair in several passages that appear almost
too fictional to be real.[13] And *Operation Shylock*, despite the author's protes-
tations of verisimilitude – "The book is true," Roth claimed to a reporter
at the time of publication – is nothing more than a false confession.[14] In it,
Roth claims to have met an exact double of himself in Israel during the John
Demjanjuk trials of the 1980s. What is more, he also claims to have gone
on undercover operations for the Mossad. To say the least, such a yarn is
difficult for most readers to accept, and in fact, the very structure of the book
betrays Roth's mischievous efforts at textual duplicity. Bracketing the novel
proper are two narrative qualifiers, each of which stands in stark contrast to
the other. In the "Preface," Roth states outright that "I've drawn *Operation
Shylock* from notebook journals. The book is as accurate an account as I
am able to give of actual occurrences that I lived through during my middle fifties and that culminated, early in 1988, in my agreeing to undertake
an intelligence-gathering operation for Israel's foreign intelligence service,
the Mossad."[15] As he does in *The Facts*, Roth claims that he is pulling his
story straight from his notebooks and without the varnish of fiction. The
only "facts" altered are for legal reasons, and "these are minor changes that
mainly involve details of identification and locale and are of little significance
to the overall story and its verisimilitude" (*Operation Shylock*, 13). In stark
contrast to this is his "Note to the Reader," a disclosure which ends the
book.[16] The Note includes the standard disclaimer that Simon and Schuster,
his publisher at the time, inserted in all of their fiction: "This book is a work
of fiction. Names, characters, places, and incidents are either products of
the author's imagination or are used fictitiously. Any resemblance to actual
events or locales or persons, living or dead, is entirely coincidental." However, Roth qualifies this disclaimer by noting two nonfictional exceptions to
the "fiction" – the interview with Appelfeld and minutes from the Demjanjuk trial – and then ends his "Note to the Reader" with the words, "This
confession is false" (399).

In addition to the obvious discrepancy between *Operation Shylock*'s fram-
ing paratexts – the Preface's claims to truth and the Note's assertion of fiction – these two qualifying statements raise other questions that are difficult
to ignore. For instance, the wording in the Preface should raise suspicion
in the astute reader: "The book is *as accurate an account as I am able to
give* of actual occurrences" (emphasis added). Coming from a writer who
generates metafictional facades, these words suggest more of a creative pre-
disposition than a limitation of style. If we read between the lines, we may
see this as a backhanded admission to narrative equivocation, and coupled
with the "minor changes" that are of "little significance," they should leave
us guarded. Furthermore, there is the ambiguous meaning behind the final
admission, "This confession is false." Is it the "confession" of fiction as
expressed in the Note that is false, or is the entire text itself, one that pro-
fesses verisimilitude and whose subtitle bears the word "confession," that
is false? Roth gives the reader no indication of which reading to take. With
Operation Shylock, as with all the other works within the autobiographical
tetralogy, Roth does not require that we ultimately distinguish fact from
fiction. In fact, he seems to be arguing against any comfortable differentiation between the two. Instead of trying to determine what is "fabricated"
and what is "true," readers should approach the text as part of a larger
metafictional project: Roth's ambitious attempt to write in the crossroads of
autobiography and fiction.

During the last part of the 1990s, and into the next century, Roth has
continued to foreground the fragmented, and highly contingent, nature of
narrative production. All three works in the American Trilogy – *American
Pastoral, I Married a Communist*, and *The Human Stain* – reveal the narrative uses of memory and show how the text of the self is inextricably
linked to its cultural times. And in *The Plot Against America*, Roth uses an
uncharacteristic generic mode, the science fiction form of alternate history,
to problematize any formal distinctions between fiction and history. So given
the author's tendencies to create these kinds of narrative conundrums, questions surrounding Roth's literary influences become suspect, at best. A more
productive way of approaching Roth's work would be to account for the
different ways he incorporates a variety of texts into the fabric of his own
fiction, specifically through means of metafiction and intertextuality. Many
of these texts make up the core of our traditional Western canon, others are a
part of the "common" cultural air we all breathe, and still others are the very
works of fiction that have established Roth as one of America's most important living authors. However he may use these texts, and whatever legacy he
may inherit in the process, one thing should be unambiguously clear: Philip

Roth has spent the better part of his career helping to show us how we structure our texts, how we construct our truths, and how we formulate our identities. Such concerns, postmodern as they are, seem considerably more vital than any question of literary patrimony.

NOTES

1 Philip Roth, *The Professor of Desire* (New York: Farrar, Straus and Giroux, 1977), p. 17.

2 See *Conversations with Philip Roth*, ed. George J. Searles: (Jackson University Press of Mississippi, 1992) and Philip Roth, *Reading Myself and Others* (New York, Farrar, Straus and Giroux, 2001). As for his Czechoslovakian experiences, Roth visited the Soviet-dominated country during the 1970s, and while there befriended such repressed authors as Milan Kundera and Ludvik Vaculik. This exposure led to the Penguin book series "Writers from the Other Europe," for which Roth served as General Editor until 1989.

3 See Harold Bloom, *The Anxiety of Influence: A Theory of Poetry*, 2nd ed. (New York: Oxford University Press, 1997) and T. S. Eliot, "Tradition and Individual Talent," in *Selected Essays, 1917–1932* (New York: Harcourt, 1950), pp. 3–11.

4 At the risk of overgeneralizing, it might be useful to differentiate between modern understandings of literary influence and postmodern concerns of textual interplay. Modern approaches would see no problem with – and indeed, may even promote – such concepts as originality, universality, self-contained authority, unity, and "genius." Postmodern readings, on the other hand, tend to problematize both originality and authenticity, emphasize indeterminacy and contingency, present subjective experience as fragmented, and subvert distinctions between "high" and "low" culture.

5 Julia Kristeva, *Desire in Language: A Semiotic Approach to Literature and Art*, ed. Leon S. Roudiez, trans. Thomas Gora, Alice Jardine, and Leon S. Roudiez (New York: Columbia University Press, 1980), p. 66.

6 Julia Kristeva, "Title," in *The Kristeva Reader*, ed. Toril Moi (New York: Columbia University Press, 1986), p. 36.

7 Michael Riffaterre, "Syllepsis," *Critical Inquiry*, 6 (1980): 626.

8 Michael Riffaterre, "Compulsory Reader Response: The Intertextual Drive," in *Intertextuality: Theories and Practices*, eds. Michael Worton and Judith Still (Manchester: Manchester University Press, 1990), p. 57.

9 See George Searles, "Salinger Redux via Roth: An Echo of *Franny and Zooey* in *My Life as a Man*," *Notes on Contemporary Literature*, 16.2 (1986): 7.

10 Patricia Waugh, *Metafiction: The Theory and Practice of Self-Conscious Fiction* (London: New Accents-Routledge, 1984), p. 2.

11 Philip Roth, *The Counterlife* (New York: Farrar, Straus and Giroux 1987), p. 145.

12 Philip Roth, *The Facts: A Novelist's Autobiography* (New York: Farrar, Straus and Giroux, 1988), p. 5.

13 See, for instance, the section where Philip unconsciously drives to his mother's cemetery (pp. 19–21), the bathroom scene where he cleans up after his father's uncontrollable bowel movement (pp. 171–76), and the account of Walter

Hermann's sexually tinged Holocaust experience (pp. 208–18). Such events may have occurred, but they are narrated in such a way that they resonate with novelistic significance.

14 Esther B. Fein, "'Believe Me,' Says Roth with a Straight Face," *New York Times*, March 9, 1993: B1.

15 Philip Roth, *Operation Shylock: A Confession* (New York: Simon and Schuster, 1993), p. 13.

16 It is significant to note that much as he does in *My Life as a Man*, Roth uses this "Note" to complicate any straightforward readings of his text. He even does something similar in the "Note" that he includes at the end of his more recent novel, *The Plot Against America*.

3

DONALD M. KARTIGANER

Zuckerman Bound: the celebrant of silence

Zuckerman Bound is one of the major achievements of post-World War II American fiction. A full-scale portrait of the artist, the trilogy invokes several of its most illustrious precursors – the "wonderful and famous stories and novels by Henry James and Thomas Mann and James Joyce about the life of the artist" – and effects a transformation, inserting between the lines of these lives and works the novelist Nathan Zuckerman and "the comedy that an artistic vocation can turn out to be in the U.S.A."[1]

While all three novels of *Zuckerman Bound* and its epilogue comment on the full range of the artistic process, each of them emphasizes a different phase. *The Ghost Writer* deals with shifting conceptions of the writer at work: from the high modernist heroic figure redeeming the real, at times appearing to abandon it for the sake of some imaginary coherence, to the postmodern comedian eager to violate clear-cut divisions of life and art, particularly if that means offending the self-appointed arbiters of both. *Zuckerman Unbound* describes the engagement of writer with reader through the published book, an act of cultural exchange in which the production of the writer is born anew as the possession of the reader. *The Anatomy Lesson* moves beyond literary creation and reception to the crisis of the renunciation of language itself: the supreme challenge to writing and reading by the body in pain. *The Prague Orgy* encapsulates the whole, extending the range of the major concerns of the trilogy: writing, reading, the cycles of process and possession, and the human suffering that limits utterance to the evocation of silence.

The Ghost Writer

Nathan Zuckerman, the novice in quest of a mentor as well as a father to replace the one with whom he has quarreled, and E. I. Lonoff, the chosen "Maestro," are, for all their mutual admiration for each other's work, opposed writers in virtually every respect. The most obvious area of difference, presented in broad parodic strokes, is the characterization of Lonoff as the selfless saint of high modernism and Zuckerman as the self-indulgent, irreverent postmodernist. Behind Lonoff's portrait, which, although written by Zuckerman in the late 1970s, reflects the attitudes toward high modernism of the 1950s, is a conception neatly summarized by Frank Kermode's *Romantic Image*, published in 1957: "These two beliefs – in the Image as a radiant truth out of space and time, and in the necessary isolation or estrangement of men who can perceive it – are inextricably associated."[2] Lonoff is the remote artist sacrificing what he calls "'[o]rdinary human pleasures'" in order to produce an art comparably remote, autonomous, cleansed of history, mass culture, the quotidian.[3]

It is an art filtered through a net of linguistic and existential prohibition: one or two laboriously chiseled sentences a day, figuring the emptiness of his life – "Nothing happens to me" (*The Ghost Writer*, 16) – into a fiction of and about emptiness. Lonoff's typical fictional character, Zuckerman tells us, is a man "thwarted, secretive, imprisoned . . . more often than not a nobody from nowhere, away from a home where he is not missed, yet to which he must return without delay" (12–14): a man whose quite unexpected willingness to risk some change in his routine only leads to a rueful confirmation of his former caution. Invariably he discovers that there is really nothing to be accomplished except to make everything worse. The climax of Lonoff's work has been a collection of stories in which there is no action at all. The most tentative consideration of a move breaks itself against "the ruling triumvirate of Sanity, Responsibility, and Self-Respect, assisted handily by their devoted underlings: the timetable, the rainstorm, the headache, the busy signal, the traffic jam, and, most loyal of all, the last-minute doubt" (15). The perfection of the stories is the perfection of a stillness, an evocation of life so finely wrought it bestows on the absence of action an eloquence of despair that a tragic action can never have.

As we soon learn, there are in fact disturbances that threaten Lonoff's tower of detachment. In addition to a wife occasionally given to outrage at his "religion of art" that rejects life, Lonoff has three children, now grown, and a guest at the house, Amy Bellette, an attractive young woman of somewhat unclear origins who may be his lover. Sufficient activity, it would appear, to distract any number of dedicated artists, yet none of these has penetrated the fiction itself. Zuckerman recalls that in Lonoff's seven volumes of stories "I could not think of a single hero who was not a bachelor, a widower, an orphan, a foundling, or a reluctant fiancé" (71). Not a single hero, in other words, who belongs to a family, who weds, fornicates, fathers, who reflects the life of Lonoff himself.

Zuckerman's fiction refuses to disengage itself from the messiness of its author's life, as first revealed to us in the story "Higher Education." Summarized, it is apparently a fairly close retelling of the battle of some of Zuckerman's relatives over an inheritance. The story dismays Zuckerman's father, who fears it will corroborate the anti-Semitic prejudices of its gentile readers. In the story Zuckerman writes in *The Ghost Writer*, "Femme Fatale," he continues to escape the impersonality of Lonoff – not, however, to the accurate reportage of "Higher Education," but to what Roth has referred to as a fiction of "impersonation." The writer need not refine himself out of existence or elide himself totally into his characters; he impersonates them, masks himself with their identities as a means not only of providing new insight into his own, but of enlarging that identity into a being of far greater interest and relevance: a "being whose existence was comparable to my own and yet registered a more powerful valence, a life more highly charged and energized, more entertaining than my own."[4] The vitality of impersonative creation, however, is owing to the abiding presence of the original imagining self who, like the ventriloquist, refuses to remain concealed while speaking the other of his performance. To put it another way, Roth's fiction stages a metamorphosis, but it is one in which transformation is never completed: opposing selves, original and successor, coexist as competing claims to an identity.[5]

The family dispute aroused by "Higher Education" is displaced in "Femme Fatale" into the details of the conversation between Lonoff and Amy Bellette that Zuckerman has overheard while in Lonoff's study, supplemented by his insertion of Anne Frank, who has been recommended to him as a model of more constructive Jewish writing. He gives the story of Anne Frank a disturbing twist, however, by suggesting that she may have actually survived the Holocaust, but has chosen to conceal her identity behind "Amy Bellette"; she is more interested in preserving the powerful effect of her "masterpiece" by remaining dead than in reuniting with her still living and mourning father. He then gives it a thoroughgoing wrench by proposing that Anne Frank *is* dead and that Amy Bellette is a writer pretending to be Anne Frank in order to appropriate the diary as her own creation.

Fueling these alternative impersonations is Zuckerman's impersonation of both Anne and Amy, as he converts the entire story into an exploration of his own artistic predicament. The conflicts of "Femme Fatale" stem directly from his ambivalence inspired by the negative response to "Higher Education": between loyalty to the father and loyalty to art, between the capacity of the artist for self-sacrificing dedication and the capacity for self-promoting unscrupulousness, between the artist as beholden to his Jewish heritage and the artist as the singular being, following, as it happens, the example of Anne

Frank, whom Zuckerman quotes: "*I don't feel in the least bit responsible to any of you*" (*The Ghost Writer*, 140). "Femme Fatale" demonstrates Zuckerman's willingness to heed the advice of his authorities to emulate a deeply admired Jewish writer, only to commit a "desecration even more vile than the one they had read" (171).

For all the differences between the strategies and productions of Lonoff and Zuckerman, however, their fictions strangely impersonate each other. Zuckerman's Amy Bellette admits to Lonoff that her life is "like one of your stories . . . You'd know how to tell it in three pages. A homeless girl comes from Europe, sits in the professor's class being clever" (124), and then reaches out for the impossible, reveals to her mentor that "of all the Jewish writers, from Franz Kafka to E. I. Lonoff, she was the most famous" (152). In other words, a "nobody from nowhere" hazards an act of daring, the upshot of which is surely to make everything worse. That Lonovian kernel expands through Zuckermanian "turbulence" into thirty-four pages of wildly improbable narrative, yet continues to survive as its miniature reflection.

The crucial bond between Lonoff and Zuckerman lies in what the latter terms the "secret," the "puzzle" (50) of Lonoff's parables. According to Zuckerman, they are free of every facet of Lonoff's life except one:

> I think of you as the Jew who got away . . . from Russia and the pogroms . . . from the purges . . . from Palestine and the homeland . . . from Brookline and the relatives . . . from New York . . . Away from all the Jews, and a story by you without a Jew in it is unthinkable . . . [A]ll you write about are Jews.
>
> (50–51)

This is the single ounce of self, the violation of modernist purity that the impersonal artist Lonoff allows into his fiction. For Zuckerman it is enough. At bottom, he decides, Lonoff is also engaged in an act of impersonation, assuming as his faint yet constant avatar the Jew whose life and destiny he has escaped and yet must always retell. The Lonoff story struggles to transcend its source – "twenty-seven drafts of a single short story" (25) – reiterates defeated desire in a jewel-like, increasingly refining prose, eliminates content by bringing life to a standstill, as if aiming at Flaubert's dream of writing a book about nothing at all. But not quite; for Lonoff's Jew remains, however distorted, the content of his creator: the Jew, *c'est moi*.

Each of Lonoff's nobodies from nowhere, it turns out, is a Jew, and thus a somebody from somewhere, representing a minimal yet indelible placement of Lonoff's art in a social and historical moment. This is the dimension of Lonoff's fiction that Zuckerman, reading modernism according to his New Critical instructors or, in Harold Bloom's terms, "misprisioning" it in order to make room for his own originality, has apparently overlooked until now. That this historical center takes the form of the Jew is an obvious yet painful irony, for the Jew became for many of the high Modernists a prominent image of what it was that Modernism needed to expunge. The Jew was the crudeness that blocked the refined sensibility, the deracinated being that threatened a purer folk consciousness, the middle-class materialist blind to the deeper values of spirit and culture – in his most extreme guises, both the Bolshevik revolutionary and the capitalist oppressor.

In reading a Jewish center into Lonoff's fiction, Zuckerman borrows or creates – most important, is unable to escape from – the image of the Jew, whatever his violent objections to his father's prescriptions for its fictional representation. In "Femme Fatale" it takes the form of the Jewish writer whose fate is always to have to confront the threat of silence: the risk of becoming, literally, a "nobody from nowhere." Zuckerman impersonates the Jewish writer, Anne Frank, who writes her private diary in and of silence, made tragically resonant by the silence that will eventually consume her. He impersonates her through Amy Bellette, herself possibly a Jewish writer who is either pretending to be the ghost writer of Anne Frank or is Anne Frank herself, determined to remain a ghost. In either case she has nothing more to write, and will be known as "Anne Frank" only to Lonoff, to whom she reveals her identity. Both Anne and Amy, however, become the fictional guises through which Zuckerman breaks out of the writing block – the threat of silence – that he experiences in the chapter "Nathan Dedalus."

In that chapter he has been unable to complete a letter to his father, who has urged him not to publish his latest story, and he refuses to write a letter to Judge Wapter, who also opposes publication. Moreover, he finds himself imaginatively blocked by the extraordinary scene between Lonoff and Amy Bellette that has just occurred in the room above him: "if only I could have imagined the scene I'd overheard! . . . If one day I could just *approach* the originality and excitement of what actually goes on!" (121). In defiance of all these barriers to writing, Zuckerman turns, in a burst of bizarre impersonation, to Anne Frank, the writer who made a book both in, and of, incarceration.

The Jew silenced is what Jewish writers make words of in *The Ghost Writer*, whether the writer be Lonoff, Anne Frank, Amy Bellette, or Zuckerman. The common theme, the common protagonist, serve to deliver the Modernist from the charge of indifference to history and the postmodernist from the charge of exploiting it. In an act of appropriation and an acknowledgment of dependency, the Rothian postmodern contrives in and from silence the semblance of a "master narrative" that, however fragile, however grotesquely it combines offense and pathos, centers the novel and the entire trilogy: an "impersonation" of the destruction of European Jewry. Taking his place in the chain of blocked voices, despite his insistence, echoing Anne Frank, that "I am on my own!" (109), Zuckerman inherits his calling and revivifies it, explodes the story of silences into a verbal flood of impersonation, yet clings to its origin: the somebody from somewhere, the murdered girl who continues to ghost-write them all.

Zuckerman Unbound

In the second novel of the trilogy Nathan Zuckerman, now the infamous author of the scandalous bestseller, *Carnovsky* – comparable in its family focus and its raucous sexuality to Philip Roth's *Portnoy's Complaint* – abandons the sacred and secluded site of the making of art and plunges into a world teeming with creativity. As "the great Durante" put it, "Everybody wants to get into the act!" The death of a mobster is the occasion of a lavish, dignitary-studded funeral; the vanished East European Jewish ghetto is reborn in the sentimentalized Broadway smash, *Fiddler on the Roof*; a big-pay-off quiz show is fixed for dramatic effect, its producers justifying corruption as integral to the creative process: "art is *controlled*, art is *managed*, art is *always* rigged. That is how it takes hold of the human heart."[6]

For Zuckerman the spread of creativity takes the form of the reader replacing the writer, the consumption of fiction superseding its production. Unlike *The Ghost Writer*, *Zuckerman Unbound* is not about how a book comes to be, but about what happens to a book in the world, how the responses to that book become a mirror of its creative mode and a fertile provocation that generates the next fiction. Consumption, that is, shifts from its dependency on production to its inspiration.

The richest example in the novel of the interdependency of reading and writing, of impersonation as the method of both, is the relationship between Zuckerman and Alvin Pepler, who as a contestant on the quiz show, *Smart Money*, was compelled, in the interests of "art," to lose to Hewlett Lincoln. Pepler has found in *Carnovsky* a representative account of his local background – "you have pinned down for all time growing up in that town [Newark] as a Jew"(*Zuckerman Unbound*, 14) – and in the writer Zuckerman a pointed image of himself: "in many ways that book is the story of my life no less than yours" (148).

They begin as genial opposites, the admiring fan and the celebrated author who happen to be from different parts of the same city. Pepler is the Jew who grew up "at the decaying heart of the old industrial city" (14) and joined the Marines in 1943, while Zuckerman lived in the newer residential area and went to college in 1949. But their differences soon shade into similarities, so that Pepler's claim of identity with Zuckerman has a validity the latter is hard put to deny. In fact he is in the process of retroactively confirming it as he begins jotting down Peplerian material: "Zuckerman found a fresh composition book and . . . began to record what he could still recall of the previous day's business. Because this *was* his business: not buying and selling, but seeing and believing . . . He wrote steadily for over an hour, every irate word of Pepler's deposition" (119). In the midst of his incessant claims that his proper place is in the study, surrounded by books, rather than in the streets being accosted by strangers, Zuckerman has been inspired by one such stranger to begin his next novel.

Pepler is a man of extraordinary memory, an inventor of wild scenarios, a pariah among the Jews of the broadcasting world, a would-be writer – in each case a sort of *Zuckermenshele*, a miniature version of the man he regards, along with Stephen Crane, as one of Newark's two greatest writers. "I wouldn't dream," Pepler says, "of comparing the two of us. An educated artist like yourself and a person who happens to be born with a photographic memory are two different things entirely" (19). And yet ultimately, of course, Pepler not only compares himself with Zuckerman but, far more audaciously, declares that Zuckerman has usurped his life, has "impersonated" him in creating the character of Carnovsky.

Zuckerman's final encounter with Pepler precipitates their most candid claims as to the nature of the fiction they equally, if opposingly, serve. Pepler insists on transforming a book back into the life that the writer's talent, the source of what Zuckerman calls the "art of depiction," has convinced him is his. Following Zuckerman's negative response to his draft of a review of *Carnovsky*, Pepler blurts out: "you only wrote that book because you could! Because of having every break in life there is! . . . those hang-ups you wrote about happen to be mine, and . . . you knew it . . . you stole it!" (155).

Zuckerman, in complete contrast, wishes to transform the life he lives – with family, lovers, readers – into a book whose art of depiction so combines impersonation and detachment as to release him from its origins. What Pepler wants to repossess, now that the action of art has fully revealed it to him, Zuckerman is ready to abandon, in his search for new life to impersonate, new impersonations to depict. As Laura has said, or rather as Zuckerman impersonates her into saying, "*having written a book like that, you had to go. That's what writing it was all about*" (162).

Fleeing to the safety of a funeral parlor from a man whose impersonation of *him* he regards as insane – "*The man is mad. . . . He thinks he's me*" (149) – Zuckerman nevertheless at once resumes writing feverishly about him. Now, more than jotting down Pepler's lines, Zuckerman also begins to theorize the dynamic of their secret sharing. The enduring difference between himself and Pepler is Zuckerman's ability to see and recreate their relationship as impersonation that maintains its dual identity. Zuckerman knows that *for the writing* he must be Pepler *and* himself: he must record that "maniacal memory," but shaped by his own "maniacal desire for comprehension"; document that "file cabinet" of a mind, but with "detachment"; recognize, with a kind of awe, this higher exponent of a familiar passion – "The brute strength, the crazy tenacity, the desperate hunger" (159) – but tamed by a talent whose essential quality is the skill of the impersonative mode itself. His impulsive note-taking, even while hiding from a man he believes may be ready, à la Oswald, to kill him, is the beginning of the movement toward the "re-binding" of Zuckerman: his withdrawal from the world precisely in order to reimagine it as a fiction in which Alvin Pepler will become – as he is in this novel – the vividly conceived other of Nathan Zuckerman.

The gains and losses of writer and reader who find themselves so deeply joined in fictional representation are comparably great. Pepler gains his life, but with the painful evidence of his inability to articulate it, his dependency on Zuckerman to impersonate him. Possessed of the "unstoppable energy, the flypaper brain," but with a memory that "coheres around nothing," Pepler lacks the talent to imagine his own reality: "It's the talentlessness that's driving him nuts" (159). Zuckerman's talent, however, must lead him inevitably to the loss of whatever life he has chosen to make use of, his own and the lives of those around him.

This loss of the now written life drives the novel to its major theme. Despite the inspiration to fresh writing provided by the astonishing Pepler, the chief effect of publication in *Zuckerman Unbound* is to silence the writer, essentially by removing the book from his sovereignty. Readers claim the work as their own, reversing the writer's impersonation of the real into a mask of himself into their appropriation of that mask into versions of themselves. A book transforms, as the actress Caesara O'Shea puts it, into "'Everything that says 'me'" (92). As for the original reality, Zuckerman is now unbound from it: origin has disappeared into its fiction.

The last section of the novel, "Look Homeward, Angel," describes the process of unbinding. For his final words to his dying father Zuckerman delivers a characteristically ambiguous speech. On the one hand, it is one more piece of information he thinks his father requires – "Last chance to tell the man what he still doesn't know" (187) – this time on the creation and future prospects of the universe. On the other hand, it is an improbable reading of those phenomena – "the chances for no ending didn't look good" (192) – calculated to soothe the father (and himself) into the delusion that life is eternal, that what is happening here, to both of them, is not the definitive end of something but another phase of the world's continuing pattern of contraction and explosion: "A universe being reborn and reborn and reborn, without end" (192). Purveyor of arcane facts, novelist of fictional cosmic symmetry, Zuckerman is maintaining the dual stance of a lifetime, only to hear his father respond – cryptically? pointedly? – "Bastard" (193).

The epithet is apt. For both father and son now know the self-declared illegitimacy of the son, a verdict Zuckerman's younger brother Henry will later make harshly explicit. These are the wages of *Carnovsky*, as Zuckerman knew they must be. Books, as Henry angrily insists, as it is the whole point of *Zuckerman Unbound* to demonstrate, have "*real consequences*": "he knew, he knew, he knew, he'd known it all along . . . He'd known when he was writing the book. But he'd written it anyway" (217–18). One might almost say he not only knew but hoped. For even as Zuckerman-as-son struggles to reread his father's last utterance into "faster" or "vaster" or "better," Zuckerman-as-novelist prefers the more striking option: "'Bastard' was the writer's wishful thinking, if not quite the son's. Better scene, stronger medicine, a final repudiation by Father" (200). Writing the real is the growing distance from it. Laura, Pepler, Zuckerman's family recede from him like discarded worksheets: "You are no longer any man's son, you are no longer some good woman's husband, you are no longer your brother's brother, and you don't come from anywhere anymore, either" (224–25).

Like *The Ghost Writer*, *Zuckerman Unbound*, for all its exuberant comedy, grounds itself in death and silence, narrowed once more to a historical particular, the silencing of Jews. The most vivid image of the Jew silenced is not the writer but the reader, Alvin Pepler. Initially as a quiz show contestant, when he was forced to lose to Hewlett Lincoln: "To break the bank you had to be a goy like Hewlett. The bigger the goy the bigger the haul. This is on programs *run* by Jews" (35). Then as the writer manqué trying to publish the story of his victimization, which has been rejected twenty-two times. Finally as the self-appointed reviewer of *Carnovsky*, resoundingly put down by none other than Zuckerman himself.

Each member of the immediate Zuckerman family participates in what appear to be no more and no less than the inevitable silences of ordinary life. Victor Zuckerman's letters to President Johnson arguing against the Vietnam War, a correspondence "nearly as fat as *War and Peace*" (177), have elicited not a single reply – almost as if they had never been written; Selma Zuckerman receives elaborate coaching from her son Nathan on how *not* to respond to reporters' questions; and Nathan's brother Henry has systematically silenced himself, foregoing a career in theater in deference to his father's wishes, enduring first an engagement and then a marriage he wishes futilely to dissolve. In these almost incidental examples the theme of the proscribed voice achieves a cumulative power, completing itself in the larger story of Zuckerman, silenced, ironically, by his impassioned readers, who impersonate the writer's book beyond his own imposed boundaries, deprive his words of their intended meaning, make the book say more and other than he wishes it to say. From the obsessive, meticulous, remorselessly disciplined act of writing comes a book whose publication releases it to its readers' unappeasable rage for possession: "A book, a piece of fiction bound between two covers, breeding living fiction exempt from all the subjugations of the page, breeding fiction unwritten, unreadable, unaccountable and uncontainable" (198).

In this new fiction no longer his, Zuckerman is left without an impersonation in which to "be": "he's most himself by simultaneously being someone else, neither of whom he 'is' once the curtain is down" (*Reading Myself and Others*, 144). The curtain is now down; the performance belongs to its audience. At the end of the novel, sitting in his chauffeured limousine, protected from the world by an armed driver, Zuckerman is accosted once more, this time by a young black man who now lives on the street Nathan Zuckerman once walked on his way to school:

> "Who you supposed to be?" he said.
> "No one," replied Zuckerman, and that was the end of that.
>
> (*Zuckerman Unbound*, 224)

The Anatomy Lesson

From its focus on first the creation, then the reception of words, the *Zuckerman Bound* trilogy descends in *The Anatomy Lesson* to the body, the "mindless matter" on which everything depends.[7] But not just to the body; rather to that order of body when it blocks out all that is not body: the body in pain, where art, cultures high and low, language itself give way before the onslaught of physical suffering.

In July of 1972, three years after the publication of *Carnovsky*, which may have helped precipitate Zuckerman's father's fatal heart attack, and a year and a half after the death of his mother, Zuckerman finds himself experiencing severe upper back, shoulder, and neck pains. So severe is the pain that not only is he unable to write, he cannot do anything except indulge in the drugs, drink, and sex that will either reduce or make momentarily bearable his suffering. Paramount is the pure "selfness of pain" (*The Anatomy Lesson*, 10), pain driving out all but the sentience of it, the self's private and inexpressible feeling: "Had he kept a pain diary, the only entry would have been one word: Myself" (232).

Not a sign of something deeper, some psychic if not somatic cause that converts pain into symptom, dilutes pain by dividing it between signifier and signified, Zuckerman's pain is simply itself. "Too elementary for understanding" (23), it is the enemy of language. Elaine Scarry writes, "Physical pain does not simply resist language but actively destroys it, bringing about an immediate reversion to a state anterior to language, to the sounds and cries a human being makes before language is learned"; "[it] has no referential content. It is not *of* or *for* anything."[8]

Locked in this self-filled state of pain, Zuckerman no longer has the need for impersonation, that tension of self and other that is the creative core of his fiction – and that is also the route to any authentic understanding of himself:

> If he wasn't cultivating hypothetical Zuckermans he really had no more means than a fire hydrant to decipher his existence. But either there was no existence left to decipher or he was without sufficient imaginative power to convert into his fiction of seeming self-exposure what existence had now become. There was no rhetorical overlay left: he was bound and gagged by the real raw thing, ground down to his own unhypothetical nub. He could no longer pretend to be anyone else, and as a medium for his books he had ceased to be.
>
> (*The Anatomy Lesson*, 149)

No longer able to fantasize otherness, Zuckerman allows himself the privilege of unrestrained sensual pleasure – his fourfold harem of obliging women, an ample supply of Percodan and vodka – as the entitlement of pain: "to what end? To *no* end? To the end of ends? To escape completely the clutches of self-justification? To learn to lead a wholly indefensible, unjustified life – and to learn to like it?" (37–38).

But Nathan Zuckerman will not rest comfortably in the unjustified life; rather, he will pursue the body's own discipline. He decides, at the age of forty, to go to medical school, giving up the art of doubleness for the art of the resolutely singular: "The bilge, the ooze, the gooey drip. The stuff. No words, just stuff. Everything the word's in place of" (103). The physician listens all day to stories freed from ambiguous meaning: "stories intending to lead to a definite, useful, authoritative conclusion. Stories with a clear and practical purpose: *Cure me*" (109). Above all, he frees himself from the writer's incessant doubt; the physician "knows *how* to be right – how to be right *quickly*," and with the stakes always perfectly clear: "Life vs. Death. Health vs. Disease. Anesthesia vs. Pain" (202).

Zuckerman, however, always remains the writer, not so much despite but because of the threatening silences of censorship, of creative readers, and now of debilitating pain. His new silencer, who succeeds in arousing his passion for impersonation even beyond his physical pain, is the literary critic, Milton Appel, who has dismissed Zuckerman's entire oeuvre, *Carnovsky* as well as the previous fiction he had earlier praised. The self-assigned task of the critic, according to Zuckerman, is to practice the literary equivalent of the physician. What in the realm of bodily pain, however, is the single goal of relief becomes in the realm of language the refusal to acknowledge human or literary complexity and the impersonative mode that spans it. The task of the critic is to be right in and about a medium that does not allow it: "Right then, and now that he's changed his mind, right again" (92).

The mode of the novelist is not correctness but doubt and doubleness: not to know but to explore, not to come down on one side or another of an issue but to straddle the gap – the wider the better – between. As critic, Milton Appel exemplifies those people who, in Roth's terms, "hide the places where they're split" (*Reading Myself and Others*, 143), whereas Zuckerman, as novelist, must not only expose his divisions but reveal just how richly wedded they are. Essentially, this is what the novelist offers readers: the opportunity to engage in transformations of their own, recognizing in the novelist's impersonations their once unknown selves. For Zuckerman, the critic – at least Milton Appel – is the reader who refuses that recognition and resents most the writer who most insists on it.

Accused by Appel of fictional oversimplification of Jews rather than "social accuracy," and in *Carnovsky* of near anti-Semitic vulgarity in pursuit of an "audience" as opposed to "readers" (*The Anatomy Lesson*, 69), Zuckerman identifies an ambivalence in Appel as deep as his own: the tension between a Jewish immigrant father and a native-born son, between a desire to support the Jews and a contempt for their assimilationism and ignorant, mawkish nostalgia. For Zuckerman the split in Appel, repressed in his writing, compels him to "charge . . . you with his crime and castigate . . . himself in you" (78).

Debate, however, with its winners and losers, offers no consolation to Zuckerman, despite his fierce indulgence in it. Zuckerman's talent is not to debate Milton Appel, but to impersonate him. And so, without apparent premeditation, Zuckerman – while aboard the plane to Chicago in order to begin his medical studies – casually identifies himself to a fellow passenger as Milton Appel, editor of the pornographic magazine *Lickety Split*: "*everything's* in it" (181). The thrust of Zuckerman's parody is an Appel whose commercial vulgarity is also marked by "social accuracy" (exclusively concerning American sex habits) and literary integrity. *Lickety Split* is not a "mass-distribution publication because it's too dirty" (173); Appel shuns the hypocrisy of *Playboy*, which glosses porn with high culture. Unlike Hugh Hefner (and Zuckerman), Appel has chosen "readers" over "audience."

The upshot is that Zuckerman projects a Milton Appel who duplicates the sins of vulgarity of which he has accused the writer, redeems those sins by justifying them as a vehicle for serious social criticism, all the time revealing the whole enterprise – sin and redemption – as ridiculous since *Lickety Split* doesn't exist in the first place and would hardly warrant such heady appraisal if it did. Zuckerman confirms Appel's charges in this latest creation *and* refutes them: pornographer Appel serves the highest causes by pandering to the lowest desires.

For all of the hilarious enactment of impersonation, at once "subliterary shenanigan" and rich exemplum of Roth's metamorphic mode, *The Anatomy Lesson* remains true to its title. Neither fiction nor medicine, the vocation of doubt or of single-mindedness, can permanently resist the ultimate demands of the body. The final lesson of anatomy is death: "Illness is a message from the grave. Greetings: You and your body are one – it goes, you follow" (254). "Pain," Scarry writes, "is the equivalent in felt-experience of what is unfeelable in death. Each only happens because of the body. In each the contents of consciousness are destroyed . . .Regardless, then, of the context in which it occurs, physical pain always mimes death and the infliction of physical pain is always a mock execution" (*The Body in Pain*, 31).

Death is a presence throughout the *Zuckerman Bound* trilogy, especially so in this final volume: in Mr. Freytag's grief over the recent death of his wife, Julie, and in Zuckerman's recollection of his mother's death, which occurred eighteen months earlier. Memory of her comes to Zuckerman now as part of everything else that has abandoned him – his health and his subject – but chiefly as the body that is gone and that he cannot give up. In the immediate aftermath of her death, Zuckerman has sought her in the possible fragrance of hair still left in a silk hood, in her folded Kleenex, a stack of her hand-written knitting instructions, in a book in which she made a record of Zuckerman's earliest weeks, a page of which is stained with what he decides is a drop of her milk: "Closing his eyes, he put his tongue to the page" (*The Anatomy Lesson*, 65). More than anything else Zuckerman wants the reality of her body; there is no ritual of mourning, no words, that will overcome this loss.

Now, in the present, his own ceaseless physical pain is the relic of self, the guarantee of his identity upon the demise of vocation, and the reminder of annihilation. Pain recalls to him the death of that body that was both the source of his life and the unmistakable sign of its transience. But is the body all? Are its twin messages of birth and death the alpha and omega of existence? And if so, what is the value of writing? Is the writing of fiction, with its impersonation of the other into a mask of the self, anything more than subjectivity? And is it a legitimate route to those who have "disappeared into the enormity of death?" (45). For Zuckerman, writer not critic, these are questions to explore, not resolve. Subjectivity "is also dying like the body is dying, this remnant of her spirit is dying too" (229).

A few pages later Zuckerman, still arming himself against pain with Percodan and vodka, goes with Mr. Freytag to the cemetery to visit his wife's freshly dug grave. Zuckerman, surrounded by the Jewish dead, begins raving madly at the silencing whose source is the buried fathers: "*We* are the dead! These bones in boxes are the Jewish living! These are the people running the show!" (262) – following which he falls face forward on a headstone, cracking open his chin and breaking his teeth.

The novel concludes with Zuckerman in the hospital, his former pain of neck, back, and shoulders rendered negligible by the pain of his mouth: "at long last he found out just what pain could really do. He'd had no idea" (276). The site of sound, of language, Zuckerman's mouth is wired shut – total silence – as the difficulty of being a writer now comes down to its crudest bodily manifestation short of death itself. "[H]e himself had become his mouth . . . In that hole was his being" (266).

Eventually, in the course of convalescence, he makes rounds with the interns, seeing case after case of dreadful illness, hearing doctors' confident prognoses, still believing that "he could unchain himself from a future as a man apart and escape the corpus that was his" (291). The concluding pun keeps intact Zuckerman's coexistent, unreconciled poles: without the body there will be no books; but without the books there is no reason for him to be a body: "The burden isn't that everything has to be a book. It's that everything *can* be a book. And doesn't count as life until it is" (281).

Shadowing all, darkest in *The Anatomy Lesson*, remains the trilogy's constant threat of silence: from the condemning critic, the ancestors, the writer's fear that he has nothing more to say, climaxed by the inevitable prospect of the body in pain and eventual death. Again that silence grounds itself in a specific Jewish history. As a test of cognition following an apparent stroke, Zuckerman's mother had been asked by her doctor to write her name: "instead of 'Selma' [she] wrote the word 'Holocaust,' perfectly spelled . . . Zuckerman was pretty sure that before that morning she'd never even spoken that word aloud" (41). Zuckerman takes the piece of paper and keeps it, a single written word, transforming her death by brain tumor in a Miami hospital into the mass executions in Europe thirty years earlier.

A year and a half and two hundred pages later, the referent reappears: improbable yet not really surprising, like a nameless anxiety that, almost in relief, one finally puts an image to. As Zuckerman, Freytag, and the chauffeur Ricky approach the cemetery, "across the road, beyond a high black fence of iron palings, the gravestones began, miles and miles of treeless cemetery, ending at the far horizon in a large boxlike structure that was probably nothing but a factory, but that smoking foully away through the gray of the storm looked like something far worse" (257–58).

The Prague Orgy

In the epilogue to *Zuckerman Bound* the silences imposed by angry fathers, creative readers, and chronic back pain assume the horrific shape of the police state: 1976 Soviet-occupied Prague, thirty-one years after the end of its occupation by the Nazis – in both eras far removed from the world of Nathan Zuckerman, American-Jewish comic novelist. In Prague the risk of breaking silence is a jail sentence or worse; impersonation is not a strategy of fiction, a rhetorical projection of oneself into one's "vividly transforming heroes" (*Reading Myself and Others*, 170), but the writer's literal transformation into a janitor, a street-cleaner, or an emigré in America. Zuckerman fantasizes a Kafkaesque fate that would be neither symbolic nor surreal: "*As Nathan Zuckerman awoke one morning from uneasy dreams he found himself transformed in his bed into a sweeper of floors in a railway café.*" In the face of brutally imposed censorship, the only free expression, the only resistance, however desperate and ultimately futile, is obscenity and sex: "You think to sign a petition will save Czechoslovakia, *but what will save Czechoslovakia would be to fuck Olga* . . . [It] is all we have left that they cannot stop."[9]

Zuckerman's mission in Prague is to recover the unpublished Yiddish stories of a deceased Czech writer. Given the political situation, the mission is doomed from the outset. Fifteen minutes after he has finally acquired the stories from the above-mentioned Olga, they are confiscated by the police. Knowing no Yiddish, Zuckerman has not even been able to read them, and he is quickly expelled from the country as a Zionist agent. Nevertheless, he has touched the core of his connection to the current situation and to the tragic history that precedes him. In the course of his wandering through Prague, he is reminded of a childhood fantasy, a city he imagined as the "homeland" of the Jews for which he once solicited contributions door to door. Suffering in 1976 under the silence imposed by the Soviets, Prague becomes the embodiment of that "homeland," whose deterioration, whose uninhabitability he pictured as the secret joke of its survival, "a used city, a broken city," a city only Jews could value as the site for their "endless stories" – not knowing in 1942 that even this vision is impossible, its prospective citizens already in the process of annihilation.

What you smell are centuries and what you hear are voices and what you see are Jews, wild with lament and rippling with amusement, their voices tremulous with rancor and vibrating with pain, a choral society proclaiming vehemently, "Do you believe it? Can you imagine it?" even as they affirm with every wizardly trick in the book by a thousand acoustical fluctuations of tempo, tone, inflection, and pitch, "Yet this is exactly what happened!" That such things can happen – there's the moral of the stories – that such things happen to me, to him, to her, to you, to us. That is the national anthem of the Jewish homeland.

(*The Prague Orgy*, 63–64)

The significance of the loss of the stories is that "Another Jewish writer who might have been is not going to be" (84). That grimly familiar sentence resonates through the whole of *Zuckerman Bound*. "The difficulties of telling a Jewish story," Roth has said, "was finally to become *The Ghost Writer's* theme" (*Reading Myself and Others*, 166), ultimately pointing to the supreme difficulty: that no one will be left alive to write it.

The tens of thousands of words of the trilogy are a vast memorial of silence, as Nathan Zuckerman impersonates himself into history, links himself with the victimized, the muted, the dead as the vehicle for his voice, writes on and on, of and as the nightmare of his own potential silence. As remote as anyone can be from the primal event itself, Zuckerman knows first-hand the writing and silence that are the twin terms, the metamorphic dynamic, of his profession. He is the center of a trilogy of novels about that tension, establishing it as the condition of every writer, of all writing, seizing it as his only means of taking hold of what he cannot, yet must, understand. Born and raised in New Jersey, educated in Chicago, and made a millionaire in New York, Zuckerman assumes the roles of silenced Jewry: from the writer born in Frankfurt, raised in Amsterdam, and murdered at Belsen, to the quiz-show contestant forced out for the sake of the genteel gentile, to the "correct" critic whose attempted silencing of the writer is the outrage of his own guilt, to the dead Czech Jew whose Yiddish stories will never be read. They all become part of the masquerade of Zuckerman, who gives them a voice through the continual reinvention of himself: "most himself by simultaneously being someone else" (*Reading Myself and Others*, 144).

That Nathan Zuckerman should become the writer of the Holocaust must strike us as a fictional tactic as unseemly as anything else in Roth, who has never hesitated to shock his readers, particularly the Jews. And yet this is the underlying thrust of *Zuckerman Bound*, proposed by Roth in an interview shortly before the publication of the trilogy as a single volume. Commenting on the incident in *The Anatomy Lesson* in which Zuckerman's mother writes the word "Holocaust" instead of her name, Roth identifies that historical moment as the indispensable word of the trilogy:

Without this word there would be no Nathan Zuckerman, not in Zuckerman's fix. No chiropodist father and his deathbed curse, no dentist brother with his ferocious chastisement. There'd of course be no Amy Bellette, the young woman in *The Ghost Writer* who he likes to think could have been Anne Frank. There'd be no Milton Appel with his moral ordinances and literary imperatives. And Zuckerman wouldn't be in his cage. If you take away that word – and with it the fact – none of these Zuckerman books would exist.

(Reading Myself and Others, 136)

Roth quickly qualifies his statement, as if restoring a decorum that even he will not violate: "No, no, of course not" – the subject of *Zuckerman Bound* is not the Holocaust. In much the same way, however, that Rothian characters are simultaneously themselves and others, living their lives on the dual planes of surface and shadow, the subject *is* the Holocaust. This is the powerful yet ghostly force that darkly imbues a trilogy of novels about comic writing in America, a metamorphic fiction for our time:

it is simply there, hidden, submerged, emerging, disappearing, unforgotten. You don't make use of it – it makes use of you. It certainly makes use of Zuckerman. There is a certain thematic architecture to these three books that I hope will make itself felt when they're published in one volume . . . [T]he little piece of paper in Zuckerman's wallet might not seem quite so small.

(Reading Myself and Others, 136–37)

NOTES

1 Philip Roth, *Reading Myself and Others* (New York: Penguin Books, 1985), p. 162.
2 Frank Kermode, *Romantic Image* (New York: Vintage, 1964), p. 2.
3 Philip Roth, *The Ghost Writer* (New York: Farrar, Straus and Giroux, 1979), p. 40.
4 Philip Roth, *The Facts: A Novelist's Autobiography* (New York: Farrar, Straus and Giroux, 1988), p. 6.
5 See my essay, "Fictions of Metamorphosis: From *Goodbye Columbus* to *Portnoy's Complaint*," in *Reading Philip Roth*, eds. Asher Z. Milbauer and Donald G. Watson (London: Macmillan, 1988), pp. 82–104.
6 Philip Roth, *Zuckerman Unbound* (New York: Farrar, Straus and Giroux, 1981), p. 38.
7 Philip Roth, *The Anatomy Lesson* (New York: Farrar, Straus and Giroux, 1983), p. 238.
8 Elaine Scarry, *The Body in Pain: The Making and Unmaking of the World* (Oxford: Oxford University Press, 1985), pp. 4–5.
9 Philip Roth, *The Prague Orgy* (New York: Farrar, Straus and Giroux, 1996), pp. 80, 37, 73.

4

MICHAEL ROTHBERG

Roth and the Holocaust

For most reflective American Jews, I would think, it is simply there, hidden,
submerged, emerging, disappearing, unforgotten. You don't make use of it –
it makes use of you.[1]

The Holocaust, American-style

In Philip Roth's 1983 novel *The Anatomy Lesson*, the mother of Nathan
Zuckerman, Roth's alter ego, develops a brain tumor. Admitted into the
hospital for the second time, Zuckerman's mother

> was able to recognize her neurologist when he came by the room, but when
> he asked if she would write her name for him on a piece of paper, she took
> the pen from his hand and instead of "Selma" wrote the word "Holocaust,"
> perfectly spelled. This was in Miami Beach in 1970, inscribed by a woman
> whose writings otherwise consisted of recipes on index cards, several thousand
> thank-you notes, and a voluminous file of knitting instructions. Zuckerman
> was pretty sure that before that morning she'd never even spoken the word
> aloud.[2]

In succinct, enigmatic fashion, this passage captures the complex form that
memory of the Holocaust has taken in American life and in Roth's work.
The carefully situated mother's death – in Miami Beach in 1970 – testifies
to the belated and displaced effect of the European catastrophe on Jewish-
American identity. Alternately "disappearing" from and "emerging" into
Jewish-American consciousness, as Roth once remarked in an interview,
Holocaust memory has a history that Roth's fiction both reflects and anato-
mizes.

Although the Holocaust is present as either a "submerged" or concrete
presence in the early, middle, and late stages of Roth's work, from *Goodbye,
Columbus* (1959), by way of *The Ghost Writer* (1979), to *Operation Shylock* (1993) and *The Plot Against America* (2004), that does not necessarily
mean that it is a constant presence or that critics have always considered that
presence an important component of his work. As Steven Milowitz points
out, books on Roth published before 1990 rarely treated the Holocaust at
all. This critical climate has begun to change, however, especially since the

publication of *Operation Shylock*, Roth's most sustained and direct engagement to date with the Nazi genocide and its implications.[3] Milowitz himself is dedicated to revealing a more fundamental relation between Roth's writing and the Holocaust. He argues that "the issue of the Holocaust and its impact on twentieth-century American life" is "a central obsessional issue" for Roth, and that "any reading of Roth's oeuvre that ignores his primary impetus cannot truly locate Roth's place in American letters."[4] Milowitz overstates the case and misses the paradoxical status of Holocaust in Roth's work.

In this essay, I argue that it is less the Holocaust and its impact on American life that obsesses Roth than the unbridgeable distance between the Holocaust and American life – and the inauthenticity of most attempts to lessen that distance. Such an observation does not mean that Roth minimizes or relativizes the significance of the Holocaust. To the contrary, he has been, as Milowitz suggests, one of the earliest and most articulate writers to address the genocide's devastating singularity. But its singularity is precisely not American. To use a term inspired by Roth, the Holocaust is something like the "counter-history" of American life. Emphasizing the Holocaust's distance rather than its overwhelming proximity leads to a formulation of the central paradox of Roth's quite original perspective on the Shoah: the greater the significance accorded to the Holocaust as an event of modern history, the more distant a role it plays in the lives of American Jews.

To understand why Roth's approach to the Nazi genocide takes such a paradoxical form requires situating his oeuvre in the postwar American culture of the Holocaust. Most critical work on Roth has failed to historicize his responses to the Holocaust, and yet his works are inevitably in dialogue with the larger context and changing patterns of Holocaust reception in the United States (as the passage from *The Anatomy Lesson* already suggests). Indeed, Roth's life and work correspond in fascinating ways with the narrative of the Holocaust's reception in the United States that can be found in Peter Novick's authoritative history *The Holocaust in American Life*.[5] Roth happened to be born in 1933, the year that Hitler took power in Germany. He published his first book, which includes subtle explorations of the legacies of World War II, in 1959, a year in which the transition of the Holocaust from a seldom openly discussed topic into a public matter is marked by the release of the first Anne Frank movie. Two years later, the Eichmann trial in Jerusalem would be an epochal turning point, leading to the rise of survivor testimony and the use of "Holocaust" as the proper name for the events of the genocide. Roth's next significant literary grappling with the Holocaust, the publication of *The Ghost Writer* in 1979, takes place in the immediate shadow of the 1978 television mini-series *Holocaust*, which marks the entry of the Shoah into mainstream American popular culture.[6] Finally, his major Holocaust novel, *Operation Shylock* was published in 1993, a year that ABC's late-night news show *Nightline* dubbed "The Year of the Holocaust" because of the opening of *Schindler's List* and the United States Holocaust Memorial Museum and the sense that genocide was re-emerging in Europe with the Yugoslavian wars.[7] Written during the first Palestinian intifada, *Operation Shylock* also addresses head-on the convergence of Holocaust memory, American identity politics, and the Middle Eastern conflict – a convergence that had been brewing since the Israeli–Arab wars of 1967 and 1973.[8]

Although partly accidental, this series of parallels between Roth's career and the career of Holocaust memory in the United States helps to illuminate both Roth's oeuvre and the contexts out of which it has emerged.[9] Paying attention to the responses of writers such as Roth can offset one of the significant shortcomings of Novick's *The Holocaust in American Life* – its almost complete lack of discussion of literary and artistic responses to the genocide. On the one hand, Roth's work could be seen as confirming Novick's controversial thesis that the Holocaust has become central to American Jews because it guarantees them a winning hand in the game of ethnic competition over victim status. On the other hand, the fact that Roth (among others) has consistently satirized such identity politics, while still recognizing the enormity of the event itself, suggests that the terrain of American Holocaust memory is not as monolithic as Novick would have it. In each of his significant Holocaust writings, Roth responds to and rewrites the stages of Jewish consciousness that Novick identifies.

Displaced persons: Roth's early fiction

Roth achieved early celebrity when his first book, *Goodbye, Columbus*, won the National Book Award. While the title story of the collection consists of a lampooning of the suburbanization and "whitening" of American Jews during the increasingly prosperous 1950s, two of the other stories confront, albeit in somewhat indirect fashion, the catastrophe of European Jews. As is fitting for the period, the word "Holocaust" is never mentioned. Nevertheless, Roth demonstrates an early understanding of the significance of the Nazi genocide as a caesura between worlds.[10] These worlds are not primarily divided historically, however, but geographically and culturally. That is, while much discussion of the Holocaust focuses on the very different meanings of life "before" and "after Auschwitz," Roth focuses, as he will throughout his oeuvre, especially on the division between European and American experiences.

"Eli, the Fanatic" demonstrates clearly the dualistic approach that echoes throughout Roth's Holocaust writing. While written at one moment of transition for Holocaust memory, the story is set at another transitional moment – in the immediate aftermath of the war, when American Jews were rapidly integrating themselves into mainstream gentile culture. In "Eli," the Jewish residents of Woodenton, a New York suburb, find themselves confronted with the uncanny presence of displaced persons: eighteen Jewish orphans from Europe and the two Orthodox Jewish men who have established a yeshiva for them. The story is focalized through the perspective of Eli Peck, a lawyer with a history of nervous breakdowns who has been sent to dispense with the yeshiva before the town's Christian residents are moved to an anti-Semitic backlash against their newly suburbanized neighbors. Especially unsettling for the anxious Jewish-Americans is the sight of one of the "greenhorns" in particular, who strolls around town in the traditional attire of Hasidic Eastern Jews. As Eli approaches the man, hoping to find a "more reasonable" interlocutor than the school's stubborn director has proven to be, he is instead taken aback:

> He was stopped by the sight of the black coat that fell down below the man's knees, and the hands which held each other in his lap. By the round-topped, wide-brimmed Talmudic hat, pushed onto the back of his head. And by the beard, which hid his neck . . . He was asleep, his sidelocks curled loose on his cheeks. His face was no older than Eli's.[11]

Narrated from the perspective of an assimilated Jew, this passage evokes a sense both of the extreme otherness of the traditional, religious Jew and, in the last line, of the danger of identification with otherness that haunts Eli. And indeed, after deciding that the solution to the town's problems would be the simple updating of the immigrants' dress, Eli ends up "becoming" the Hasid: he dons the black suit and hat himself and parades around town like a "fanatic" in front of his neighbors and wife.

The difference between secular, modern Jews and *Ostjuden*, with their supposedly out-of-date habits, is a stock trope of "Enlightened" Jewish discourse both in Europe and the United States. But Roth is not simply repeating stereotypes here: instead, he makes the reader aware of how different that discourse sounds after the Nazis have all but eliminated both modern and traditional Jewish cultures from their homelands in Europe. When Eli proposes to the school head Tzuref that the Hasid could wear a new suit, Tzuref replies, "That's all he's got." Eli, assuming that the problem is a simple matter of poverty, proposes replacing the suit, but is rebuffed again:

"But I tell you he has nothing. *Nothing.* You have that word in English? *Nicht?*
Gornisht? . . . A mother and a father?" Tzuref said. "No. A wife? No. A baby? A
little ten-month-old baby? No! A village full of friends? A synagogue where you
knew the feel of every seat under your pants? . . . And a medical experiment they
performed on him yet! That leaves nothing, Mr. Peck. Absolutely nothing! . . .
No news reached Woodenton?"   (*Goodbye, Columbus*, 191)

In this passage, the traditional attire of the Hasid becomes a material index of
genocide, a remnant that by its very displaced nature suggests the entire context or lifeworld that has been destroyed in the Holocaust. The destruction
Tzuref evokes contrasts directly with Eli's evocation of his own town: "What
peace. What incredible peace. Have children ever been so safe in their beds?
Parents – Eli wondered – so full in their stomachs? . . . No wonder then they
would keep things just as they were. Here, after all, were peace and safety –
what civilization had been working toward for centuries" (202). While the
residents of Woodenton are aware of the catastrophe that has occurred in
Europe, they refuse to let it threaten their well-being and progressive world-
view. As Tzuref's ironic final question indicates, the distinction between the
yeshiva's displaced persons and the Jews of Woodenton is not one of information – the news has indeed reached Woodenton – but one of knowledge
and understanding.

In "Eli, the Fanatic," Roth describes a moment when, for American Jews,
knowledge of the fact of the Nazi genocide has not yet become consciousness of the rupture the Holocaust would soon represent. But the proximity
of the yeshiva to the town and Eli's deluded attempt to take over the identity of the Hasidic man also prophetically suggest that that consciousness is
about to erupt and that, when it does, the results will sometimes be troubling. While "Eli" primarily concerns the failure to acknowledge Jewish
suffering (even by other Jews), "Defender of the Faith," the other story from
Goodbye, Columbus in which the Holocaust makes itself felt, begins Roth's
exploration of the potential for the exploitation of Jewish suffering. Like
"Eli," this story also concerns intra-Jewish conflict, this time between two
Jewish soldiers during the last months of World War II when Nazi Germany
has been defeated but the Pacific war remains in its last throes. Sergeant
Nathan Marx has finished "racing across Germany" to defeat the Nazis,
and has now returned to the United States in order to oversee a group of
trainees (*Goodbye, Columbus*, 116). Among them is a trio of young Jews,
one of whom, Sheldon Grossbart, is determined to exploit ethnic solidarity
to extort favors from Nathan. While apparently straightforward, the story –
which garnered great controversy among those who read it as the product of
Jewish "self-hatred" – treats moral and ethical dilemmas with great subtlety.

Nathan finds himself in a situation without easy answers, caught between the clearly disagreeable Grossbart and a dawning recognition of the real, if relatively benign, anti-Semitism of his Christian commanding officer and of the US Army in general. Furthermore, the events take place against the backdrop of Nathan's struggles to formulate a sense of self in relation to ethnic ties, national identity, and an inchoate sense of the scale of the European catastrophe.

Grossbart's professed desire to celebrate the Sabbath, which later proves to have been insincere, provokes a telling Proustian reflection in Nathan:

> I indulged myself in a reverie so strong that I felt as though a hand were reaching down inside me. It had to reach so very far to touch me! It had to reach past those days in the forests of Belgium, and past the dying I'd refused to weep over; past the nights in German farmhouses whose books we'd burned to warm us; past endless stretches where I had shut off all softness I might feel for my fellows, and had managed even to deny myself the posture of a conqueror – the swagger that I, as a Jew, might well have worn as my boots whacked against the rubble of Wesel, Münster, and Braunschweig.
>
> But now one night noise, one rumor of home and time past, and memory plunged down through all I had anesthetized, and came to what I suddenly remembered was myself. (122)

This passage ingeniously suggests both the force of Nathan's experience in the war and the degree to which it remains unprocessed. The burning of German books that Nathan reports can only echo ironically the auto-da-fés of the Nazi era and, seemingly without Nathan's awareness, hint at the burning of flesh that is nowhere directly evoked in the story. While Nathan recognizes the extent of hardening that was required in order to avoid confrontation with the horrors of the war, both what is said and what is not said imply that a more complete confrontation lies somewhere in the future. The self Nathan remembers will not ultimately be the same as the one he reconstructs after the war. The story suggests that consciousness of the extremes of the Holocaust would only emerge belatedly for American Jews and, more generally, for Europeans and Americans who did not experience the war or witness the genocide directly. What probably made the story so disturbing for some members of the Jewish community was the supplementary, anticipatory suggestion, incarnated in Grossbart, that the emergence of consciousness of the extreme could so easily become the occasion for sentimental, politically interested claims to ethnic solidarity. In both "Eli, the Fanatic" and "Defender of the Faith" there is a call to recognize the specificity of a genocide that does not yet have a proper name and, especially in the second story, a warning to avoid turning that event into ethnic property and cultural capital.

From Anne Frank to Holocaust pornography

Between 1959, when Roth published *Goodbye, Columbus,* and 1979, when he published *The Ghost Writer,* the shift in the status of the Holocaust suggested presciently by his early stories took place. No longer a marginal and threatening presence at the outskirts of Jewish consciousness, the Holocaust had moved to the center of Jewish-Americans' self-conception. Writing in the wake of this transformation prompts Roth to sharpen the satiric edge of his response to the Shoah. While Roth had initially taken pains to evoke with subtlety the overwhelming horrors of the Holocaust – through the presence of the orphans and Hasidim, through Nathan's unspoken experiences in Europe – by 1979 recognition of the Holocaust's uniqueness had become widespread, at least among Jews. The problem to which he addresses himself with greater force at this point is the other side of the issue he'd already sensed: that once recognized the seemingly shattering tragedy of the Holocaust could easily be incorporated into other agendas.

The Ghost Writer is a novella that inaugurates a series of fictions featuring Roth's alter ego Nathan Zuckerman (another Nathan!). While self-consciously staged as a *Bildungsroman,* in this case a *Künstlerroman* or story of the birth of an artist, the text also contains at its center a hilarious and provocative satire of the newfound Holocaust piety. The premise of the novella (clearly based on the negative response to "Defender of the Faith") is that Nathan, a promising young writer, is suffering the wrath of his family for having written a short autobiographical story that is "bad for the Jews." Although the transgression involves the revelation of family secrets, the shame is a public one, and involves, like "Eli, the Fanatic," the image of Jews among their Christian neighbors. As Nathan's father complains, "your story, as far as Gentiles are concerned, is about one thing and one thing only . . . It is about kikes. Kikes and their love of money. That is all our good Christian friends will see, I guarantee you" (*Zuckerman Bound* 57). Since his son refuses to renounce his story, Nathan's father asks an esteemed, if self-righteous, judge to appeal to Nathan's sense of obligation and responsibility for his maligned people. The judge writes to Nathan and includes a questionnaire to spark his moral self-interrogation that poses questions such as, "Can you honestly say that there is anything in your short story that would not warm the heart of a Julius Streicher or a Joseph Goebbels?" (63).[12] As an antidote to Nathan's alleged self-hatred, Judge Wapter suggests a dose of mid-1950s Holocaust culture: "If you have not yet seen the Broadway production of *The Diary of Anne Frank,* I strongly advise you to do so. Mrs. Wapter and I were in the audience on opening night; we wish that Nathan Zuckerman could have been with us to benefit from that unforgettable experience" (62). It is this therapeutic and sentimental version of Holocaust memory that Roth had already anticipated in 1959 and against which he now turns his considerable satiric powers.[13]

As *The Ghost Writer* makes clear, the moral authority that Nathan's parents and Judge Wapter evoke involves a confusion between the situation of the Jewish victims of Europe and the Jews situated, more or less comfortably, in the United States. In response to his mother's accusations of immodesty, Nathan points out the absurdity of the judge's position:

> "The Big Three, Mama! Streicher, Goebbels, and your son! What about the judge's humility? Where's his modesty?"
> "He only meant that what happened to the Jews – "
> "In Europe – not in Newark! We are not the wretched of Belsen! We were not the victims of that crime!" (64)

Mainstream Jewish America, Roth wants to point out, has come a long way from Eli's ode to the "peace and safety" of suburbia. It is now the "unforgettable experience" of the Holocaust that grounds Jewish identity as much as does the urge to fit in with the gentiles. Indeed, instead of warding off the specters of the genocide, it is identification with the martyred innocence of Anne Frank that seems to provide the ticket of admission to the mainstream.[14]

Faced with the conflicting demands of family and art, Nathan seeks solace by literalizing the fantasies of his elders and imaginatively appropriating the icon of Jewish innocence. He brings Anne Frank to America "in the flesh" – and not just in the theatrical version favored by the Wapters. In Nathan's late-night fantasy, the mysterious Amy, assistant and lover of Nathan's idol, the great writer E. I. Lonoff, becomes Anne Frank. Having survived against all odds, Anne makes her way to America, where she assumes the identity of Amy. The transformation of a victim of the Holocaust into a living American immigrant provides the fantasy space for Nathan's comic resolution to his identity crisis – he'll marry Anne Frank! He imagines the redemption he'll obtain when he announces his surprising engagement: " 'Married? But so fast? Nathan, is she Jewish?' 'Yes, she is.' 'But who is she?' 'Anne Frank' " (95). Nathan's absurd fantasy reveals how the Holocaust, far from evoking anxiety, as it did in the Jews of Woodenton, has come to fortify an acceptable Jewish identity. And it suggests that the saintly image of Anne Frank – too universal and optimistic in her Broadway and Hollywood incarnations to be threatening to Jews or Gentiles – has helped to transform the genocide's status. In *The Ghost Writer*, Roth daringly deploys comedy to expose

Jewish-Americans' ambiguous position as a "well-off" minority related through cultural and kinship ties to a deeply tragic, recent history that is ultimately not their own.

Roth's fictions say at least as much about the realities of their moment of composition as about the recent past that they reconstruct. Just as his invocation of the victims and exploiters of the not-yet named Holocaust had responded to the uncertain status of the genocide on the eve of the Eichmann trial, so his attention to the inflation of the image of Anne Frank responds to the growing importance of popular cultural representations of the Holocaust in the 1970s.[15] In his 1991 memoir *Patrimony* he submits that inflation to even more outrageous parody in a hilarious passage. After considerable cajoling, Philip agrees to read a manuscript of the Holocaust memoirs of one of his father's buddies. It turns out to be rather different from what one would expect. According to Walter, the survivor, he was "the only man left in Berlin," and his memoirs are the graphic depictions of his sexual exploits with the women who hid him – quite a twist on the usual plot of Holocaust testimonies. "My book is not a book like Elie Wiesel writes," Walter honestly remarks. "I couldn't write such a tragic book. Until the camps, I had a very happy war."[16] Between his many girlfriends, Walter's war turns out to have been more an orgy than one of the greatest tragedies of the century.[17] This odd episode suggests that there might be something *pornographic* about making images and ultimately commodities out of the Holocaust. It is as if the fundamental obscenity of the events themselves cannot be represented without a pornographic contamination of the person doing the representing.[18]

This negative lesson about the possibilities of Holocaust representation is not an easy one to maintain, however, and even Roth occasionally falls victim to the forces he so compellingly satirizes. The desacralization of the Holocaust in an American context – implicit in *The Ghost Writer*'s parody of sentimental constructions of Jewishness and *Patrimony*'s ironic story of Holocaust pornography – is partially forgotten in *Patrimony*. Although the Nazi genocide itself is peripheral to his memoir, the Holocaust's legacies form the metaphorical background against which Roth frames the story of his father's losing battle with cancer. Roth uses figures of speech that call upon both timeless Jewish themes of memory and historically specific evocations of the Nazis and their victims. Despite the father's obstinate "survivor" mentality, Herman Roth's tumor, Roth writes, "would in the end be as merciless as a blind mass of anything on the march" (*Patrimony*, 136). In its slight but powerful invocation of the tropes of the Holocaust, Roth's moving portrait of his father demonstrates the extent to which the Holocaust has penetrated American culture as an archetype of innocent suffering.[19] As an archetype, the Holocaust can serve as a powerful resource for expressing personal and historical tragedy, but it can also facilitate the erosion of the distance between history's victims and those who grow up in the relative peace and security of America.

Triangulating the Holocaust

Operation Shylock (1993) represents Roth's most sustained and complex meditation on the ethical, historical, and cultural implications of the Nazi genocide. Bringing together Roth's habitual self-consciousness about writing in general and his tragi-comic recognition of the inevitable contamination of representing the Holocaust, the metafictional pyrotechnics of *Operation Shylock* expand the scope of Roth's engagement with Holocaust memory into an international sphere. *Operation Shylock* is the story of what happens when the writer Philip Roth discovers that someone posing as him in Israel is attending the trial of alleged Treblinka guard John Demjanjuk and espousing in the media a theory of Diasporism, which encourages Ashkenazi Jews to re-emigrate from Israel back to their European homelands. Since he is already planning a trip to Israel to interview Holocaust survivor and novelist Aharon Appelfeld for *The New York Times*, Philip decides to investigate the impostor, whom he names, in an attempt to reappropriate his stolen identity, Moishe Pipik (or "Moses Bellybutton"). Philip's pursuit of Pipik leads him into a tangled conspiracy involving, it would seem, PLO agents, Israeli intelligence operatives, Holocaust survivors, recovering anti-Semites, and various other eccentrics. At the end, Philip agrees to go undercover in an Israeli intelligence operation code-named "Shylock," although the details of his actions are, for "security reasons," removed.

As this all too brief synopsis of the extremely complex novel makes clear, *Operation Shylock* does not directly represent the Holocaust; yet the text probes Holocaust memory at different levels and suggests how Jewish-American identity intersects with these modes of remembrance.[20] At the level of plot, *Shylock* turns on the importance of Philip's and Pipik's attendance at the Demjanjuk trial. This contemporary legal staging of the Holocaust calls upon its epoch-making ancestor, the Eichmann trial, an event which, as I've suggested, first brought the continued suffering of Holocaust survivors into a public space. The text also incorporates Roth's actual *New York Times* conversations with Appelfeld about representing the Holocaust and includes allusions to various other Holocaust texts, including Roth's own *The Ghost Writer* and Saul Bellow's *The Bellarosa Connection*. And, as a novel of ideas, Roth simultaneously espouses and ridicules a post-Holocaust philosophy of Diasporism, which insists that a second Holocaust can only be averted through a reversal of Zionism and a reoccupation of Europe.[21]

As in Roth's earlier fictions of the Holocaust, *Operation Shylock* is at pains to establish the distance between Jewish-American security and European tragedy. The figure central to this aspect of the novel is the "real" survivor Appelfeld, who serves as Philip's "counterself." Roth contrasts Appelfeld's experience to Philip's: "Hiding as a child from his murderers in the Ukrainian woods while I was still on a Newark playground playing fly-catcher's-up had clearly made him less of a stranger than I to life in its more immoderate manifestations."[22] The contrast between Appelfeld and Roth's namesake in the novel is further complicated by the presence of Pipik, the Philip Roth impostor. When, eager for Philip's attention, the impostor asks, "Why should you converse with Aharon Appelfeld . . . and not with me!," Philip answers by meditating on their "drastically *bifurcated* legacy":

> Because . . . of Aharon's and my distinctly radical *twoness* . . . [B]ecause we are anything *but* the duplicates that everyone is supposed to believe you and me to be . . . because each recognizes in the other the Jewish man he is *not*; because of the all but incompatible orientations that shape our very different lives and very different books and that result from *antithetical* twentieth-century Jewish biographies. (*Operation Shylock*, 200–01)

Like Eli and the displaced persons in *Goodbye, Columbus*, like the Jews of Newark and the Jews of Belsen evoked in *The Ghost Writer*, Appelfeld and Philip Roth represent the extremes of Jewish history in the twentieth century. Through such contrasts, Roth explores the riddles of a history that could simultaneously produce unprecedented wealth and success on one shore and unprecedented destruction on another.[23]

In *Operation Shylock*, Roth's exploration of the Holocaust's meanings also extends beyond the America/Europe duality that has anchored so much of his fiction. Roth carefully sets his novel at various temporal and spatial crossroads, and, crucially, triangulates the opposition between Europe and America by including sustained consideration of Israel and Middle Eastern politics.[24] He makes a point of telling the reader that upon arriving in Jerusalem, Philip stayed not in his usual guest house, but "at the American Colony, a hotel staffed by Arabs and situated at the other end of Jerusalem, virtually on the pre-1968 borderline between Jordanian Jerusalem and Israeli Jerusalem" (51). The historical resonance of this location is reinforced by the restricted time and place in which most of the novel takes place:

> It felt like a May afternoon, warm, breezy, lullingly serene, even though it was January of 1988 and we happened to be only a few hundred yards from where Israeli soldiers had teargassed a rock-throwing mob of young Arab boys just

the day before. Demjanjuk was on trial for murdering close to a million Jews at Treblinka, Arabs were rising up against the Jewish authorities all over the Occupied Territories, and yet from where I was seated amid the shrubbery, between a lemon tree and an orange tree, the world could not have seemed any more enticing. (88–89)

By inscribing history into a hotel courtyard, Roth creates an allegory in which a series of temporal turning points – the Holocaust, the occupation of the West Bank, the beginnings of the intifada – structures a geographical locale and an ethnic identity. Philip's particular American Jewishness is determined, this setting implies, both by his implication in the aftermath of the Holocaust and in the crises of Zionism *and* by his comfortable, tourist's remove from them. He is simultaneously caught between Demjanjuk, Arafat, and the Israeli Defense Forces, and sitting safely between two fruit trees. As with the rest of his literary oeuvre, the political meaning of these juxtapositions is not explicit, although it's difficult not to hear the echo of dissent in the Israeli soldiers' use of gas and in the name of Philip's hotel. What is significant about *Operation Shylock*, as about Roth's other Holocaust-related texts, is not the conclusions to which it might come, however, but the map it provides – in this case, one that acknowledges how the state of Israel has insinuated itself into American-Jewish consciousness in close proximity to the catastrophe in Europe. Notably sensitive to the currents that define Holocaust memory in the United States, Roth probes the cultural spaces where history, ethnicity, and politics intersect and exposes the sometimes comic, sometimes tragic outcomes.

Conclusion: Roth's new plot?

After publishing *Operation Shylock* and celebrating his sixtieth birthday, Roth entered one of the most productive phases of his career. In rapid succession he published powerful and provocative novels such as *Sabbath's Theater* (1995), *American Pastoral* (1997), and *The Human Stain* (2000). Yet, at least until *The Plot Against America* (2004), memory of the Nazi genocide played little role in his recent work. In the meantime, with the attacks of September 11, 2001, it seems likely that Holocaust consciousness in American life has entered a new phase. How memory of the Shoah will mutate in the coming years remains to be seen, as does the question of how Roth will respond. In conclusion, I would like briefly to consider whether *The Plot Against America* represents a significant transformation in Roth's approach to the past.

Told, like *Shylock*, from the perspective of "Philip Roth" and set predominantly in the author's hometown, *Plot* is an alternate history that explores the question of what would have happened if Charles Lindbergh had run for president on an anti-war platform in 1940 and defeated Roosevelt.[25] Once in power, in Roth's telling, Lindbergh allies himself with Nazi Germany and inaugurates anti-Semitic policies, including ones meant to separate Jewish children from their families and turn them into "real Americans." The Roth family finds itself split apart as each member responds differently to the social and political pressures of the new era. How can we evaluate this imaginative but dark retelling of the recent past? Ironically, *Plot* seems to take up the conjunction that, in *The Ghost Writer*, Roth had Nathan Zuckerman definitively reject: in this new novel it is almost as if the Jews of Newark *are* the wretched of Belsen (although things never proceed that far in Roth's alternate history)! At least one prominent critic has pursued this angle and read *The Plot Against America* as a competitive attempt to displace historically verifiable American racism against African Americans by overstating the significance of anti-Semitism and the Holocaust in US history.[26] Is such a reading credible? If so, it would indicate an almost total reversal in Roth's approach to anti-Semitism and the Holocaust.

As always with Roth, however, historical referentiality is a good deal more complicated than such a straightforward conclusion would suggest. Despite its success in recreating a realistic version of a history that never was, the novel has a deliberately paradoxical and tantalizing relationship to contemporary political conditions. President Charles Lindbergh's folksy populism and patriotism have reminded more than a few readers of President George W. Bush; yet, the central conflict of the novel – whether to engage in war on foreign soil – has precisely the opposite valence as it does today, with Bush's interventionism contrasted to Lindbergh's pro-fascist isolationism. Such provocative historical reversals – common to many of Roth's works – frustrate attempts to draw too straight a line between the novel and any given political context. The novel's evocation of anti-Semitism gone wild might be read, for example, less as a literal commentary on the social position of Jews – either now or in the past – than as an indirect indictment of the contemporary resurgence of right-wing Christianity in American public life.

There is no telling in what directions Roth's work will move in the coming years, but this essay has attempted to show that significant continuities have defined his responses to the Holocaust since the late 1950s. While always aware of the shifting contexts through which the Holocaust first entered and then permeated American life, Roth has proven himself consistently skeptical about the historically understandable Jewish tendency to see enemies everywhere and to embrace the Holocaust as a pillar of identity. Such a perspective, we have also seen, does not entail denying either that anti-Semitism has played a significant role in America or that the Holocaust was a particularly, even uniquely, traumatic event. Rather, Roth seems to be saying, the more seriously we take the Holocaust as history, the more important it is to distinguish the multiple legacies – comic as well as tragic, everyday as well as extreme – that define the present.

NOTES

I am grateful to Amanda Dysart for research assistance.

1 Philip Roth, *Reading Myself and Others*, new expanded ed. (New York: Penguin, 1985), p. 136.
2 Philip Roth, *Zuckerman Bound* (New York: Farrar, Straus and Giroux, 1985), p. 269.
3 See, for example, Andrew Furman, "The Ineluctable Holocaust in the Fiction of Philip Roth," *Studies in American Jewish Literature*, 12 (1993): 109–21.
4 Steven Milowitz, *Philip Roth Considered: The Concentrationary Universe of the American Writer* (New York: Garland, 2000), p. ix.
5 As numerous critics have pointed out, there are various aspects of Novick's book that can be disputed. Nevertheless, his periodization of the stages through which Holocaust remembrance has passed in the United States remains helpful and the wealth of details he provides is an invaluable resource. See Peter Novick, *The Holocaust in American Life* (Boston: Houghton Mifflin, 1999).
6 See Mintz's excellent discussion of the Holocaust and popular culture. Alan L. Mintz, *Popular Culture and the Shaping of Holocaust Memory in America* (Seattle: University of Washington Press, 2001).
7 In *Traumatic Realism* I discuss "The Year of the Holocaust" and the significance of 1993 as a turning point in US Holocaust consciousness with reference to Roth's oeuvre. See Michael Rothberg, *Traumatic Realism: The Demands of Holocaust Representation* (Minneapolis: University of Minnesota Press, 2000), pp. 181–263.
8 See Novick on America, Israel, and the Holocaust: Peter Novick, *The Holocaust in American Life*, pp. 146–69. On Israel and the Holocaust more generally, see Tom Segev, *The Seventh Million: The Israelis and the Holocaust* (New York: Hill and Wang, 1993).
9 Additional aspects of Roth's relationship to the Holocaust, touched on only briefly here, include his efforts in the "Writers from the Other Europe" series to publish Eastern European authors such as Bruno Schulz and Tadeusz Borowski, both of whom were victims of the Nazis, and his friendships with survivor-writers such as Primo Levi and Aharon Appelfeld. See his interviews with Levi and Appelfeld, originally published in *The New York Times Book Review* and available, respectively, in Primo Levi, *The Voice of Memory: Interviews 1961–1987* (New York: New Press, 2001), pp. 13–22; Aharon Appelfeld, *Beyond Despair: Three Lectures and a Conversation with Philip Roth*, trans. Jeffrey M. Green (New York: Fromm International, 1994), pp. 59–80.
10 Baumgarten and Gottfried describe one of the stories, "Eli, the Fanatic," as "the first major story about the Holocaust written by an American writer after the first wave of reporting that succeeded the end of World War II had come to a

close." See Murray Baumgarten and Barbara Gottfried, *Understanding Philip Roth* (Columbia: University of South Carolina Press, 1990), p. 54.

11 Philip Roth, *Goodbye, Columbus* (New York: Bantam, 1968), p. 183.

12 In *The Facts*, Roth writes that Wapter's questions were inspired by the response he received after speaking at a 1962 Yeshiva University panel on "The Crisis of Conscience in Minority Writers of Fiction." See Philip Roth, *The Facts: A Novelist's Autobiography* (New York: Penguin Books, 1989), p. 127.

13 Spargo provides a detailed consideration of *The Ghost Writer* in relation to the "cultural memory" of Anne Frank in the 1950s. See R. Clifton Spargo, "To Invent as Presumptuously as Real Life: Parody and the Cultural Memory of Anne Frank in Roth's *The Ghost Writer*," *Representations*, 76 (Fall 2001): 88–119.

14 The ever self-reflexive Roth will go on to parody his own parody of the Holocaust's excessive significance. In *The Counterlife*, the outrageous Jimmy Lustig tells Nathan Zuckerman he's going to highjack an El Al flight to get across his message that Jews should "FORGET REMEMBERING!" and "Dismantle Yad Vashem!," Israel's Holocaust remembrance authority. See Philip Roth, *The Counterlife* (New York: Farrar, Straus and Giroux, 1986), pp. 165–66. This passage also anticipates sections of *Operation Shylock*.

15 Shostak shows that Roth's interest in Anne Frank goes back at least to the early 1970s, when he was writing an early draft of *American Pastoral*. See Debra Shostak, *Philip Roth – Countertexts, Counterlives* (Columbia: University of South Carolina Press, 2004), pp. 123–25.

16 Philip Roth, *Patrimony: A True Story* (New York: Vintage Books, 1996), pp. 212–13.

17 The odd association between Holocaust and orgy appears also in *The Prague Orgy*, the epilogue to *Zuckerman Bound*, the trilogy that began with *The Ghost Writer*. In that short story, Zuckerman travels to a decadent Communist-era Prague in an unsuccessful attempt to locate the Yiddish stories of a Czech Jew (possibly) killed by the Nazis. Among other things, *The Prague Orgy* illustrates the gap between the unrecoverable story of the Holocaust and pre-Holocaust Europe, on the one hand, and the good intentions of the American literary celebrity, on the other. The story of the lost manuscript is inspired in part by the life of Bruno Schulz.

18 See the critique of the tendency to associate Holocaust representation and memory with pornography in Carolyn J. Dean, *The Fragility of Empathy after the Holocaust* (Ithaca, NY: Cornell University Press, 2004), pp. 16–42. My purpose here is not to affirm Roth's particular association but to reveal its logic, which I believe is more subversive than Dean's analysis allows.

19 See the discussion of the transformation of the Holocaust into an archetype in James E. Young, *Writing and Rewriting the Holocaust: Narrative and the Consequences of Interpretation* (Bloomington: Indiana University Press, 1988), pp. 99–116.

20 See the discussion of Jewish identity in *Operation Shylock* in Timothy L. Parrish, "Imagining Jews in Philip Roth's *Operation Shylock*," *Contemporary Literature*, 40.4 (1999): 575–602. More generally, see Alan Cooper, *Philip Roth and the Jews* (Albany, NY: SUNY Press, 1996); Ranen Omer-Sherman, *Diaspora and Zionism in Jewish-American Literature: Lazarus, Syrkin, Reznikoff, Roth* (Hanover, NH: Brandeis University Press, 2002).

21 See the excellent reading of the tensions of Diasporism and Zinoism in the novel in Sidra DeKoven Ezrahi, *Booking Passage: Exile and Homecoming in the Modern Jewish Imagination* (Berkeley: University of California Press, 2000), pp. 221–33.

22 Philip Roth, *Operation Shylock: A Confession* (New York: Vintage Books, 1994), p. 111.

23 The theme of doubling and the contrast between American normality and European extremity is repeated and complicated in the sections of the novel dealing with the Demjanjuk trial, a topic that cannot be dealt with here.

24 On Roth's fictions of Israel, with some attention to the question of Holocaust memory, see the chapter on Roth in Andrew Furman, *Israel through the Jewish-American Imagination: A Survey of Jewish-American Literature on Israel* (Albany, NY: SUNY Press, 1997). See also Omer-Sherman, *Diaspora and Zionism*.

25 Philip Roth, *The Plot Against America* (Boston: Houghton Mifflin, 2004).

26 See Walter Benn Michaels, "Plots against America: Neo-Liberalism and Anti-Racism," *American Literary History*, (forthcomming 2006). I respond to Michaels in Michael Rothberg, "Against Zero-Sum Logic: A Response to Walter Benn Michaels," *American Literary History*, 18.2 (2006): 288–302. See also the more measured account of the novel's relationship to African–American history in Timothy L. Parrish, "Review of *The Plot Against America*," *Philip Roth Studies*, 1.1 (2005): 93–101.

5

EMILY MILLER BUDICK

Roth and Israel

In *The Anatomy Lesson* (1983), Roth has his authorial alter ego, Nathan Zuckerman, explicitly blame the loss of his writerly subject on the creation of the Jewish state. In the wake of Israel, Zuckerman has exhausted the subject of being an American Jew. While "the great Jewish struggle was with the Arab states," Zuckerman's own great struggle was with "the Jersey side of the Hudson, his West Bank." His difficulty was to portray how this conflict had ended with his territory "occupied now by an alien tribe."[1] Zuckerman's despair is that with his parents dead and his neighborhood lost, he must confront the recognition that "no new Newark was going to spring up again for" him (*Zuckerman Bound*, 445).

One might well imagine that when Zuckerman does, in *The Counterlife*, recover his "posture for writing" –or perhaps his *imposture* for writing – it is because Israel has finally been launched into the position of "homeland" and, thereby, Oedipal father. "There's a world outside the Oedipal swamp," Nathan's brother Henry angrily responds in *The Counterlife*, when Nathan questions Henry's new-found home in a right-wing Israeli settlement.[2] "Tell me something, is it at all possible, at least outside of those books, for you to have a frame of reference slightly larger than the kitchen table in Newark?" (*Counterlife*, 138). Nathan's response amounts to an honest and resounding no. "The kitchen table in Newark," he lectures Henry, "happens to be the source of your Jewish memories, Henry – this is the stuff we were raised on. It *is* Dad," he goes on to say of the settlement leader Lippman who has taken Henry under his wing; "It's Dad, but the dream-Dad, supersized, raised to the hundredth power" (138). For Roth the draining of the Israeli swamps, which is one of those sacred images of the early "pioneering Jewish fathers," might have seemed to seriously have muddied the waters of the Jewish family romance. From beginning to end, for Roth the only "homeland" that matters is "desire's homeland" (322). And Israel, now that it has become the "homeland of Jewish abnormality" (73), is no longer a source of impotency, as it was for Nathan in *The Anatomy Lesson* or for Portnoy in *Portnoy's Complaint* (Portnoy twice fails to achieve an erection in Tel Aviv). Rather it has become fit ground for Roth for the staging of archetypical familial conflicts and hence for the production of fiction.

Using Israel this way in his fiction marks an important change in the trajectory of Roth's, indeed American-Jewish literature's, relation to the Jewish state. As Andrew Furman has pointed out, "it would be difficult to overstate [the] impact of the Jewish state in forging the ethos of Jewish-Americans." Nonetheless, "while Jewish-American writers have written prolifically since the 1960s about the Holocaust (the other central Jewish event of the twentieth century), it would be disingenuous to suggest that Israel has carved out an equally substantial niche for itself in the Jewish-American writer's imagination."[3] Roth, Furman notes, is the large exception to this. And Roth's exceptionality in this regard, I suggest, may well have to do with the fact that, from his earliest works of fiction, Roth has been primarily concerned, not only with Jewish-American identity but with Jewish identity as such. This Jewish identity emerges for Roth through an Oedipal swamp that extends back centuries in time and over several continents, though what Roth, as what Freud meant by the Oedipal struggle is far more complex and rich than either the young Nathan or even, later on, his older brother Henry could even begin to imagine. That Freud too was a Jew makes his theory of mental process especially relevant to the historically specific dimensions of Roth's subject. Jewish identity for Roth also has everything to do with the Jewish writer as the one who documents and even produces such identity. How one constructs a fiction may not be so very different from how one constructs an identity. At least in Roth's later writings, identity, too, is a fiction of sorts.

Heretofore protected, like so much else in Jewish history, from the uninhibited scourge of the writer's own Oedipal rages by the events of the Holocaust, Israel had, in the aftermath of its victory in the June 1967 war, finally, it seems, become a fitting subject for the art of a writer like Philip Roth. This is so even though Roth is quick to voice the self-awareness and self-criticism that had also accompanied his earlier satires of the American (rather than the Israeli) Jew. In *The Counterlife* this important self-conscious awareness of the limitations and even dangers of his literary approach is voiced through Roth's alter ego's alter ego, the leftist Israeli academic Shuki. In this book that not only produces counter lives but tends to turn lives and realities inside out, Shuki serves as none other than a kind of Israeli Philip Roth, countering the American Roth, Nathan Zuckerman. Shuki is no less than *The Counterlife's* "P. R. man," as he himself puts it, and as the text reminds us more than once. He expresses and protests the voice of that other P. R. man who is writing the book and whose voice is being more directly and familiarly expressed by the American Nathan.

Shuki and Roth are not only P. R. men in the sense that they are both versions of the author. They also serve, albeit in highly subversive, Philip Rothian ways, the public relations both of the Jewish people and of the Jewish state. Lest we miss the significance of those initials and how they play out in the text, Roth repeats them twice (he later signs the introduction to *Operation Shylock* P. R.). The first time is early in the book when Zuckerman and Shuki first meet up. Shuki describes to Zuckerman an anti-Semitic BBC interviewer, concluding "I'm not known around here as this country's leading P. R. man, but if I'd had a gun I would have shot him" (66). The defender of the faith in England is a role that Zuckerman himself will take up later in the book, inspired, perhaps, by Shuki's conversation with him.

The second time Shuki refers to himself as a P. R. man is in the letter he sends Nathan after Nathan's visit to the right-wing West Bank fanatic Mordecai Lippman, who has taken brother Henry under his wing (in *The Counterlife* Nathan finally makes good on his wish to enter Jewish history from some place other than the "Jersey side of the Hudson"). Earlier in that letter Shuki had voiced his worries concerning Zuckerman's penchant for comic fiction and the high stakes for the state of Israel of what might seem to Roth no more than fodder for the literary mill. "There is . . . a little more to this country," writes Shuki, "than what you hear out at Agor from Lippman, or even what you heard in Tel Aviv from me (another peripheral character – the peripheral crank, wasted down to his grievances); remember, if you take as your subject his diatribe – or mine – you will be playing with an argument for which people *die*" (158). By the end of the letter, Shuki has turned comedy itself inside out:

> The comedy is obvious. Shuki the Patriot and P. R. man – the call for Jewish solidarity, for Jewish responsibility, from your perverse old guide to Yarkon Street. So be it – I am a ridiculously twisted freak, as hopelessly torqued by the demands of this predicament as anybody else in our original history. But that's a character even more up your alley. Write about an Israeli malcontent like me, politically impotent, morally torn apart, and weary to death of being angry with everyone. But be careful representing Lippman. (161)

Insofar as Shuki is Roth's P. R. man, his advice to Roth is to represent himself, which advice Roth, I think, takes. Roth, through Zuckerman, is the major protagonist in *The Counterlife*, and the novel becomes nothing less than a call for Jewish solidarity.

The rather counter-intuitive, almost comical idea of Roth and his fiction serving as PR for the Jewish state recurs in *Operation Shylock*, where it is represented in what initially takes on the more recognizable, subversive register of Roth's writing. There it is suggested, with undisguised anti-Semitic intention and yet despite that, some truth, that Jews "are born with the PR gene."[4] This idea of the self-serving self-protectiveness of Jews is developed at length in the anti-Semitic tape Roth recovers from his double in the novel, the other Philip Roth, whom Roth, acknowledging his double's kinship to him, calls Moishe Pipik. Pipik is Roth's imp of the perverse, and like all of Roth's characters, he represents at least some dimension of the author himself. This is true as well of the earlier character in his career, who does seem to have been born with the defective PR gene: the manipulative Jewish recruit in "The Defender of the Faith." The idea of this character trait is picked up later in *Operation Shylock* when Roth imagines the thoughts of his Palestinian friend George Ziad at the trial of John Demjanjuk: "why he is lying?" thinks Ziad of one of the witnesses against Demjanjuk (or rather Roth thinks, imagining what Ziad is thinking); "Because that's what public relations is . . . Marlboro has the Marlboro Man, Israel has its Holocaust Man . . . Or," Roth continues, "was George thinking about me and my usefulness, about making me into *his* PR man" (*Operation Shylock*, 296).

Making Roth into a PR man is clearly what Smilesburger, Roth's Mossad handler, intends for Roth to become for him and the Jewish state at the end of the novel, producing a new Israeli version of the American-Jewish community's expectations of Roth earlier in his career. In every way, the new (old) Israel would seem to be a replay of the old (new) Israel as represented by new-ark New Jersey – especially in this matter of Jewish "responsibility" and PR. As Roth makes very clear in his critical essays, he has never taken well to this idea of doing Jewish PR. Yet, part of what all this discussion of PR in *The Counterlife* and *Operation Shylock* is for is to suggest that the case *for* Israel, in a very straightforward even political way, is (like the case *for* Jewry, American and otherwise) not absent from Roth's thoughts, perhaps even his authorial intentions. This is the case, however much his fiction would seem to be rejecting any such simplistic notion of "responsibility" – to pick up Shuki's highly charged word. This is the very word, as we shall soon see, that comes to dominate the final chapter of *Operation Shylock*, where we know to resist what Smilesburger is attempting to impose on Roth and his writing. What constitutes responsibility as what constitutes public relations or, to complete the play of words, what (as who) constitutes P. R., are very much at issue in Roth's two Israel-centered novels. Indeed, from his earliest fiction Roth indicates that he is quite aware that being Jewish, while it can – indeed while it *must* – become the object of the novelist's craft, including his humor, is, in and of itself, no joke. It is quite true what Shuki says, that Roth may well be playing with an argument for which people die. Shuki should know. Roth gives Shuki a brother who dies in a particularly grisly way in one of Israel's battles with the Arabs; Shuki's father has died of the grief of this. Roth also gives Shuki a son who is about to go into the army.

Roth would remain the loyal Jew if he could, but what constitutes loyalty, who is the true defender of any faith, his fiction insists, is not to be assumed beforehand, although PR is clearly *not* served by adopting the official government or community line. "Why do you persist," Smilesburger asks him, "in maintaining that you undertook this operation [i.e., operation shylock] as a writer only, when in your heart you know as well as I now do, having only recently enjoyed all your books, that you undertook and carried it out as a loyal Jew?" (*Operation Shylock*, 388). That, as an Israeli, unthreatened by the concerns of American Jewry and at some years' remove from the site of Roth's early writings, Smilesburger can say this about Roth's American novels says something about the different investments of American Jews in the 1960s and Israeli Jews in the 1990s. I must confess to being myself an example of such suspect partisan politics: although I had never been the least troubled by any of the early Roth that had so incensed the American-Jewish community, and while I found their response to Roth quite ridiculous, I did take offense at *The Counterlife* when it first came out. It seemed to me indelicate, to say the least, and perhaps even endangering to me and my family personally living in Israel, for Roth to use the dire political reality of Israel in order to play frivolous postmodernist games with Jewish identity. It took me a few years' distance to understand that Roth knew full well what he and Shuki articulate, that Israel was a reality for which people gave their lives. And for that very reason, Roth would risk the reader's wrath. That is the brilliant genius of this work and why it is a novel and not a political tract. For all of its dangerous and brilliant critique of the Jewish people, I came to see that *Operation Shylock*, like Roth's earlier works, is in every way a work of literary genius.

Smilesburger's reference to the "operation" Roth has undertaken, uttered as it is in the context of what Smilesburger believes that the writer knows in his "heart" about his Jewish loyalties, serves to remind us of the existence in the novel of another operation also having to do with the heart: the heart surgeries of both *The Counterlife* and *Operation Shylock*, as well as the knee surgery that more directly propels the second novel into action. Like these other surgical operations, operation shylock has something to do for Roth (both the author and the fictional character) with Jewish survival, most especially his own. Indeed, as both books are associated as well with psychotic breakdown, they go right to the heart of the matter of (Jewish) identity.

Smilesburger, therefore, is not off the mark in designating Roth a loyal Jew, in his earlier works of fiction as well. From his earliest writings, Roth has been (like his character Nathan Marx) his own sort of creative, artistic, and even comedic defender of the faith (hence the play of Marxes – from political ideologue to stand-up comic).[5] Such faith is not for Roth a faith *in* anything. It is rather a faithfulness or fidelity or loyalty *to* something; namely, to Jews and Jewish history; specifically to Jewish survival, in the fullest possible, bodily as well as spiritual terms. This loyalty continues to operate in *Operation Shylock* – where he is still, we might want to say, also trying to perform the operation that will alleviate (not cure) the "Jewish disease" from which he as other Jews suffer.

Or, rather, more precisely, he would operate to express what might more accurately be represented as his (and the Jewish people's) Jewish *dis-ease*. *Dis-ease* is not *disease* exactly, either organic or psychological. It is *not* a pathology or illness, and it is certainly not in search of a cure. It does not, therefore, require performing surgery or any other operation of that sort. Rather, in the oft-repeated expression in *The Counterlife*, such dis-ease is itself a performance. It is an *operation* of the mind by which we humans express that conflict and pain that define all of us as human beings and some of us as Jewish human beings. It is, we might say, a "symptom," as Freud initially used the term and as it has been developed by later psychoanalytic critics such as Slavoj Žižek. It is a symptom of our specialized, specific, and (for those of us who are Jews) Jewish humanness.[6]

To place Roth's writing under the lens of a Freudian or any other sort of psychoanalytic reading is to risk putting his work in an all-too-familiar and, potentially at least, all-too-reductive place. It's not that the Oedipal dimensions aren't there. It's that they are all too obviously there. From Alexander Portnoy to Nathan and Henry Zuckerman to the two Philip Roths of *Operation Shylock* (and a lot of characters in between), Roth's characters are neurotics of a highly visible and juicy sort. Zuckerman's physical ailments in *The Anatomy Lesson*, which land the writer flat on his back, prefigure the failure of heart in *The Counterlife*. This cardiac condition, when treated by drugs, only serves to produce in the two afflicted Zuckerman brothers the even more severe and literal impotency of which the heart ailment is only, paradoxically, a milder (if more life-threatening) expression (Shuki also claims to be spiritually or emotionally impotent in *The Counterlife*). When the heart problem is treated surgically the brothers become more than sexually impotent: they actually die in a very non-metaphorical sense.

The problem with analyzing Roth's characters' diseases, which, even if we grant them a non-psychosomatic status for the characters, nonetheless serve symbolically within the texts themselves as symptoms of psychological ailments, is that Roth's characters so closely conform to the contours of the archetypical Freudian hysteric (despite their being men rather than women) that the diagnosis seems suspect. To add suspicion to suspicion, they enact their hysteria by precisely following *the* Freudian plot in all of its classical Oedipal details. Roth's characters seem less to be acting from a Freudian unconscious than to be consciously, even self-consciously, performing what they take to be the "truth" of Freud's model of mind. This truth, further-more, seems to conform to the particular plot through which Freud described human psychosexual development. It is as if Freud serves as a kind of Bible for Roth's characters, perhaps even for Roth himself. Given that Freud him-self was Jewish, this may be simply a way of putting him in the line of Jewish dis-ease – a move that Roth might well be intending, albeit not in the frivolous manner of the characters themselves. Without, for the moment, saying how Roth's Freudianism differs from that of his characters, we might want to call this strict observance of Freud halakhic Freudianism: to practice or perform one's life according to the Bible of Freudian theory.

We are specifically invited in *Operation Shylock* to think about this pos-sibility when Roth's intelligence handler Smilesburger juxtaposes the wis-dom of the Chofetz Chaim to the more tawdry "talking cure" of Freud, thereby recalling Henry's own rebuttal of his brother's tendency to flounder in the Oedipal swamp. The Chofetz Chaim, explains Smilesburger, advo-cated silence and the restraint from *loshon hora*, i.e., speaking ill of others or gossiping. "They came to Freud," he goes on, "the talking Jews, and what did Freud tell them? Keep talking" (*Operation Shylock*, 335). If the ability to say anything is taken away from the Jews, then instead of Jews all that remains is "nice goyim" (336). By this logic, "speaking *loshon hora* is what makes Jews Jews" (336). Israel, according to Smilesburger, is "the full flowering of the Jewish *genius* for *loshon hora*" (337).

From Smilesburger's perspective, and perhaps Roth's as well, Israel has become one more brilliant and quintessentially Jewish expression of the Jew-ish disease of *loshon hora* – a disease, which Roth is suggesting with a barely contained smile of his own, he himself clearly knows something about. This is none other than the disease of Freudianism from which so many of Roth's characters suffer. Yet Roth is no Smilesburger. Nor is he identical to any of his fictional creations. If Freud is also Roth's Bible, not only his license for speaking ill of the Jewish people but the commandment (or mitzvah) that he do so, then it is a much more sophisticated Freud than Smilesburger can comprehend.

By making themselves a part of a tradition of writing about and thus pro-ducing Jewish identity, Roth's fictions express the author's Jewish loyalty and his fidelity to the Jewish subject. It is in the name of such responsibility differently defined that Smilesburger (echoing the earlier complaints of Roth's American Jewish audience) would have Roth in *Operation Shylock* perform the simple operation of excision or omission on his text. Roth both rejects this operation *and* performs a different operation of his own. *Operation Shylock*, or rather the chapter entitled "Operation Shylock," which is excised from the book, represents, as it were, a textual circumcision, expressing fidelity or loyalty to Jewish history and tradition through the same trope of covenant or *brith* with which *The Counterlife* also concludes.

Smilesburger would have Roth cut chapter 11, the chapter describing operation shylock, from his book. Rather than wholly removing chapter 11, however, castrating the book, as it were, Roth, following the trajectory of his response to the American-Jewish community's pressure earlier on in his career, will produce in his writings, as their very subject, just that pressure to un-write the text and his resistance to it. What Roth gives us instead of "Operation Shylock" is *Operation Shylock*. Instead of a chapter 11 we get an "epilogue." This epilogue isn't chapter 11 exactly, either in terms of its content or in terms of its technical relation to the text. Following chapter 10, however, it is as close to a chapter 11 as this book will ever get (to echo the words written by Zuckerman to Maria concerning the birth of their as yet unborn child at the end of *The Counterlife* – [324, the words close the book]). This non-chapter 11 is aptly entitled "Words Only Spoil Things." It is, as it were, chapter 11 under erasure, surgically operated on, and yet still there, in so many words. In so doing and undoing chapter 11, Roth concedes the need to avoid wantonly publishing materials detrimental to the Jewish state. At the same time, however, he also avoids fashioning the novel according to the demands of his ever-censoring Jewish public, now represented by Israel rather than America.

Roth, in other words, avoids spoiling the novel completely by spoiling it a little. He avoids completely bankrupting it by bankrupting it a bit. He makes his "failed 'responsibility'" to the Jewish people "the leitmotif" of this text as of his entire "career with the Jews" (*Operation Shylock*, 377) and thus elevates the idea of failed responsibility into its own form of specifically Jewish responsibility-taking. This is the Jewish subject of Roth's family of Jewish writers, from Aharon Appelfeld, Anne Frank, Isaac Babel, Franz Kafka, Bruno Schultz to his own Nathan Zuckerman (and himself). There is among all these writers and their characters what Nathan in *The Ghost Writer* calls a "family resemblance."[7] They are all, in this sense, P.R./PR men. They all suffer from the same Jewish dis-ease. They all perform (and produce) Jewish identity.

The most important contemporary Israeli figure in this tradition of Jewish abnormality (*Counterlife*, 162) is Aharon Appelfeld. There are several reasons for the inclusion of Appelfeld on the scene of *Operation Shylock*. Like the appearance of John Demjanjuk, Appelfeld establishes the real contexts in which the fiction is written, which is to say as well, the fiction's real-life stakes. Lest there be any doubts about this, many excerpts of the Roth–Appelfeld interview, which appear elsewhere, are repeated verbatim in the novel. Insofar as both Appelfeld and Demjanjuk are also associated with the Holocaust, Demjanjuk as (possibly) Ivan the Terrible, Appelfeld as most definitely a survivor and Israel's premier writer of Holocaust fiction, the references to both of them also import the extraterritorial, extratextual, historical reality of the Holocaust into the novel. Roth has done this elsewhere in his fiction: in "The Defender of the Faith" and *The Ghost Writer*, for example.

But Roth's primary reason for introducing Appelfeld into his novel has to do with his own relationship to Jewish history and Jewish writing. Appelfeld is for Philip Roth one more P. R. person, in the right sense of the word. On the surface of it, Appelfeld's writing would seem to be the very opposite of Roth's. Appelfeld writes about just that European Jew in the throes of anti-Semitism, often on the brink of the Holocaust and very often caught in its aftermath, whom the American-Jewish community would throw in the face of its upstart Jewish American writer Roth, or his surrogate Zuckerman. And indeed Appelfeld has been warmly embraced by an American-Jewish readership, as well he ought to be, although not perhaps for these reasons. Yet, Appelfeld's Jews are in many ways more like Roth's than the Jews fantasized by the sentimental American-Jewish community.[8] Furthermore, like Anne Frank (as she emerges in Roth's *Ghost Writer* and as the recent publication of the unexpurgated *Diary* affirms), Nathan Zuckerman, and Roth himself, Appelfeld is a writer at odds with his (Jewish) community. For the Israeli writing establishment of the 1940s and 1950s, when Appelfeld first took up the challenges of authorship, the dominant political and aesthetic imperative had to do with the new Hebrew (i.e, Israeli Jew) and not the old (Diaspora) Jew. Almost the mirror reversal of the American community, it demanded that the writer *not* write about the European Jew and the Holocaust in any form whatsoever. It especially did not want to be reminded of Eastern European Jewish weakness and suffering. For those swamp-clearing Jewish pioneers, whom Roth alludes to in *The Anatomy Lesson*, and who have been replaced in *The Counterlife* by the new pioneers, the settlers, Israel would be the repudiation of everything that defined Diaspora Jewry. Its literature would both reflect and even help give birth to the new reality of the new Jew in his new promised land. Hebrew literature, with the notable exception of Appelfeld, meant to throw out a lot more than the kitchen table in Newark, New Jersey.

The family resemblance between Roth and Appelfeld has everything to do with what are for Roth the hard distinctions fiction makes in the face of difficult to interpret and ambiguous realities. Because the state of Israel changes the course of Jewish history and the definition of the Jew is, in Roth's view, no reason to forget the Jews' origins in Eastern European Jewish history; because the Holocaust happened does *not* mean that there isn't also something called Holocaustomania, which is its own form of exploitation of the historical reality. "Did six million really die?" the anti-Semitic Diasporist anti-Roth asks in his infamous tape. He argues, "the Jews pulled a fast one on us again, keeping alive their new religion. Holocaustomania. Read the revisionists. What it really comes down to is *there were no gas chambers*" (*Operation Shylock*, 253). Roth II is clearly distorting the truth here. Yet, as in so much of Roth's fiction, the malicious manipulation of the truth cannot be permitted to occlude the truths on which those distortions are malevolently based. Whatever might be the truth of Freud's own revisionism, psychoanalytic theory might still be valid. By the same token, the scientific revisionism of anti-Semitic historians may be only an expression of anti-Semitism pure and simple.

Discovering the truth of anything is perilously difficult. And even if the Holocaust did, quite horrifically, indisputably occur, there might still be a disease called Holocaustomania, which is not the Jewish dis-ease of which Freud and others – such as Appelfeld – are the authors but the chapter eleven, the bankruptcy of Jewish culture. Ironically, Appelfeld is the most popular of the Israeli writers in the United States, perhaps, in part, because of their Holocaustomania. This is *not* to conclude that Appelfeld is not a great Jewish writer. It is only to recognize that public applause does not necessarily correspond to authorial genius. It is also to suggest that such greatness as Appelfeld does possess has to do with his conflictual, confrontational, even Oedipal relationship to the Jewish culture he in so opposing perpetuates and strengthens. The quirky, distorted, grotesque and quite human and even humane "old Jews" of Appelfeld's fiction (who might just seem to Roth II to fit his anti-Semitic stereotype of them) suffer as much as Roth's from age-old Jewish dis-eases, including the quite Oedipal conflicts of children and their parents. The "real" Roth plays the anti-Semitic tape by mistake, when he goes to play a tape of one of his conversations with Appelfeld, thus drawing the connection that points to the difference between the anti-Semitic Diasporist and the loyal Jewish writer of Jewish grotesque fiction. Such Jewish *loshon hora* as Appelfeld or Roth (or Kafka or Shultz) write, furthermore, is not the same as Holocaust denial, or Nazism, or anti-Semitism, or even auto-anti-Semitism – a subject in both Roth's and Appelfeld's fiction. And by the same token, that other protest against Freud uttered by Smilesburger, which is uttered in the name of Jewish tradition and the Chofetz Chaim, is by no means to be confused with the anti-Semitism of Moishe Pipik, even if it too constitutes a misreading of Freud.

For Roth the moral life has to do with making difficult fine distinctions. The accusation (not completely unfounded) that the Demjanjuk trial is a P.R. event revives an old controversy in Holocaust history, which is also not to be set aside lightly. In the Eichmann trial the identity of the defendant was not under doubt. Nonetheless, the purposes of the trial were. It was this other trial of another Nazi war criminal that first introduced the Holocaust full-scale into the American imagination. It is also the trial that put Zuckerman (and Roth) in bad odor with the Jewish community. Does Roth's fiction, or Appelfeld's for that matter, in presenting the Jew as a figure of considerable neurotic energy (Roth) and considerable neurotic suffering (Appelfeld) serve the purposes of anti-Semites, as the American community protested concerning Roth or the Hebrew literature establishment implied concerning Appelfeld? Or do these writers write Jewish P. R. of another, more complex literary sort?

One of the reasons *Operation Shylock* is made to recall the most famous anti-Semitic archetype of the avaricious, bloodthirsty Jew is that it recalls the tradition of anti-Semitic literature, in which even a Shakespeare can create a Shylock. Shakespeare's play itself knows something about the conditions that produced Jewish abnormality. And yet Shylock is villainous in ways that far exceed what even the conditions of anti-Semitism can condone. Invoking Shakespeare's Shylock in a text in which some of the characters do indeed, at various moments, behave like Shylocks and in which a major Israeli security operation is named after Shakespeare's character, Roth would present himself as unintimidated by Christian paradigms of the Jew. He would also mount his own operation Shylock, in defense of Jewish autonomy and authority.

The shadow of Shakespeare's Shylock hovers over the Jews of *Operation Shylock*. Even Roth the character is seen as bearing some affinity to Shylock, as when he tries to buy off his impersonator Philip Roth II in a stereotypically money-grubbing way: "How much would it take for you to leave me alone? Name a figure" (316). This kind of haggling, which Roth the character quickly abandons, is picked up once again when the Mossad agent Smilesburger tries to get Roth to eliminate "Operation Shylock" from the book: "Show some gratitude," Smilesburger counsels him (388). He reminds Roth that historically tithing has been a custom among Jews. Smilesburger suggests that Roth "cede to the Jews" chapter 11 (388).

But it is precisely this kind of cost-accounting that distinguishes Shakespeare's Shylock from Roth's idea of the Jew. In dealing not in words (like Roth and Zuckerman) but in the flesh, Shylock is, from the perspective of

Roth's fiction, the anti-Jew, the goy's misconception of the Jew. In fact, Portia is more properly the Talmudist of Shakespeare's play. She is the expert in *pilpul*, the "Supposnik" of Shakespeare's text (Supposnik is another Mossad agent). Smilesburger, when he tries to Jew Roth down, is also not the authentic Jew but more like a sort of *trayfeh* fast food operator, offering a "bum steer" (384). Smilesburger, for all his appreciation of Roth's fiction, is the anti-writer of this text, and hence its Shylock. That role is given to Lippman in *The Counterlife* and to Nathan's brother Henry.

Roth's Jewish writers are not usurers like Shylock. They are not ideologues like Henry, Lippman, and Smilesburger, who in their somewhat different way protect investments and demand interest. Rather, they are babblers, speaking *loshon hora*. They rant and rave and even (given the frequency of their sexual escapades) may be said to pound their flesh, but they do *not* demand their pound of flesh, and certainly not from non-Jews. What they do demand, what Roth's Zuckerman demands at the end of *The Counterlife*, is the much more slender foreskin of circumcision.

"That delicate surgery," which is "performed upon the penis of a brand-new boy" is the operation whereby Zuckerman the son takes on the responsibilities (to once again invoke that leitmotif of Roth's writings) of Zuckerman the father, with all of the Oedipal tensions of that quite intact. Throughout *The Counterlife* and *Operation Shylock* one response to Jewish dis-ease has been to operate to surgically remove it. If "Shylock" is one clue as to the meaning of *Operation Shylock*; the word "operation" is the other. *Operation Shylock*, we are told, comes instead of "a Zuckerman sequel to *The Counterlife*" (*Operation Shylock*, 359). It is the Zuckerman sequel in a very real sense. In point of fact, Roth's surgeries (one the knee surgery, which is followed by a nervous breakdown, the other heart surgery) span the period of the publication of *The Counterlife* in 1987 and *Operation Shylock* in 1993. The fictions merge and blend the two surgeries, thus linking the two stories as *counterlives* of each other not to mention of Roth himself, whose "counterlife," he tells us, is the basis for *The Facts*.[9] *The Facts* is the novel actually published in the period between the two other novels. The post-operative "Halcion madness," from which the character Roth suffers in *Operation Shylock*, in some form or other shadows his entire experience in Israel. It is, we might say, the Israeli counterpart of his American disease, impotency. "I am back in America," Roth says at the end of *Shylock*; "I'm no longer recovering from that Halcion madness" (383). This new Israeli disease of "Halcion madness" also recalls and displaces what we might label the "halcyon daze" of pastoralism, which threatens to overtake Nathan in one version of the end of *The Counterlife*. That pastoralism is associated not only with Christian England and the fantasy of immaculate conception, but, Roth makes clear in

The Counterlife, also with the more phallic (gun-toting) militancy of Israeli settlers as well (322).

Zuckerman resists the urge to pastoralism when he decides to circumcise his as-yet unborn (not necessarily male) child – the operation by which Nathan seeks to save himself, not to become simply a father, but to become a *Jewish* father – with all of the Oedipal dangers (to himself) that that involves: "What's our unborn offspring meant to me, right up to tonight in fact," he writes to his wife Maria, to whom he is also expressing his disdain of the Christian idea of nativity, "but something perfectly programmed to be my little redeemer? . . . Well, that's over. The pastoral stops here and it stops with circumcision . . . Circumcision is everything that the pastoral is not" since it "gives the lie to the womb-dream of life in the beautiful state of innocent prehistory . . . To be born is to lose all that. The heavy hand of human values falls upon you right at the start, marking your genitals as its own" (*Counterlife*, 323).

Whether Zuckerman has this son and has him circumcised, we'll never know (his wife Maria is still pregnant when *The Facts* is published some years later). But the Halcion madness that carries forward the severe physical disability, including, in particular, the impotency of Roth's characters from Portnoy and the Zuckermans onward, reaches its culmination in the post-operative condition of *Operation Shylock* itself – which is no cure, but rather a new, Israeli, Jewish dis-ease. "You think in the *Diaspora* it's abnormal? Come live here. This is the *homeland* of Jewish abnormality," exclaims Shuki (*Counterlife*, 73) and thus provides Roth with his license for using Israel as a homeland in which to wage his Jewish Oedipal struggles, trading one West Bank for another.

For Roth Israel is no promised land; no more a new covenant or a new ark than Newark, New Jersey is a New American Israel. It is rather, like all human places, including the kitchen table in Newark and the West Bank settlement of Agor, a compromised land. "I signed no contract. I made no promises" (*Operation Shylock*, 381)," Roth says concerning the compromising chapter Smilesburger would have him remove. Toward the end of *Operation Shylock*, Roth reproduces in Hebrew the words that appear, once in English and once in Hebrew, as one of two quotations at the beginning of the novel. "This is what I painstakingly copied down," Roth tells us, "thinking that afterward, if there was an afterward, these markings might provide the clue to exactly where I'd been held captive and by whom" (315). "So Jacob was left alone, and a man wrestled with him until daybreak." Struggle, "contradiction," and "debate" (the terms of the other epigram from Kierkegaard) – these are the "terms" of Roth's art, the terms on which he will produce fiction ("This time the terms are mine," writes Roth of his authorial decisions in relation to

Operation Shylock [378]). These are also the terms of Jewish consciousness: to struggle "alone" and to record that struggle.

Roth inscribes this essential Jewish dis-ease of solitary wrestling in both Hebrew and in English in order to suggest how much the American-Jewish writer is quintessentially a part of a Jewish tradition going back to the biblical text itself. In so doing he also suggests, however, not only the origins of his own art in the tradition of Jewish language and thought, but the counter-influence of the American-Jewish writer on the Hebrew literary tradition (represented in the novel, perhaps, by Appelfeld). Roth's *Operation Shylock* intends to restore potency and power to the tradition of Jewish authorship in Israel as much as in America, and as that tradition is expressed in the Hebrew language and not only in English. Had brother Henry made *aliyah* to Israel because he'd fallen in love with the language, then, Nathan tells us in *The Counterlife*, he could have understood and forgiven. In that novel and in *Operation Shylock* Roth makes himself a son of that other Jewish community, and an elder, both continuing his own Oedipal struggle of loyal opposition to the past, and accepting, indeed inviting, the sons' struggle against himself.

NOTES

1 Philip Roth, *Zuckerman Bound: A Trilogy and Epilogue* (New York: Farrar, Straus and Giroux, 1985), pp. 445–46.
2 Philip Roth, *The Counterlife* (New York: Farrar, Straus and Giroux, 1986), 140.
3 Andrew Furman, *Israel Through the Jewish-American Imagination: A Survey of Jewish-American Literature on Israel 1928–1995* (Albany: State University of New York, 1997), pp. 1–2.
4 Philip Roth, *Operation Shylock: A Confession* (London: Jonathan Cape, 1993), p. 260.
5 See my essay "Philip Roth's Jewish Family Marx and the Defense of Faith," *Arizona Quarterly*, 52 (1996): 55–70.
6 Slavoj Žižek. "The Truth Arises from Misrecognition," in *Lacan and the Subject of Language*, eds. Ellie Ragland-Sullivan and Mark Bracher (New York: Routledge, 1991), pp. 188–212.
7 Philip Roth, *The Ghost Writer* (New York: Vintage Books, 1995), p. 47.
8 For more on Appelfeld and the tradition of Jewish writing, see my book *Aharon Appelfeld's Fiction: Acknowledging the Holocaust* (Bloomington: Indiana University Press, 2004).
9 Philip Roth, *The Facts: A Novelist's Autobiography* (New York: Penguin, 1988), p. 6.

6

JOSH COHEN

Roth's doubles

Writing as deception

The title of Roth's 1990 novel, *Deception*, is instructively deceptive. Its evident reference is to the erotic deception practiced and endlessly discussed by its protagonists, the writer "Philip" and his unnamed married mistress (among others). Yet the penultimate chapter sees this sense of "deception" overlain by another. Here, Philip's (also unnamed) wife confronts him with the notebook she's discovered, containing the very transcripts of post-coital chatter we've just read. Philip counters her furious charge of deception with the insistence that it's his notebook rather than himself that's deceived her; the affair is fictive, not real, and the Philip of its pages is "*far* from myself – it's play, it's a game, it is an *impersonation* of myself!"[1] Philip's defense, in other words, is an appeal to the clear distinction between his real self and its fictive double.

The problem for Philip and his readers, spousal and otherwise, is that once it rears its head, the specter of deception refuses to be contained in this way. Designed to quell suspicion, his insistence on the fictionality of the affair only intensifies it: what if this insistence is part of the same deception? What if, as his wife, no doubt speaking for many readers, charges, "You are caught and you are trying to confuse me!"(*Deception*, 183) Nor is there any way of resolving this predicament – the affair remains permanently suspended between fiction and reality, such that to read the novel is to be condemned irremediably to deception.

In this chapter, I will read Roth's abiding preoccupation with fictive alter egos, counter-selves, and doubles as an effect of this logic of endless deception. Drawing on psychoanalysis,[2] one of Roth's key imaginative resources, I will argue that his fictive doubles are means of dramatizing the fundamental predicament of selfhood. As *Operation Shylock*'s "emphysemic old Jew" intimates to Roth, the human animal is above all deceiving and deceived. Its irrevocable destiny is "[e]rror, misprision, fakery, fantasy, ignorance, falsification and mischief . . ."[3] As *Deception* shows, this destiny is brought to light above all at the meeting-point of the erotic and the literary, modes of experience that share the same structure of deception. And for Roth, of course, erotic and literary error is perpetually bound up with *Jewish* error. Indeed, the vertiginous mirror play of such texts as *The Counterlife* and *Operation Shylock* is thoroughly continuous with the preoccupations of the early Roth. The vicissitudes of the erotic life and the dilemmas of the Diaspora Jew, comically anatomized in the early texts, are in the later texts – as we shall see – the means through which the self divides and multiplies itself.

Psychoanalysis and "someone else"

The affinity between doubling and erotic life is a key premise of psychoanalytic theory. For Freud, sexuality is above all what divides us from ourselves, what prevents the self from becoming fully present and knowable to itself. Consciousness comes into being by means of repressing the clamorous demands made by the erotic drives from infancy. However, as Roth's fiction repeatedly confirms, repression by no means frees adult consciousness of these demands. On the contrary, it produces the *unconscious* – a repository of repressed wishes which, denied direct expression, assert themselves in the indirect and devious forms of dreams, jokes, slips, and neurotic symptoms. These manifestations of the unconscious confront the known and knowing self of everyday life with a strange internal other or double. As Freud puts it in his famous 1915 essay, "The Unconscious": "all the acts and manifestations which I notice in myself and do not know how to link up with the rest of my mental life must be judged as if they belonged to someone else: they are to be explained by a mental life ascribed to this other person."[4]

It is the idea of this "someone else" that accounts for the abiding fascination in Freud and his disciple Otto Rank for the literary narratives of the double, in which a protagonist is shadowed by a duplicate self. The double, writes Rank, is the "detached personification of instincts and desires which were once felt to be unacceptable, but which can be satisfied without responsibility in this indirect way" (*Double*, 76). The double personifies Freud's "return of the repressed"; it confronts the protagonist with impulses which disturb his sense of who he is. This is what renders the double, in Freud's famous term, "uncanny," that is, so simultaneously strange and familiar. The protagonist's frequent terror in narratives of the double stems from the perception of his tormenting copy as both his intimately known self *and* his radically estranged other. The double, to invoke a famous formulation of Freud's, is the self I both know and don't want to know.

For Freud as for many of his psychoanalytic successors, this doubleness of the self is inextricable from the doubleness of language. Not for nothing are dreams, jokes, and slips the means by which the unconscious irrupts into conscious life. Each of these forms works by mining the peculiar capacity of words to mean more than one thing. Discussing the intricate ambiguities of dream imagery, Freud writes that "[w]ords, since they are the nodal points of numerous ideas, may be regarded as predestined to ambiguity."[5] By signifying meanings beyond our conscious intention or control, words reveal our irreducible doubleness.

This insight can be seen as the basis for the dense theoretical edifice built by Freud's most controversial successor, the French psychoanalyst Jacques Lacan. For Lacan, to be a speaking being is to be consigned to a kind of constitutional mendacity – not the conscious mendacity of the deliberate liar, but the mendacity that belongs to speech itself. As fiction above all reveals, words can exist in full independence of any reality. "[I]t is only with speech," says Lacan in his 1954 *Seminar* "that there are things which are . . . and things which are not."[6] Speech introduces the possibility of falsehood, of "making things up," without which there exist only brute facts – "there is neither true nor false prior to speech" (*Seminar I*, 228). Echoing Freud, Lacan concludes "[s]peech is in essence ambiguous" (229).

"Words generally only spoil things"

Similar thoughts occur to the Philip Roth of *Operation Shylock* as he contemplates the madness to which his double forever consigns him. Even if he should never again meet the double he renames "Moishe Pipik," the very thought of his presence in the world condemns him to "insufferable sieges of confusion" (*Operation Shylock*, 307) and the malevolent inversion of Psalm 23's consolatory conclusion: "Pipik will follow me all the days of my life, and I will dwell in the house of Ambiguity forever" (307). Roth, in other words, no longer needs the presence of an actual double to feel doubled. The disappearance of his external double can't rid him of his far more insistent internal double. Roth, after all, was a prisoner in the house of ambiguity long before Pipik came on the scene.[7] What placed him there was not Pipik but his insistence on following the slippery trails of speech. Like so much of Roth's fiction, *Operation Shylock* is a masterclass in the seductions of rhetoric. Its contending voices constantly attest to the inventive power of language, its capacity, rooted in the essential ambiguity of speech, to produce and perform, rather than merely represent, truth. This accounts for the vertiginous quality of reading Roth, his prose's capacity to carry us along on waves of rhetorical persuasion, regardless of the inner logic or content of its argument.

It is not the least of the novel's ironies that perhaps its most potent rhetorical tour de force is ostensibly an elaborate warning against the corrupt and dangerous pleasures of rhetoric. Smilesburger, the (apparently) crippled and elderly spymaster, recruits Roth to the novel's eponymous operation by means of a long disquisition on the corrosive effects of *loshon hora*, or evil speech. Jewish tradition, Smilesburger argues, so solemnly enjoins silence precisely because of its intimate understanding of the temptation to speak. Jewish history is an unending record of internal conflicts: "inside every Jew there is a *mob* of Jews. The good Jew, the bad Jew. The new Jew, the old Jew. The lover of Jews, the hater of Jews. The friend of the goy, the enemy of the goy. The arrogant Jew, the wounded Jew" (334).

Smilesburger's rather more expansive inventory of this inner mob, "a three-thousand-year amassment of mirrored fragments," attests above all to a deep historical intimacy with doubleness (334). Jews talk a lot, he suggests, because words are the natural medium for their perpetually doubled condition. Always suspended between the lures of acceptance and rejection, segregation and assimilation, tradition and modernity, doubling is integral to the Jews' historical wiring. It is this insight that inspires Smilesburger's identification of the exemplary doubles of modern Jewish history: the Chofetz Chaim and Sigmund Freud. The revered Polish rabbinical scholar is famed above all for his painstaking elaboration of the intricate network of prohibitions around *loshon hora*.

This intricacy stems from the difficulty of containing the unintended effects of even the most minimal of speech. But these effects multiply in the mouths of Jews, who seem somehow constitutionally driven to maximal speech: "inside each Jew were *so many speakers*! Shut up one and the other talks. Shut him up and there is a third, a fourth, a fifth Jew with something more to say" (335). Jewishness, then, is on this account a kind of internal proliferation of selves made through words. The Chofetz Chaim's regulative ideal of silence is a recognition of this condition: history has destined the Jew never to stop talking once he starts. From this perspective, Freud's profane injunction to "say everything" through the rule of "free association," his lifting of every prohibition on speech however perverse, venal, or devious, can be understood as double to the Chofetz Chaim, a malevolent inversion in precisely the sense of Roth's Moishe Pipik (*Operation Shylock*, 335). Freud and the Chofetz Chaim are exactly opposed manifestations of the same Jewish insight into the corruptive force of verbal ambiguity, expressed in the "admirably simple sentence" Smilesburger quotes from the Talmud: "Words generally only spoil things" (335). To live in and through words is to be condemned to deceive and be deceived.

As Smilesburger implies, however, Freud is rather less negative than his rabbinical counterpart about the consequences of ambiguity. For if ambiguity gives rise to error, error itself, as Lacan provocatively suggests, is the paradoxical path to truth: "error is the habitual incarnation of truth . . . as long as the truth isn't entirely revealed, that is to say in all probability until the end of time, its nature will be to propagate itself in the form of error" (*Seminar 1*, 263). This is the very insight at the heart of Freud's exhaustive inquiries into dreams, jokes, and slips. Each of these modes of speech seeks simultaneously to reveal and conceal the truth, to communicate it by the contrary means of "error, misprision, fakery . . ." This is a paradox acutely dramatized early on in *Operation Shylock*, when Roth phones his double in Jerusalem. In fact, Roth decides he can most effectively probe his double's intentions by doubling himself. Posing as a French journalist, he perpetrates a fraud in order to expose one. As a result, he is caught off guard when his interviewee momentarily reverses roles and asks, "Who is this, please?" Roth's reply, "plucked seemingly out of nowhere", is an exemplary slip: "I am Pierre Roget." The double significance of this apparently arbitrary pseudonym strikes Roth immediately. Not only are its initials the same as his own (and his double's) – "[w]orse, it happened also to be the barely transmogrified name of the nineteenth-century word cataloguer who is known to virtually everyone as the author of the famous thesaurus. I hadn't realized that either – the author of the definitive book on synonyms!" (40).

Roth's slip, in line with Freud's understanding, is also an irruption of unconscious truth. He disguises himself in order to establish his other as the fake, and himself as the authentic "Roth." And yet in so doing, he not only fakes himself, but chooses a pseudonym that betrays his uncanny sense that his double is closer to him than he wants to acknowledge – his synonym, not his antonym. The scandalized victim of identity theft, seeking to assert that his fraudulent double has nothing to do with him, ends up alluding unwittingly to their likeness. Look one Roth up in the thesaurus, and one might be referred to the other. Little wonder that his double responds to the confirmation of Pierre's last name at the end of the conversation with a loud eruption of laughter: "He knows, I thought, hanging up. He knows perfectly well who I am" (48). Words have only spoiled things; Roth's ambiguous speech has blown the very cover it was meant to provide.

The self and/as its double: *The Counterlife*

Roth, then, may seek to rid himself of his external double; but in so doing, he becomes all the more helplessly enslaved to the will of his no less alien internal double. Roth spends the entirety of the novel slipping, being led inexorably down paths of word and deed he neither controls nor understands. In this, he is thoroughly in keeping with his other fictional protagonists, doomed to speak as "someone else" at the very moment he wishes to speak and act as himself.

No novel by Roth more determinedly interrogates this doubled logic of selfhood than *The Counterlife*. In all the Zuckerman novels, but especially in the *Zuckerman Bound* trilogy and epilogue, Roth famously plays on his protagonist as fictive alter ego. Details recognizably belonging to Roth's own biography are displaced onto Zuckerman's, teasingly shifting the boundaries of art and life. *The Counterlife*, however, is not simply another instance of this self-doubling, but a meditation on the very process of doubling, on the self as its own ineradicable double.

The novel imagines different destinies or "counterlives" for both Zuckerman and his brother Henry ("the double," writes Rank, "is often identified with the brother" [*Double*, 75]). The succession and interplay of counterlives frustrates any attempt to identify any one of them as more authoritative than the others. Indeed, the novel repeatedly alludes to this desire to establish a clear boundary between reality and fiction. In the fourth chapter, Henry is imagined as a version of the wife of *Deception*. Like her, he happens upon a stray manuscript, in this case that of the recently deceased Zuckerman, which for him too reveals the depths of his betrayal. And as in *Deception*, what he reads appears to be the very chapters preceding this one (as well as the chapter following it).

Henry reads Zuckerman's now posthumous novel in a frenzy of mounting disgust, as he discovers his own life retold through the distorted lens of his brother's invention. Nathan has simultaneously appropriated and betrayed Henry's life through a duplicitous weaving of truth and fakery. "Basel" takes Henry's intimate confidences of adultery and filters them through the fantasies and vicissitudes of Nathan's own life (and death), whilst "Judea" inserts him, "a Jew who didn't think twice about Israel or being a Jew" into a delirious fantasy of transformation into a West Bank militant.[8] Not the least enraging aspect of these distortions is the disguised appearance of Nathan himself "*as* himself, as *responsible*, as *sane*," and the concomitant displacement of his erotic and Jewish obsessions onto Henry (*Counterlife*, 230). In one of the novel's slyest moments of its ongoing auto-commentary, he remarks, "The son of a bitch seemingly abandons the disguise *at the very moment he's lying most!*" (231).

Henry, then, unmasks Nathan's absence of disguise as merely another, yet more deceptive disguise. But in so doing, he baits the reader into further error and misprision, for the temptation here is to imagine that with Henry we are burrowing down to the authoritative truth to set against the imaginative distortions – the life, so to speak, to the counterlives. But problems immediately attach to this reading. Most obviously, it raises the question of just who is writing this account of Zuckerman's posthumous life? It is after all structurally integral to the book we're reading, and as such partakes of the same devious logic of "counterlife." Indeed, the singular form of the word in the novel's title is instructive in this respect. What we are reading is not an assortment of fictional counterlives to set against the truth of a real life, but a meditation on life as always and necessarily counterlife – always, that is, doubled, haunted by the specter of the "someone else" leading it alongside the self.[9] Henry's lifting of the veil of fiction is itself a fiction, his broadside against Nathan's "deliberate deception" part of the novel's elaborate play of deception (236).

Once again, this play is staged in large part through the novel's interlacing of carnality, Jewishness, and writing. For Roth, as we've already seen, these three themes are adjoining stages on which to play out the unending drama of doubled selfhood. Erotic, Jewish, and literary life are all forms of counterliving, of experiencing oneself as more than one self. Indeed, each of the places alluded to in the chapter titles – "Basel," "Judea," "Aloft," "Gloucesteshire," "Christendom," become names for the self-defeating struggle to forget this condition. Basel and Judea become alternate sites for Henry of promised redemption from the "fakery" of his life, the concealed emptiness, whether erotic ("Basel") or spiritual ("Judea"), of his work and marriage. Henry is lured in each case by the promise of integrating the scattered parts of his selfhood. Erotic fulfillment with Maria in Basel and messianic fulfillment with Lippman in Agor are polarized images of the same fantasy of wholeness. Henry's transmogrification into Agor's Hanoch, heroically sacrificing his inessential past self to the authentic historical destiny of the settlers, points up the essential violence of this fantasy. Contemplating the aura of aggressive self-assertion emanating from Lippman's young wife as she sings in the Sabbath:

> Ronit looked as contented with her lot as any woman could be, her eyes shining with love for a life free of Jewish cringing, deference, diplomacy, apprehension, alienation, self-pity, self-mistrust, depression, clowning, bitterness, nervousness, inward-ness, hypercriticalness, hypertouchiness, social anxiety,

social assimilation – a way of life absolved, in short, of all the Jewish "abnormalities," those peculiarities of self-division whose traces remained imprinted in just about every engaging Jew I knew. (124)

Lippman's militant territorialism is intimately bound up with his drive to purge Jewish experience of its ambiguity. Common to all the items in Zuckerman's exhaustive inventory of Jewish self-division is a sense of distance between the self and its disguises. For all their differences, deference, alienation, and clowning are all modes through which the self both divides and multiplies itself. Lippman's messianic dream offers the dubious promise of an end to this self-proliferation, to what Smilesburger will call "the *mob* of Jews" in every Jew (*Operation Shylock*, 334).

As the novel's final chapter shows, not the least difficulty with such a dream is its uncannily close accordance with the fantasies of anti-Semitism. "Christendom" narrates the collapse, over the course of one night, of the foundations of Zuckerman's marriage to the gentile (and genteel) Maria under the pressure of the insidious anti-Semitism of English society in general and Maria's family in particular. Subjected firstly to the malevolent probing of Maria's sister Sarah, and then to the more flagrant bigotry of an elderly fellow restaurant diner complaining about his "terrible smell," Zuckerman provokes an epic showdown with his new bride over the question of his Jewishness (*Counterlife*, 295).

It is to Sarah that he first intimates the thesis of his concluding address to Maria. Approaching him after the church carol service, Sarah asks him if he enjoys the "strutting" assigned to him in his role as "moral guinea pig" – that is, as New York Jew in High Church. "Not enough," he replies – "I'm not a sufficiently shameless exhibitionist . . . I can only exhibit myself in disguise. All my audacity derives from masks" (274). Once again, Zuckerman provocatively inverts conventional understanding. The genteel English sensibility defines exhibitionism as the vulgar exposure of what the elaborate codes of etiquette conceal, namely the raw, unadorned inner life. For Zuckerman, however, to exhibit the self is not to expose but to perform, not to reveal but to dissimulate.

The "undisguised" self, then, is merely another disguise. As Zuckerman's climactic address to Maria will argue, the self is not an irreducible essence, but a potentially infinite sum of disguises. As he wonders following their initial row, "Is an intelligent human being likely to be more than a large-scale manufacturer of misunderstanding?" (310). If selfhood is never more than the sum of its disguises, misunderstanding becomes the paradoxical essence of the human being.[10] As we recall from Lacan, "the paths of truth are in essence the paths of error" (*Seminar I*, 263). Human relations are never more authentic than when caught in the net of misunderstanding, "error, misprision, fakery . . ."

It is against this insight that Maria, in the novel's most explicit gesture of literary self-consciousness, protests to Zuckerman in announcing her departure from him and "the book." Her life as his fictive creation has become intolerable, a state of constant guardedness against the possibility of one kind of deception or another: "I can't take a lifetime of never knowing if you're fooling" (*Counterlife*, 316–17). For Maria, Zuckerman's "preoccupation with irresolvable conflict," and the incessant self-division that results, is a willfully perverse choice, a rejection of the simpler and more satisfying imaginative possibility of "life *working out*" (317). Zuckerman's insistence on dramatizing his own Jewishness as an ongoing problem setting him willy-nilly against the world undoes the possibility of their peaceful coexistence. To her husband's faith in "art and its strength," Maria thus opposes "my stand for something far less important than axing everything open – it's called tranquillity" (321).

One of *The Counterlife*'s richest provocations, then, is the way its apparently polarized voices come to take on an uncanny resemblance to one another. Maria's caricaturally English ideal of tranquillity involves the same silencing of the inner Jewish mob striven for by Lippman. Both Maria and Lippman, like Henry before them, are invested in the escapist fantasy of an undivided self. It is this fantasy which becomes the object of Zuckerman's climactic manifesto for selfhood as performance. Alluding, perhaps, to the various protagonists of his counterlives,[11] he targets first of all the illusion of "*being oneself*" (323), and more particularly the blindness of some to the essentially imitative nature of this being oneself: "If there *is* a natural being, an irreducible self, it is rather small, I think, and may even be the root of all impersonation – the natural being may be the skill itself, the innate capacity to impersonate" (324). Little wonder that the figure Zuckerman finally chooses to embody this performative conception of selfhood is one which signifies Jewishness and carnality simultaneously, namely "my erection, the circumcised erection of the Jewish father" (328). What makes circumcision quintessentially Jewish is its stark refutation of the Edenic fantasy of innocence and wholeness. It "gives the lie to the womb-dream of life in the beautiful state of innocent prehistory," since "to be born is to lose all that" (327). Circumcision attests that the human being is destined to disguise. Roth writes, "the heavy hand of human ritual falls upon you right at the start, marking your genitals as its own" (327). The human being *is* only insofar as he is inscribed by the intricate codes and practices to which he is submitted from the very first. Nowhere is this insight realized more potently than in erotic life – where else are self-exposure and self-concealment, vulnerability and guile, so indissociable? Zuckerman invokes as the book's coda Maria's bemused comment on handling his circumcised erection for the first time: " it's fine . . . but it's the phenomenon itself: it just seems a rather rapid transition" (328). To what transition is Maria referring? To Zuckerman's newly restored potency? Or to the mark that differentiates him from her former gentile husband? Another, no doubt unintended, resonance is the transition from the natural to the human body, and so from the unitary to the doubled self. Doubleness has emerged at the precise intersection of Jewishness, carnality, and writing – and it is with this emergence that the book ends itself.

Pipikism

With *Operation Shylock* Zuckerman's internal double has become Philip Roth's undeniably external one. The fictional Roth's reaction to his double's appearance in Jerusalem suggests more than a hint of self-satire; the author whose novels have so insistently explored and embraced the creative possibilities of psychic and literary doubleness is scandalized by the appearance of actual doubleness. In denouncing his double's fraudulence, he echoes ironically Henry's disingenuous protests against writerly deception.

Understandably, the Diasporist leader's claim to be the authentic spiritual distillation of Roth's fiction, converting his page-bound verbal pyrotechnics into global action, is an intolerable provocation. The attempt to deduce a determinate program for political action from a corpus of fiction is not simply absurd – it is, as Roth exasperatedly describes it, "Pipikist," a manifestation of "the antitragic force that inconsequentializes everything – farcical-izes everything, trivializes everything, superficalizes everything" (*Operation Shylock*, 389). The Pipikist double seems to divest his original of all substance, inducing a kind of delirious dispossession of mind and body. Roth finds himself ventriloquized by Pipik, even as he scorns his grandiose claim to be "YOUR GOOD NAME" and "THE YOU THAT IS NOT WORDS" (87). In one of the novel's many abyssal ironies, the fraudulent Roth continually promises to purge the real one of his inauthenticity, to liberate him from the falsifying grip of words.

The novel narrates Roth's increasing possession by his double's words and desires – accepting the million-dollar donation tendered to the leader of the Diasporist cause, assuming the identity of the Diasporist zealot to his Palestinian hosts, and above all seducing his double's lover. With her voluptuous body and "reformed" anti-Semitic mind, Wanda Jane "Jinx"

Possesski is a kind of Pipikized parody of any in Roth's extensive fictive gallery of *"shiksa"* fantasies. "You go around pretending to be me," Roth charges his double, only to receive the "loathsome" reply, "You go around pretending to be *me*" (72). Yet loathsome or not, the reply is more incisive than Roth cares to know – for the more he strives to differentiate himself from his false counterpart, the more undifferentiated they become. There is more than a trace of justice in Pipik's anguished climactic cry against Roth: *"He's the fake, that's the irony, he's the fucking double,* a dishonest impostor and fucking hypocritical fake" (367). After all, where the alleged double stands for meaningful intervention in the state of the world, the original stands only for the evasions and convolutions of fiction.

By conferring the disparaging pseudonym of Moishe Pipik on his double, Roth hopes somehow to contain his mischief. A Moishe Pipik, or Moses Bellybutton, is "that little folkloric fall guy whose surname designated the *thing* that for most children was neither here nor there . . . as meaningless as it was without function – the sole archaeological evidence of the fairy tale of one's origins" (116). By naming his double after this thing without meaning or function, Roth imagines he can stem the diffusion of his presence.

Rather than impose himself on Pipikism, however, Pipikism insinuates itself into him – an irony acutely attested to by the book itself. *Operation Shylock* is an exemplary document and expression of Pipikism's farcicalizing, trivializing force. Does not its title function like the bellybutton of Roth's childhood imagination, a meaningless trace of an absent origin? The Mossad operation which Roth undertakes, and whose account he agrees to excise from the book, is the nothingness, or Pipik, around which the book orbits. The novel becomes a kind of self-canceling act of inconsequentialization, with its Zeno-like bracketing by mutually canceling declarations of its truth and falsehood.[12]

In spite of Roth's apparent triumph, the double has, in accordance with his famed literary predecessors, taken his vengeance – not by killing his original, but by voiding his claim to truth. Indeed, isn't this the ultimate effect of all Roth's doubles? The double's doubling is at the same time an annihilation of the self. As the novels attest, however, this is a profoundly generative annihilation; the loss of one's self is infinitely rich in creative possibilities.

NOTES

1 Philip Roth, *Deception: A Novel* (New York: Simon and Schuster, 1990), p. 190.
2 Roth's use of the double motif is a self-conscious literary gesture insinuating him into the company of Goethe, Dostoevsky, Poe, Hawthorne, Wilde, and E. T. A. Hoffman amongst others. That this motif was an early and insistent preoccupation of psychoanalytic theorists can be no coincidence. See Otto Rank's 1925

The Double: A Psychoanalytic Study (trans. Harry Tucker, Jr., London: Karnac Books, 1989).

3 Philip Roth, Operation Shylock: A Confession (New York: Simon and Schuster, 1993), p. 209.

4 Sigmund Freud, "The Unconscious," in The Standard Edition of the Complete Psychological Works of Sigmund Freud, 24 vols., trans. and ed. James Strachey (London: Vintage 2001), vol. XIV, p. 179.

5 Sigmund Freud, The Interpretation of Dreams, in The Standard Edition, vol. V, p.340.

6 Jacques Lacan, Seminar I: Freud's Papers on Technique, ed. J-A. Miller, trans. J. Forrester (New York: W. W. Norton, 1988), p. 228.

7 The slippage here between Roth the fictional protagonist of Operation Shylock and Roth the real-world author of the same text is both unavoidable and instructive.

8 Philip Roth, The Counterlife (New York: Farrar, Straus and Giroux, 1986), p. 231.

9 Deborah Shostak's comment on the relationship between selfhood and narrative in the novel is particularly apposite here: "Where the interpretive act tends to fix a subject into stasis, the speculative narrative, by its resistance to interpretation, opens up the self to its own power of self-creation." See Philip Roth: Countertexts, Counterlives (Columbia: University of South Carolina Press, 2004), p. 216.

10 "That's how we know we're alive: we're wrong," Zuckerman will go on to write, in Philip Roth, American Pastoral (London: Vintage, 1998), p. 35.

11 One of the protagonists being, of course, himself; the Zuckerman of "Gloucestershire" submits to bypass surgery in order to escape the loss of sexual function with Maria. For Nathan, erotic life without an erection is one irresolvable conflict too many.

12 In interviews to publicize the novel, Roth insisted on its veracity with some irritation towards those who doubted it. As he was undoubtedly aware, this only exacerbated the taunting unreliability of the book itself.

7

JEFFREY BERMAN

Revisiting Roth's psychoanalysts

> I write fiction and I'm told it's autobiography, I write autobiography and I'm told it's fiction, so since I'm so dim and they're so smart, let *them* decide what it is or it isn't.[1]

The distinction between autobiography and fiction is always problematic, and no writer poses a greater challenge to untangling the threads of life and art than does Philip Roth, who goes out of his way to bedevil his readers. Like Nabokov, who sets traps in *Lolita* for psychoanalytically oriented readers who try to understand the source of Humbert's obsession, Roth both encourages and discourages public scrutiny of his life. He frequently uses real characters' names in his novels while contending at the same time that he is imagining events that never happened. Even in his memoirs, like *The Facts: A Novelist's Autobiography*,[2] he creates a countervoice, his fictional alter ego Nathan Zuckerman, who insists that "Philip Roth" is lying about his life. What, then, should a reader do to find the figure behind the veil – or the ventriloquist behind his fictional voices?

I cannot answer these questions definitively, but I can make a start. While writing *The Talking Cure*,[3] I began to suspect, on the basis of reading *Portnoy's Complaint*[4] and *My Life as a Man*,[5] that both novels dealt with Roth's own psychoanalysis. Readers familiar with *Portnoy's Complaint* will remember Spielvogel's celebrated punch line at the end of the novel: "So [*said the doctor*]. Now vee may perhaps to begin. Yes?" (274) – Roth's comic suggestion that his eponymous hero's embattled psychoanalytic odyssey is only beginning. This is Spielvogel's only utterance in *Portnoy's Complaint*, the novel that brought psychoanalysis into the homes of millions of readers, but Roth greatly expands his character and role in *My Life as a Man*, which explores in painstaking detail the five-year analysis of Peter Tarnopol, the fictional novelist who is a thinly disguised version of Roth himself. Whereas Roth's comic hero refers to Spielvogel as "Your Honor" and "Your Holiness" in *Portnoy's Complaint*, Tarnopol describes him as "Warden Spielvogel" in *My Life as a Man*, which reveals a much darker view of psychoanalysis.

My Life as a Man dramatizes a bitter argument occurring during Tarnopol's third year of analysis when he sees a psychoanalytic journal lying in Spielvogel's office, reads it, and then becomes incensed when he realizes that the analyst has written about Tarnopol's life. Spielvogel's article is called "Creativity: The Narcissism of the Artist," and although only two pages of the essay pertain to Tarnopol, he is enraged by the biographically transparent discussion and by its rhetorical and interpretive crudities. What most horrifies Tarnopol is that the publication of Spielvogel's article in a prominent journal devoted to psychoanalysis and art seriously compromises his privacy, since the analyst has related a highly personal and embarrassing incident that Tarnopol used in an autobiographical story published a month earlier in *The New Yorker*. Tarnopol fears that anyone who reads the psychoanalytic case study and the novelist's story will be able to infer that he is Spielvogel's patient.

Tarnopol immediately confronts Spielvogel, who denies steadfastly any wrongdoing. The analyst's refusal to acknowledge the breach of confidence and unauthorized use of his patient's words further infuriates Tarnopol. After arguing for several sessions, Spielvogel gives Tarnopol an ultimatum. "'Look,' he said, "this has gone far enough. I think either you will have now to forget this article of mine, or leave me. But we cannot proceed with treatment under these conditions" (*My Life as a Man*, 247). "What kind of choice is that?" Tarnopol responds in disbelief, and the two continue to battle. The novel clearly favors Tarnopol's point of view, and Spielvogel exacerbates the situation when he interprets his patient's anger as another symptom of his "narcissistic defenses." When Tarnopol's girlfriend tells her analyst, Dr. Golding, about Spielvogel's behavior, Dr. Golding is "appalled." Tarnopol continues in analysis for another two years, but his faith in Spielvogel is shattered permanently. Nevertheless, Tarnopol grudgingly acknowledges that there is something affirmative about Spielvogel's closemindedness.

> I must say, his immunity to criticism *was* sort of dazzling. Indeed, the imperviousness of this pallid doctor with the limping gait seemed to me, in those days of uncertainty and self-doubt, a condition to aspire to: *I am right and you are wrong, and even if I'm not, I'll just hold out and hold out and not give a single inch, and that will make it so.* (259; italics in original)

After reading *My Life as a Man*, which is autobiographical in so many ways, I began to wonder whether Tarnopol's experiences with Spielvogel reflected Roth's. If so, would it be possible to locate the psychoanalytic journal in which Roth's analyst discusses his famous patient? Roth supplies several clues in *My Life as a Man*. The article, Tarnopol reveals, is published in the mid 1960s in a special issue of the *American Forum for Psychoanalytic Studies* exploring "The Riddle of Creativity." Forty years ago there were fewer psychoanalytic journals than there are today, and when I read the spring–summer 1967 issue of *American Imago*, focusing on "Genius,

Psychopathology, and Creativity," I found what I was searching for: a thirty-page essay by Hans J. Kleinschmidt called "The Angry Act: The Role of Aggression in Creativity,"[6] two pages of which describe a patient unmistakably similar to Tarnopol.

Indeed, the parallels between the fictional and real patient–analyst relationships are astonishing. In *My Life as a Man* Spielvogel describes Tarnopol in the following way: "A successful Italian-American poet in his forties entered into therapy because of anxiety states experienced as a result of his enormous ambivalence about leaving his wife"(239). In "The Angry Act" Dr. Kleinschmidt speaks about his patient in the following way: "A successful Southern playwright in his early forties illustrates the interplay of narcissism and aggression. . . He came into therapy because of anxiety states experienced as a result of his tremendous ambivalence about leaving his wife, three years his senior" (123). Castration anxiety figures in the interpretations of both the fictional and real analysts. "It soon became clear that the poet's central problem here as elsewhere was his castration anxiety vis-à-vis a phallic mother figure," writes Roth's fictional analyst in *My Life as a Man* (240–41); "It soon became apparent that his main problem was his castration anxiety vis-à-vis a phallic mother figure," writes Dr. Kleinschmidt in "The Angry Act" (124). There are many other parallels, including the identical characterization of the father. "His father was a harassed man, ineffectual and submissive to his mother" (*My Life*, 241); "His father was ineffectual and submissive to the mother" ("Angry Act," 124). Finally, the fictional and real psychoanalysts offer the identical interpretation of their patients' hostility toward women. "The poet acted out his anger in his relationships with women, reducing all women to masturbatory sexual objects" (*My Life*, 242); "The playwright acted out his anger in his relationships with women, reducing all of them to masturbatory sexual objects and by using his hostile masturbatory fantasies in his literary output" ("Angry Act," 125).

I had found the evidence for which I had been searching. The smoking gun, it turns out, was a statement that Roth disclosed to Dr. Kleinschmidt about a "castrating" mother who shames her young son.

> He was eleven years old when he went with his mother to a store to buy a bathing suit. When trying on several of them, he voiced his desire for bathing trunks with a jock strap. To his great embarrassment his mother said in the presence of the saleslady: "You don't need one. You have such a little one that it makes no difference." He felt ashamed, angry, betrayed and utterly helpless.
>
> ("Angry Act," 124)

In *Portnoy's Complaint*, Sophie and Jack Portnoy take their eleven-year-old son to his uncle's clothing store to buy a bathing suit. Alex's "secret," which he is too embarrassed to tell his parents or uncle, is that he wants a bathing suit with a built-in athletic support. Rejecting the type of little boy's trunks that he has always worn, Alex turns scarlet with embarrassment and finally blurts to his uncle,

> "I don't want that suit any more," and oh, I can smell humiliation in the wind, hear it rumbling in the distance – any minute now it is going to crash upon my prepubescent head. "Why not?" my father asks. "Didn't you hear your uncle, this is the best –" "I want one with a jockstrap in it!" Yes, sir, this just breaks my mother up. "For *your* little thing?" she asks, with an amused smile. Yes, Mother, imagine: for my little thing. (*Portnoy's Complaint*, 51)

I realized instantly that the discovery thrust me into an ethical dilemma: the publication of my finding would reinvade Roth's privacy. I felt uneasy about this, and for several months I did not know what to do. Most of my friends and colleagues to whom I showed the Roth chapter, one of many in a book devoted to literary representations of psychoanalysis, urged me to publish it, but one person said that to do so would be in bad taste since it would revictimize Roth. Had I made the discovery on the basis of reading "The Angry Act" and an early chapter of *Portnoy's Complaint* called "The Jewish Blues," published in the first issue of *New American Review* in 1967, in which Roth reveals the bathing suit incident, I would not have publicized my discovery. After much soul-searching, I decided in favor of publication, believing then, as I believe now, that I was justified because Roth had left enough fictional clues in *My Life as a Man* for a psychoanalytically oriented literary sleuth to piece together the story. Without these clues, it would have been much more difficult to make the connection. Had Roth *not* wanted this incident to become publicized, he would not have left so many clues. To remain silent about his relationship to Dr. Kleinschmidt would be to avoid examining the spectacular ways in which Roth transmuted his own case study material into the stuff of art.

Quite simply, Roth's early fictional characters are the most thoroughly psychoanalyzed in literature, and *My Life as a Man* remains, to my knowledge, the most intense investigation of the relationship between a writer's psychoanalysis and art. Additionally, *Portnoy's Complaint*, *My Life as a Man*, and "The Angry Act" are perhaps the most striking examples of the symbiotic relationship between literature and therapy. However angered Roth must have been by the publication of Dr. Kleinschmidt's essay – and no one could have chosen a more prophetically ironic title than "The Angry Act" – the novelist exploited the imaginative possibilities of stealing back his own words – and using the analyst's words as well. For example, Roth quotes in the epigraph to his novel Spielvogel's definition of "Portnoy's Complaint" as a disorder in which "Acts of exhibitionism, voyeurism, fetishism, auto-eroticism and oral coitus are plentiful" – a description that recalls Dr. Klein-schmidt's words in "The Angry Act": "Practices of voyeurism, exhibitionism and fetishism abound" (125).

Curiously, I felt more protective of Roth's analyst than of Roth himself, perhaps because of the latter's decision to exploit the argument that had arisen with Dr. Kleinschmidt. I knew that Roth would be displeased with my discovery, despite the fact that he had ambivalently led me to it, and therefore I did not send him a copy of my chapter, entitled "Philip Roth's Psychoanalysts," which I completed in 1980; but I did send Dr. Kleinschmidt a copy and invited him to comment on it before I submitted *The Talking Cure* for publication. I doubted that the psychoanalyst would welcome my finding, but I was not prepared for his telephone call to me three days after I mailed the manuscript to him. The author of "The Angry Act" was furious at me for linking his case study to Roth's novels. Far from wishing to comment on the chapter, he threatened to sue me if I submitted it for publication, claiming I was using "privileged" material, that I hadn't "proven anything" in my argument, and that the publication of the chapter would irreparably damage his reputation. Whatever protectiveness I had felt toward him soon vanished! I told him that I had made the discovery on the basis of published rather than confidential material and that, moreover, I was not interested in assigning blame for the simultaneous publication of his article and Roth's story. Nor did I believe that the publication of my book would damage his reputation. In fact, I did not accuse Dr. Kleinschmidt of a breach of confidentiality or plagiarizing his patient's words. We argued back and forth over the phone, and finally he withdrew his threat and asked me to make minor revisions, which I did, including deleting the reference to Golding's characterization of Spielvogel's behavior.

There was one moment during our telephone conversation when I felt chagrined. I almost always asked my wife to proofread important letters, but I failed to do so when I mailed my letter to Dr. Kleinschmidt, perhaps because she shared my ambivalence over publication and was not happy about my decision to include the link to "The Angry Act." (I was a newly tenured associate professor, but we barely had enough money to pay our pediatrician, and the possibility of an expensive legal fight was chilling.) After a few minutes Dr. Kleinschmidt accused me of being "aggressive," and when I asked him what he meant, he followed with his own question: "Do you remember how you opened your letter to me?" I hadn't. "Instead of beginning, 'Dear Dr. Kleinschmidt,' you wrote, 'Dear Kleinschmidt.' Tell me that wasn't aggressive." He had a point.

In a follow-up letter to me, Dr. Kleinschmidt once again went on the attack, denying that I had proved he was Roth's analyst.

> Since in my article I introduce the brief case history of a Southern playwright, I in no way allude to or reveal the identity of the patient. Your assumption that Roth's use of lines from my paper is proof positive that my case history relates to him, is inconclusive since authors habitually take material from a wide variety of sources for their fiction.
>
> (personal correspondence, December 6, 1980)

He also claimed that I had quoted his words in "The Angry Act" without his permission – a strange statement in light of his own appropriation of Roth's words without permission. He ended his letter by warning me that unless I deleted all references to him in my otherwise "excellent and extremely well written chapter," I would be faced with an "onerous lawsuit." I promptly wrote him back and reminded him that I had every legal right to publish the chapter. I also cited Freud's justification for publishing the Schreber case, which was a psychoanalytic study of a published memoir.

I brought the revised chapter to Dr. Kleinschmidt's office on East 67th Street a few weeks later, and he continued to threaten a lawsuit, claiming that he had been "too easy" with me over the phone. I found him menacing and overbearing. The interview had both serious and comic moments. When he ushered me into his lavishly decorated office and invited me to sit down, I felt like asking him if I could lie down; despite the fact that I was enrolled at the time in a psychoanalytic institute as a research scholar, I had never been in analysis, and now it seemed as if I had an opportunity to be analyzed by an avatar of Freud. I was awed by this imposing Germanic analyst who seemed to speak so authoritatively about the riddle of art. When he started calling me "narcissistic" and "aggressive" in my pursuit of scholarly publication, I felt as if I had somehow become Philip Roth. Fortunately – or perhaps unfortunately – I did not feel as if I had been metamorphosed into a giant mammary gland, as Roth describes in his wildly comic story, *The Breast*,[7] in which another fictional analyst, Dr. Klinger, tries unsuccessfully to treat a literature professor whose reality has turned into a Kafkaesque nightmare.

Yet if I wanted to be Dr. Kleinschmidt's analysand, I also resented being placed on the defensive. I felt like asking *him* to lie down, since I had possession of disturbing knowledge that he was resisting vainly. Like Spielvogel in *My Life as a Man*, he never conceded any wrongdoing about the publication of his apparent article on Roth. Also like Spielvogel, he seemed impervious to criticism. We argued for several minutes over the accuracy of my discussion of "Philip Roth's Psychoanalysts," and even after he admitted that the facts were correct, he demanded that I omit the chapter from my book. I told him that although I could not prevent him from filing a nuisance lawsuit, he would not only lose but would attract precisely the kind of attention we both wished to avoid. Finally he relented and gave me additional details of his shock upon learning that the material he used in "The Angry Act" was identical to that in *Portnoy's Complaint*. He had declined Roth's invitation to read the as-yet unpublished manuscript of *Portnoy's Complaint* while the writer was still in analysis. He told me that Roth was furious and said that he could write whatever he wanted to about his psychoanalyst but the latter could write nothing about him without permission. Toward the end of my interview, Dr. Kleinschmidt stated that he hoped I would not publish my book for another five years, at which time, he hinted ominously, he would no longer be around to be troubled by it – a prophecy that underestimated his longevity: he died in 1997. As I was leaving his office, he exclaimed, in a tone that struck me as unapologetically defiant and proud, "Incidentally, I'm Klinger too!"[8]

Roth has never commented publicly on his bruising experience with Dr. Kleinschmidt, nor has he commented on my chapter in *The Talking Cure*. I suspect he regards me, if at all, as a minor irritant. His detestation of "marginal 'literary' journalists" is well known, referring to them in Charles Dickens's words as the "lice of literature."[9] I don't mean to dismiss the possibility that critics, especially psychoanalytic ones, can harm living authors, not only by invading their privacy but also by "diagnosing" their characters. This was Ernest Hemingway's complaint about Philip Young's book,[10] which implied that it would not be inconsistent if Hemingway suffered the same fate as his self-destructive characters. But Roth, unlike Hemingway, invites his readers to scrutinize his characters, all the time denying that they are autobiographical.

Apart from the ways in which "The Angry Act" remains a cautionary tale about the dangers of breaching confidentiality, we may ask ourselves how Roth's approach to psychological conflict differs from Dr. Kleinschmidt's. As I suggest in *The Talking Cure*,

> Roth's patients, who are generally writers or professors of literature, maintain the belief that reality is intractable: Human passions are unruly, suffering cannot be explained or alleviated, and reality seems impervious to understanding. Roth's analysts, by contrast, believe that psychological illness derives from childhood experiences, that conflict can be understood psychodynamically, and that guilt and rage can be worked through. (240–41)

In his nonfictional writings, Roth has remained evasive or flippant about his psychoanalysis, despite frequent questions from literary critics who have interviewed him. If he had not been psychoanalyzed, he told Hermione Lee in 1984, *Portnoy's Complaint*, *My Life as a Man*, and *The Breast* would not resemble the stories that he published. "Nor would I resemble myself. The experience of psychoanalysis was probably more useful to me as a writer than as a neurotic, although there may be a false distinction there" (*Conversations*, 170). He was able to condense the "eight hundred or so hours that it took to be psychoanalyzed" into the "eight or so hours" that it takes to read *Portnoy's Complaint*" (171). When asked in a 1988 interview, following the publication of *The Facts*, whether his treatment was a "traditional five-days-a-week analysis," Roth replied, "I think there were eight days a week." He then compared psychoanalysis to the process of writing *The Facts*:

> In analysis you organize your life according to the perspective of psychoanalysis. You are a willing patient. This is not the work of a patient. The analysis isn't interested in the facts so much as the associations to the facts . . . Writing leads to controlled investigation. The object of analysis is uncontrolled investigation. The goal was to write about things that strike me as tedious without being tedious. (*Conversations*, 224)

He refers to Freud as the "all-time influential misreader of imaginative literature" (*Conversations*, 243).

The Facts purports to be Roth's most autobiographical work, "A Novelist's Autobiography," as it is subtitled. The book is divided into two sections. The first section, one hundred and fifty pages long, begins with a seven-page letter that "Philip Roth" writes to Nathan Zuckerman, his fictional alter ego with whom he has often been confused. "Roth" must convince his counter-self – and his readers – that he is now writing the *real* truth:

> If while writing I couldn't see exactly what I was up to, I do now: this manuscript embodies *my* counterlife, the antidote and answer to all those fictions that culminated in the fiction of you. If in one way *The Counterlife* can be read as fiction about structure, then this is the bare bones, the structure of a life without the fiction. (*The Facts*, 6)

"Roth" then describes his feelings about his childhood and parents, his life as a student, the notoriety arising from the bestselling *Portnoy's Complaint*, and his disastrous marriage to "Josie Jensen," his pseudonym for his real-life wife, Margaret Martinson Williams, who died in a car accident in 1968. ("How could she be dead if I didn't do it?" [151]). "Roth" recounts his life in a measured and mellow voice, largely devoid of his characteristic self-lacerating irony.

The second section of the book, only thirty-five pages long, is written in the form of Zuckerman's letter to "Roth," advising him not to publish the manuscript because of its distortions, omissions, and idealizations.

> Is this really "you" or is it what you want to look like to your readers at the age of fifty-five? You tell me in your letter that the book feels like the first thing you have ever written "unconsciously." Do you mean that *The Facts* is an unconscious work of fiction? Are you not aware yourself of its fiction-making tricks? Think of the exclusions, the selective nature of it, the very pose of fact-facer. Is all this manipulation truly unconscious or is it pretending to be unconscious? (164)

The reader feels at the end that either "Roth" or Zuckerman is lying – or perhaps both of them, for they offer sharply conflicting interpretations of the writer's life. "[T]he book is fundamentally defensive," Zuckerman complains. "Just as having this letter at the end is a self-defensive trick to have it both ways. I'm not even sure any longer which of us he's set up as the straw man" (192).

"Roth" devotes only one sentence in *The Facts* to his experience with therapy, referring to his "intense psychoanalysis which, undertaken to stitch back together the confidence shredded to bits in my marriage, itself became a model for reckless narrative disclosure of a kind I hadn't learned from Henry James" (137). It is fascinating to read *The Facts* with knowledge of "The Angry Act," for we now see that the reference to the "reckless narrative disclosure" applies as much to Dr. Kleinschmidt as it does to Roth. There are no references to Dr. Spielvogel in *The Facts*, despite the fact that the last chapter of "Roth's" memoir is entitled "*Now Vee May Perhaps to Begin*," no hint of the bitter argument about which Roth wrote in *My Life as a Man*, no sign of Roth's break with psychoanalysis. Interestingly, Zuckerman points out, in a taunting voice, this conspicuous omission: "Your psychoanalysis you present in barely more than a sentence. I wonder why. Don't you remember, or are the themes too embarrassing? I'm not saying you *are* Portnoy any more than I'm saying you are me or I am Carnovsky; but come on, what did you and the doctor talk about for seven years?" (169).

Good question. So good, in fact, that Zuckerman functions as "Roth's" psychoanalyst, confronting him on issues ranging from his happy childhood, to his conflict-free relationship with his parents, to the absence of a link between "Roth's" idyllic relationship to his mother and his brutal relationship to Josie. Indeed, in creating Zuckerman, Roth imagines an even more confrontational and accusatory Dr. Kleinschmidt, demanding to know why the novelist has omitted both anger and self-hatred from the portrait of his life. Zuckerman's attack on "Roth" is so convincing, so ruthlessly satirical, so unerringly perceptive that his voice is far closer to that of Roth the novelist than "Roth" the memoirist. Calling "Roth" not an "autobiographer" but a "personificator," Zuckerman rejects his creator's coyness and revisionary family history, his "nice-guy" persona, his failure of nerve, his refusal to engage in the mode of "merciless self-evisceration" (185) that is Roth's characteristic way to expose shameful truths.

"Roth" is as much the good son in *The Facts* and in *Patrimony*, his other autobiographical work, as he is the bad son in *Portnoy's Complaint*. He acknowledges the possibility that he wrote *The Facts* "not only out of exhaustion with making fictional self-legends" but also as a "spontaneous therapeutic response" (*The Facts*, 8) to a psychological breakdown in 1987. He also wrote it as a "palliative" for the death of his mother in 1981 and the fragility of his eighty-six-year-old father. Throughout *The Facts* and *Patrimony*, Roth speaks as a loving, dutiful son, anxious to heal the minor wounds of the past. Whereas Dr. Kleinschmidt asserts that his patient's main problem was his "castration anxiety vis-à-vis a phallic mother figure," "Roth" depicts her in *The Facts* as relaxing the "exacting, sometimes fastidious strictures" as soon as her two sons began to demonstrate "signs of burgeoning independence." He concedes that his older brother, Sandy, "seems as a child to have felt more constrained by her vigilant mothering than I ever did," but he states that both sons "found more than a little sustenance in the inexhaustible maternal feeling that visibly instigated and tenderized that conscientiousness" (38–39).

Roth insists in *The Facts* that, in opposition to what Spielvogel claims in *My Life as a Man*, his mother had nothing in common with his wife. Contrasting his idyllic childhood with Josie's brutal past, "Roth" refers to himself as the "gorged beneficiary of overdevotion, overprotection, and over-surveillance within an irreproachably respectable Jewish household" (93). He describes his mother a few pages later as a "woman of deep domestic expertise and benign unworldliness reassuringly confident right up to the outermost boundaries of our social world though progressively, if respectably, uncertain anywhere beyond it" (119). She is a woman who loves both him and his stories unconditionally despite the fact that novels like *Goodbye, Columbus* and *Portnoy's Complaint* depict Jews so negatively as to earn their author the charge of being a Jewish anti-Semite. "She had no idea that there could be anything seriously offensive about them and, when she came upon articles in the Jewish press intimating that I was a traitor, couldn't understand what my detractors were talking about" (119).

Zuckerman will have none of this. "Are we to believe that this warm, comforting home portrayed there is the home that nurtured the author of *Portnoy's Complaint*? Strange lack of logic in that, but then creation is not logical" (165). Noting that the mother in *The Facts* "has no developed role either in your life or in your father's," Zuckerman concludes that "Roth's" portrayal "is a way of saying 'I was not my mother's Alexander nor was she my Sophie Portnoy,'" an assertion that may strike some readers as a denial of reality. Zuckerman's next observation is telling: "Many people don't like you as a writer just because of the ways you invite the reader to distrust those very sentiments that you now publicly embrace" (168).

One must read between the lines of *The Facts* to understand Dr. Kleinschmidt's interpretation of the patient's father as "ineffectual and submissive to the mother." Instead of emphasizing the father's business failures, "Roth" affirms his indomitable will to succeed:

> When I was a small boy, my father, then in his early thirties, was still a new Metropolitan [Life Insurance] agent, working a six-day week, including most evenings, and grateful for the steady, if modest, living this job provided, even during the Depression; a family shoe store he'd opened after marrying my mother had gone bankrupt some years before, and in between he'd had to take a variety of low-paying, unpromising jobs.　　　　　　　　　(21)

"Roth" tells us that in the mid 1940s, as he was entering high school, his father took a business risk that "wiped out the family savings" (35). Deeply in debt, the father was unable to send his sons away to college, and Philip was forced to live at home in his freshman year. Despite hints of "Oedipal" rivalry, "Roth" mythologizes his father as "hardworking, self-sacrificing" (38), a man of "prodigious energies" (45) whom no one would view as ineffectual. Nor is there the suggestion that "Roth's" father was "submissive to the mother." The fictional Zuckerman, who has been disowned by his dying father, wishes that he had a father like "Roth's": "A subdued and honorable and respectful tribute to a striving, conscientious, determined father – how can I be against that?" (166).

"Roth" and Zuckerman are both anxious to distance themselves from *Portnoy's Complaint*, so anxious, in fact, that they are in complete agreement that the novel is not autobiographical. Do they protest too much?

> What had begun as a hopped-up, semifalsified version of an analytic monologue that might have been mine, by diverging more and more from mine through its mounting hyperbole and the oddly legendary status conferred by farcical invention upon the unholy trinity of father, mother, and Jewish son, had gradually been transformed into a full-scale comical counteranalysis. Unhampered by fealty to real events and people, it was more entertaining, more graphic, and more shapely than my own analysis, if not quite to the point of my personal difficulties.　　　　　　　　　(156)

Zuckerman never seriously contradicts the factual details of "Roth's" memoir, conceding that perhaps "no more than one percent" (172) of the truth has been omitted from *The Facts*. Like "Roth," Zuckerman insists that novels are primarily works of *imagination*, and that "by projecting essentially fictional characters with manic personae out into the world, you openly invited misunderstanding about yourself" (167).

It is here that Zuckerman ceases to be a psychoanalyst. "Roth" will not concede, even in his most self-accusatory, counterfactual voice, that there is truth in the psychoanalytic assumption that a novelist's characters are grounded in the writer's experience. Nor would he concede, in Mark Twain's words, that despite an author's "wily diligences," the reader can see the "remorseless logic" of autobiographical truth.[11] Ironically, *The Facts* offers a prophetic observation that Roth might not have been able to foresee when he was writing the memoir. Zuckerman's wife, Maria – who sounds similar to the woman with whom Roth was living at the time, and whom he was soon to marry in 1990, Claire Bloom – states that one of the problems with the memoir is that "men have a root neurosis about women." She expresses this as a generalization about *all* men, not simply "Roth": "It's really a sort of suspicion, I wouldn't lay any money on it, but I think that – forgive the childish nature of this remark – but through reading all kinds of books and through experience, I do feel that men are a bit afraid of women. And that's why they behave as they do" (191).

Maria's observation is remarkably similar to Claire Bloom's statement about Philip Roth in *her* 1996 memoir, *Leaving a Doll's House*:

> Here lies a common element that appears and reappears in his later works: the need to escape from a woman at the moment when he realizes his affection makes him vulnerable to her. Implicit in this notion is the sense that, through a woman's dangerous, clandestine power, she is bearer of his physical and mental castration – possibly, even, his death.[12]

Though Bloom quickly qualifies this remark by stating that in his "near-demonic" deceased first wife, he created "the polar opposite of his own overweening mother" (169), a psychoanalytic reading would see a continuity between the phallic castrating mother in *Portnoy's Complaint* and the many femmes fatales in Roth's novels. (There is no evidence that Bloom was aware of "The Angry Act.") Bloom's memoir, balanced and nuanced as it is, calls into question Roth's demonizing not only of his wives but also of women in general. In this context, Peter Rudnytsky, the current editor of *American Imago*, argues that it is less the triangular Oedipal complex that burdens the Roth hero than the more primitive, dyadic pre-Oedipal relationship: "the

JEFFREY BERMAN

compulsive promiscuity of a Tarnopol, Kepesh, Portnoy, or Zuckerman has its roots in the mother complex."[13]

Bloom's memoir suggests that Roth's mental illness in the 1980s and 1990s was far more serious than most of his readers suspected. His suicidal depression and at times florid paranoia, along with hallucinations and wild mood swings, required him to take powerful drugs, including lithium. His erratic behavior toward Bloom, wishing to leave her but fearing abandonment by her, compelled her to wonder "which was the real Philip Roth?" (*Doll's House*, 223). Capable of great tenderness, sensitivity, and compassion, he was also raging and vindictive, with most of his fury being unleashed on women. Bloom's memoir is far more psychologically perceptive than *The Facts*, and she recalls a statement Roth made to her that his "most consequential and far-reaching relationships had always been with fatherless women." "Strange, possibly, but hardly a coincidence," she continues, since "fatherless women gravitate toward emotionally unavailable men." Even stranger, she adds, is that the women who were attracted to Roth, including herself, found him a disappointing father figure, "so austere, so conditional, so far removed from the warm and protective father of our childhood imagination. Instead, he was the fleeting shadow of the one who disappeared" (*Doll's House*, 236).

No one can say whether psychoanalysis failed Roth or whether he failed psychoanalysis. What we can say is that he never sees psychoanalysis as an intersubjective, collaborative process in which both analyst and analysand seek to arrive at a mutually agreed truth. Nor does he see psychoanalysis as a narrative strategy similar to fiction making, with both the analyst and the fiction writer creating as opposed to discovering truth. His later fictional characters visit doctors who seem to have missed all the important innovations in psychoanalytic theory and practice in the last forty years, including relational approaches and self psychology. His psychoanalysts seem frozen in time, imprisoned by a rigid Freudian ideology that most analysts have long ago abandoned or sharply revised. If art is, as Dr. Kleinschmidt claims, an angry act, it is also a reparational act, as may be seen in *Patrimony*,[14] Roth's most compassionate book.

"The Angry Act" is not the "Key to All Mythologies," the book over which Casaubon labors in George Eliot's *Middlemarch*, but it does unlock some of Roth's psychic secrets. As Sanford Pinsker observed in 1975, "More than any other contemporary writer, with the possible exception of Norman Mailer, Philip Roth has been relentless about probing the connections between his private passions (kvetches, griefs, failures) and the larger mythologies that make up contemporary American life."[15] The playwright who, according to Dr. Kleinschmidt, "acted out his anger in his relationships with women, reducing all of them to masturbatory sexual objects and by using his hostile masturbatory fantasies in his literary output," resembles many of Roth's male characters. Few writers exhibit a greater degree of narcissistic rage than does Roth. He returns repeatedly in his stories to the literary critics who have wounded him deeply, as when he pillories Milton Appel, an unmistakable portrait of Irving Howe, whose influential 1972 *Commentary* essay, "Philip Roth Reconsidered," stung the novelist.[16] After Roth's five-year marriage to Claire Bloom ended bitterly in 1995, and almost immediately following the publication of *Leaving a Doll's House*, which records her dismay over his portrayal of marital infidelity in his novel *Deception*, he published *I Married a Communist*, containing an acidic portrait of his ex-wife. Despite Zuckerman's insistence in *The Anatomy Lesson* that "life and art are distinct" and that "writing is an act of imagination"[17] – a recurrent observation in his stories – there can be little doubt that Roth obsesses over his narcissistic injuries and attacks those who have attacked him. Surely Roth knows this, which is why Roseanna's father states accurately in *Sabbath's Theater*: "How you cling to your grievance! As though in a world of persecution you alone have a grievance. Wait till you're dead – death is grievance and only grievance."[18]

Roth's comments about psychoanalysis in his later novels are increasingly hostile. In *The Anatomy Lesson*, Zuckerman, tormented by a mysterious depression, consults a psychoanalyst, who wondered aloud if his patient "hadn't given up fighting the illness to *retain* (with a fairly untroubled conscience) his 'harem of Florence Nightingales.'" Zuckerman so resented the crack he nearly walked out" (14). Zuckerman – and Roth – unambiguously reject the psychoanalyst's charge of the "secondary gains" of illness, agreeing with a "no-nonsense" doctor that "The Freudian personalization of every ache and pain is the crudest weapon to have been bequeathed to these guys since the leech pot" (25). In *The Counterlife*, an editor delivers a eulogy of Zuckerman that reads like a book review; the eulogy seems to be another rebuttal of Dr. Kleinschmidt's thesis:

> The exhibitionism of the superior artist is connected to his imagination; fiction is for him at once playful hypothesis and serious supposition, an imaginative form of inquiry – everything that exhibitionism is not. It is, if anything, closet exhibitionism, exhibitionism in hiding. Isn't it true that, contrary to the general belief, it is the *distance* between the writer's life and his novel that is the most intriguing aspect of his imagination?[19]

In *Operation Shylock*, Philip Roth's "impersonator" tells him, "You're a Freudian . . . You have the Freudian belief in the sovereign power of causality. Causeless events don't exist in your universe. To you things that aren't thinkable in intellectual terms aren't worth thinking about. A lot of smart Jews are like that."[20] To quote Roth in *Conversations*, "The tradition in ventriloquism is that the dummy is always smarter than the ventriloquist" (240).

In *Sabbath's Theater*, Roth satirizes psychiatric nosology with the suggestion, proposed in the *Journal of Medical Ethics*, that the word "happiness" be classified as a psychiatric disorder and listed as a major affective disorder: "In a review of the relevant literature it is shown that *happiness* is statistically abnormal, consists of a discrete cluster of symptoms, is associated with a range of cognitive abnormalities, and probably reflects the abnormal functioning of the central nervous system" (280). In *American Pastoral* Merry's father takes her to a psychiatrist to treat her stuttering. "The psychiatrist got Merry thinking that the stutter was a choice she made, a way of being special that she had chosen and then locked into when she realized how well it worked. The psychiatrist asked her, 'How do you think your father would feel about you if you didn't stutter? How do you think your mother would feel?'" Merry's father is so enraged by the psychiatrist's questions that "by the time he left he wanted to kill him."[21] In *The Human Stain*, Faunia Farley is sexually abused by her stepfather, and when the mother takes her fourteen-year-old daughter to a psychiatrist, to whom Faunia confides her abuse, after ten sessions he sides with the stepfather. " 'Takes the side of those who pay him,' Faunia says. 'Just like everyone.' The mother had an affair with the psychiatrist afterward."[22]

Roth's rejection of psychoanalysis is part of his rejection of a simple relationship between autobiography and fiction. As Pepler observes in *Zuckerman Unbound*, "Fiction is not autobiography, yet all fiction, I am convinced, is in some sense rooted in autobiography, though the connection to actual events may be tenuous indeed, even nonexistent. We are, after all, the total of our experiences, and experience includes not only what we in fact do but what we privately imagine."[23]

Roth emphasizes the imagination's ability to transmute experience into art, an essential truth that he criticizes Dr. Kleinschmidt for ignoring. Roth's rejection of psychoanalysis is also part of a larger rejection of humanistic knowledge, the Socratic belief that knowledge is power. Whereas his early fictional characters undergo an epical quest for self-knowledge, the later characters discover that introspection leads only to increased misery. As Madeline complains about her therapy group in *Sabbath's Theater*, "In Courage to Heal they've been trying for three weeks to get me to turn in my dad. The answer to every question is either Prozac or incest. Talk about boring. All the false introspection. It's enough in itself to make you suicidal" (287). In *American Pastoral*, it is not truth but error that Roth affirms: "The fact remains that getting people right is not what living is all about anyway. It's getting them wrong that is living, getting them wrong and wrong and wrong and then, on careful reconsideration, getting them wrong again. That's how we know we're alive: we're wrong" (35). And perhaps the clearest statement of Roth's growing pessimism about knowledge appears in *The Human Stain* when Zuckerman opines, "What we know is that, in an unclichéd way, nobody knows anything. You *can't* know anything. The things you *know* you don't know. Intention? Motive? Consequence? Meaning? All that we don't know is astonishing. Even more astonishing is what passes for knowing" (209).

Roth affirms not the talking cure but the writing cure, the only type of therapy he endorses. His sacred muse is art, not life, and he is willing to make every sacrifice, including the loss of his friends. In *The Anatomy Lesson* Zuckerman speaks for Roth when he observes, "Monstrous that all the world's suffering is good to me inasmuch as it's grist to my mill – that all I can do, when confronted with anyone's story, is to wish to turn it into *material*, but if that's the way one is possessed, that is the way one is possessed" (133). So too does Maria's letter to Zuckerman in *The Counterlife* convey Roth's position: "a life without horrible difficulties . . . is inimical to the writer you are. You actually *like* to take things hard. You can't weave your stories otherwise" (316–17). Roth's observation about Zuckerman in *The Human Stain* is self-observation: "Whatever catastrophe turns up, he transforms into writing. Catastrophe is cannon fodder for him" (170). Or as Roth states simply, "A writer needs his poisons. The antidote to his poisons is often a book" (*Conversations*, 180). Given the belief that writers need their poison for the sake of art, one wonders whether Roth would be sympathetic to any therapy – apart from writing itself – that offered to counteract life's deadly toxins.

NOTES

1 Philip Roth, *Deception* (New York: Simon and Schuster, 1990), p. 190.
2 Philip Roth, *The Facts: A Novelist's Autobiography* (New York: Farrar, Straus and Giroux, 1988).
3 Jeffrey Berman, *The Talking Cure: Literary Representations of Psychoanalysis* (New York: New York University Press, 1985).
4 Philip Roth, *Portnoy's Complaint* (New York: Random House, 1969).
5 Philip Roth, *My Life as a Man* (New York: Holt, Rinehart and Winston, 1974).
6 Hans J. Kleinschmidt, "The Angry Act: The Role of Aggression in Creativity," *American Imago*, 24 (1967): 98–128.
7 Philip Roth, *The Breast* (New York: Holt, Rinehart and Winston, 1972).
8 Part of the preceding material appears in *The Talking Cure* and in my review of *Tales from the Couch: Writers on Therapy*, ed. Jason Shinder, appearing in *Psychoanalytic Psychology*, 18 (2001): 743–55.

9 *Conversations with Philip Roth*, ed. George J. Searles (Jackson: University Press of Mississippi, 1992), p. 92.
10 Philip Young, *Ernest Hemingway: A Reconsideration* (New York: Harbinger, 1966).
11 Henry Nash Smith and William Gibson (eds.), *Mark Twain–Howell Letters: The Correspondence of Samuel L. Clemens and William D. Howells, 1872–1910*, 2 vols. (Cambridge, MA: Harvard University Press, 1960), vol. II, p. 782.
12 Claire Bloom, *Leaving a Doll's House* (Boston: Little, Brown and Company, 1996), p. 169. I am grateful to Peter Rudnytsky for alerting me to this book.
13 Peter Rudnytsky, "*Goodbye, Columbus*: Roth's Portrait of the Narcissist as a Young Man," *Twentieth-Century Literature*, 51 (Spring 2005): 7.
14 Philip Roth, *Patrimony: A True Story* (New York: Simon and Schuster, 1991).
15 Sanford Pinsker, *The Comedy that "Hoits"* (Columbia: University of Missouri Press, 1975), p. 115.
16 Irving Howe, "Philip Roth Reconsidered," *Commentary*, 54 (December 1972): 69–77.
17 Philip Roth, *The Anatomy Lesson* (New York: Farrar, Straus and Giroux, 1983), p. 44.
18 Philip Roth, *Sabbath's Theater* (New York: Vintage, 1996), p. 272.
19 Philip Roth, *The Counterlife* (New York: Farrar, Straus and Giroux, 1986), p. 210.
20 Philip Roth, *Operation Shylock* (New York: Vintage, 1994), p. 79.
21 Philip Roth, *American Pastoral* (New York: Vintage, 1997), p. 95.
22 Philip Roth, *The Human Stain* (Boston: Houghton Mifflin, 2000), p. 28.
23 Philip Roth, *Zuckerman Unbound* (New York: Farrar, Straus and Giroux, 1981), p. 150.

8

DEBRA SHOSTAK

Roth and gender

With the publication of *My Life as a Man* in 1974, Philip Roth brought into sharp focus subject matter that has continued to preoccupy him for most of his career. When his protagonist, the writer Peter Tarnopol, struggles to make sense of his anguished life by dropping the guise of fiction and telling his story "straight," words such as "man," "manly," and "manhood" recur like the restless beat of a drum. "What's the matter with men?" complains a minor female character, "What do they *want?*"[1] Echoing Freud's famous rhetorical question about women's sexuality, her peevish queries indicate that neither male heterosexual desire nor masculine identity is understood by the men who desire or the women who stand outside or as objects of such desire. Tarnopol reflects mid-twentieth-century American values when he equates legitimate selfhood with masculinity: "I wanted to be humanish: manly, a man" (*My Life as a Man*, 174). At the same time, he identifies the yoke under which he labors as an ideological construction, asserting how "strong was the myth of male inviolability, of male dominance and potency" (173). The myth – and its unmasking – propels many of Roth's plots; his concern with questions of gender has been almost wholly confined to the trials of manhood. When he confessed to an interviewer in 1997 that "the lives of men has been my subject," Roth found an apt metaphor for that subject: "the circus of being a man . . . and the ringleader is the phallus."[2]

The circus of being a man – fleshly desire, force, activity, sexual display, and all kept under masterly control – such are the features of the "myth of male inviolability" that drives Roth's men. Only within its structure do they believe they can authentically speak the "I" that constructs and confirms selfhood. Under the terms of the myth, a man's sense of power relative to other men is the key to attaining the "I," a power often expressed or signified in sexual terms. Arthur Brittan calls the myth "masculinism." The ideology underlying twentieth-century American masculinism evinces "an obsession with competition and achievement" and draws upon "the myth of the autonomous and independent penis." According to this "hydraulic model" of masculinity, Brittan asserts, "A man is only a man in so far as he is capable of using his penis as an instrument of power."[3] Michael Kimmel adds that "homophobia, men's fear of other men, is the animating condition of the dominant definition of masculinity in America, that the reigning definition of masculinity is a defensive effort to prevent being emasculated."[4] The terms that identify a man's failure to achieve the masculinist ideal – emasculation, feminization, and impotence – emerge from a stubborn opposition founded upon bodily performance. One is not a "man" when one fails to dominate or to perform sexually. Such failure, according to the myth, deprives a man of the fully vested "I" of agency in the world. The governing ideology of manhood confuses the real body of a man with the idealized body of manliness, masculinity with masculinism, sexual potency with personal power, the fleshly penis with the symbolic phallus as the central signifier of desire at the root of modern male selfhood. No wonder Roth calls the phallus the ringleader.

Thus it is that Roth's interest in the lives of twentieth-century American men has often taken shape in narratives of heterosexual pursuit. He has been fearless in challenging readers to look upon raw male desires. Roth has seemed not just to risk but even to welcome censure; at times he has written male characters as if simply to learn what they will do and whether there are reasons *not* to despise them. His attention to the insatiable, transgressive, and often stultified appetites of men has laid him open to charges of misogyny, especially in his early work. For example, Brenda Patimkin, of "Goodbye, Columbus" (1959),[5] can appear to be little more than a spoiled Jewish American princess, a delectable dish tempting Neil Klugman much as does the cornucopia of fruit in her family's refrigerator. If from a feminist perspective Brenda seems a stereotypical sexual object, Alexander Portnoy's mother in *Portnoy's Complaint*[6] offers a nightmarish Jewish mother, self-denying, overprotective, and castrating. Indeed, Roth's male characters project their fears upon women who seem to threaten their performance of masculinity. Where a female character in Roth's early work appears flattest, she is presented almost exclusively through the male character's point of view, if not literally in a first-person voice, then as mediated through the focalized consciousness of the male protagonist. That point of view moves the female characters toward objectification when Roth's men express their anxieties, even hysteria, in measuring themselves against the myth of masculinity.

For these very reasons, however, Roth's work can appear as much a prescient critique of misogynist attitudes as a purveyor of them. Even in first-person narratives, Roth gives us the opportunity to gain distance on the objectifying male, to register our own ambivalence alongside the character's. Brenda, for example, the Radcliffe girl with a nose job, epitomizes for Neil not just the promise of ripe sexuality, but also Jewish assimilation achieved through conspicuous consumption. Neil is excluded from the Patimkins' materialist success as well as the condition of American masculinity bought by that success. While Neil spends his time in the library, Brenda's brother realizes a wholly assimilated identity in sports. When Neil's narrating voice obscures Brenda's in the novella and dismisses her family's excesses with disdain, therefore, readers can discern beyond his controlled comic tone the bravado of a man maneuvering for power in a foreign land where he doesn't quite know the language.

"Goodbye, Columbus" demonstrates that, from the beginning of his career, Roth perceived the devastations of masculinism through a Jewish lens. The construction of gender is inflected by the multiple cultures in which one participates. Neil's point of view on Brenda and her family is inextricable from his position as a post-immigrant Jew in an America that, in the 1950s, promoted the melting pot as an ideal and identified prosperity as the surest route to that ideal. While the myth of masculinity in the United States has been founded upon competition and achievement in the fields of both sexual prowess and economic gain, however, the Jewish man operates under conflicting expectations forged in the European Diaspora. Broadly, these expectations take shape in two related ways. In ethical terms, the Jewish man must choose *how* to behave as a Jew; in ontological terms, he must understand *who* a Jew is in relation to non-Jews.

The conceptualizations of Jewish manhood are dichotomized in special relation to the regulation of the Jewish male body. Roth clarified the ethical opposition when he explained the development of *Portnoy's Complaint*. Portnoy speaks "in behalf of both the 'Jewboy' (with all that word signifies to Jew and Gentile alike about aggression, appetite, and marginality) and the 'nice Jewish boy' (and what that epithet implies about repression, respectability, and social acceptance)."[7] The Jewboy strives to conquer American soil on its own terms – to satisfy desires, to be as big as he might be, to eat, earn, and fornicate in a display of masculine power. The Jewboy does not concern himself with moral nicety. The nice Jewish boy, however, fearful that any show of Jewish selfhood might awaken anti-Semitism, endeavors to find a place among American gentiles by erasing himself – especially any telltale desires or differences – in irreproachable behavior. The nice Jewish boy, alert to the feelings and, especially, the judgments of others, pretends that his body simply doesn't exist.

The nice Jewish boy has a much longer tradition in Jewish culture than does the Jewboy. The Jewish Diaspora caused Jews to find ways to identify themselves as distinct from the cultures where they tried to make their homes, to maintain ethical legitimacy and cultural continuity as Jews under the condition of homelessness. The nice Jewish boy is the image of the Diaspora Jew who ideally marked himself off from non-Jews by his bookishness, his unworldliness, and his rejection of carnality and violence. In clear opposition to the images of action, power, and virility that dominate masculinist ideology, therefore, the figure of the Jewish man inevitably seems feminized. Further, as Sander Gilman has pointed out, the emasculated Jew became an enduring image in the minds of non-Jews in nineteenth- and early twentieth-century Europe as it was increasingly identified with the Jewish practice of circumcision. Ironically, circumcision was a practice initiated as a symbol of the Jew's special covenant with God, a sign of membership in a select tribal group. As a rite performed on males alone, circumcision conferred Jewish identity (traditionally conceptualized in masculine terms) and ensured patrilineage. In the Diaspora, however, because Jews were culturally peripheral rather than central, circumcision became a visible mark of Jewish difference from the norm. The "Jew" as a category thus shifted to meanings defined by non-Jews: from normative self to other, from masculine to feminine, from health to pathology.[8] Gilman notes how the medical discourses of nineteenth-century Europe constructed the circumcised Jewish body as mutilated, an image that was mistakenly conflated with castration. The male Jew was not only emasculated but linked to the hysteria associated with the feminine.[9]

Roth does not refer directly to this cultural history, but his male characters clearly carry its burdens as they confront their manhood, struggling to be American Jews, to choose between being Jewboys and nice Jewish boys. Roth shines his spotlight on men in pursuit of their desires at various stages of their lives – in fact, the ages of his male protagonists often correspond to his own at the time of writing. Roth has created his fiction during a time of radical transformations in both the social conceptions of gender and sexuality and in philosophical understandings of selfhood. As a result, as he tracks men's lives over the course of his career, the terms in which he conceives of their exertions alter in relation to developing social discourses, often capturing the ideological instabilities and contradictions that result from a world that is changing under the very feet of his characters. To the degree that the texts themselves feel unresolved, a reader's sympathies ambivalent, the novels serve as battlegrounds for competing ideas as the men in them struggle to know how to be men. Roth's inquiry into the conflicts masculinism presents to his male subjects follows a rough chronology. He starts from a largely psychoanalytic perspective that acknowledges the specificity of Jewish identity, moves toward deconstructing the oppositions according to which gender is typically conceptualized, and finally weighs the liberating notion that identity is performed rather than essential against the evidence that selfhood is situated in time – in both the life of the organism and human history. The paradigms that shape Roth's representations of men are not mutually exclusive. Rather, his portraits of men who serve the phallic master amount to an ongoing, inconclusive dialogue. Is gendered selfhood an essence or socially constructed? Are we governed by ideology or by physical fact? The path Roth follows in thinking about men therefore offers a complex history of the experience and understanding of masculinity in the late twentieth century.

Psychoanalysis and the Jew

Although early murmurings of male anxiety are audible in the characterizations of Gabe Wallach in *Letting Go* (1962) and Roy Bassart in *When She Was Good* (1967),[10] the first real cries of pain from Roth's male characters resound throughout *Portnoy's Complaint*. The cries are quite literal – under the premise that Alexander Portnoy is immersed in therapeutic sessions with a psychoanalyst, the pages are littered with exclamation points. Roth depicts a man whose illness stems from his uncritical devotion to the masculine myth. Portnoy's symptom is impotence, whose proximate cause he locates in his Jewishness: "I'm living [my life] in the middle of a Jewish joke!" he exclaims to Dr. Spielvogel. "Who made us so morbid and hysterical and weak? . . . Bless me with manhood! . . . Enough being a nice Jewish boy, publicly pleasing my parents while privately pulling my putz!" (*Portnoy's Complaint*, 39–40). Portnoy voices his alliterative "complaint" in terms of conflict between the Jewboy's appetite and the nice Jewish boy's renunciation of instinctual gratification, and he conceptualizes wholeness of selfhood in gendered terms. Manhood, as defined by the masculinist myth, is what he relentlessly seeks in taboo-breaking sexual acts, each a desperate effort to "put the id back in Yid" (139). Yet such acts as obsessive masturbation and promiscuous sex paradoxically demonstrate not his wholeness but his altogether too feminizing hysteria.

Roth steeps his representation of Alex Portnoy in Freud's theories of sexuality. Indeed, part of the novel's humor lies in the patient's anticipation of the analysis a Freudian would perform on his every symptom, memory, and dream – Portnoy, like Roth, has read his Freud. Roth refers openly to *Civilization and Its Discontents* (1930),[11] where Freud identified the root conflict of Western culture – and not just of Jewish manhood – as the struggle between instinctual satisfaction and renunciation. Portnoy describes both his Oedipal longings for his mother and his castration complex, epitomized when his mother wields a bread knife over him to gain his obedience. And Roth brilliantly parodies the sort of entry one might find in a physician's diagnostic manual when he quotes from Dr. Spielvogel's article "The Puzzled Penis" to offer a summary of "Portnoy's complaint." But psychoanalysis does not alone explain Portnoy's neurosis without the cultural context of his position as a Jew. Portnoy himself identifies the Jewish distance from the monolithic masculinist model when, recounting his mother's smothering behavior, he pleads, "And why doesn't my father stop her?" (17). If one views Sophie Portnoy's emasculating ministrations largely from the point of view of her condition as an anxious Jewish mother in America, in fact, the most important lesson she teaches the young Alex is the difference between Jew and non-Jew, expressed by her as the opposition between Jew and "goy." Although she establishes the categories of "us" and "them" to protect her son from the largely incomprehensible and threatening culture in which they live, Alex experiences the category of "Jew" as a force of repression and renunciation, defined solely in relation to the nice Jewish boy and confined by regulatory codes of behavior. For Portnoy, appetite distinguishes Jew from goy, and, by extension, Jew from "man." The goy is manly, consuming and acting; fearing to act or consume, the Jew is morbid, hysterical, and weak – hardly the ringleader of the circus.

Portnoy diagnoses his condition but fails to gain critical distance on the ideologies that have created it for him. Neo-Freudians have argued that cultural prohibitions engage a man in a dialectic of desire and repression formulated in the terms of the symbolic body – in a choice, that is, either "to be or not to be the phallus, and to have it or not to have it."[12] Accordingly, Portnoy's perfervid acts of sexual excess can be seen as efforts to be and to have the phallus: "My wang," he insists, "was all I really had that I could call my own" (35). His method is systematically to break the most significant taboos that regulate the Jewish male body, so as to cast off "diseased" Jewish masculinity in favor of "healthy" American (read goyische) manhood. If the Talmud contains proscriptions against masturbation,[13] then Portnoy's compulsive masturbation – in school, at the movies, on a bus, all over the family bathroom – expresses his penis envy, his attempts to fill the lack that, as he sees it, constitutes the feminized Jewish male. He obtains little power or pleasure from his transgressions, however, which instead intensify his fantasies of castration. He can no more free himself from the criminal guilt of the masturbatory act than he can, as it were, wear away the mark of circumcision that tells him who he is.

Portnoy discovers that he does not possess his "wang" in his mature sexual encounters, either, because he remains under the cloud of the Jew/goy opposition. He seeks to transgress against the regulation of his Jewish body by sexual pursuit of a series of gentile women whom he hopes will afford him symbolic entrée into American manhood. In Portnoy's coarse argot (his verbal mimickry of "manliness"): "I don't seem to stick my dick up these girls, as much as I stick it up their backgrounds – as though through fucking I will discover America. *Conquer* America" (265). The *shiksa*, the derogatory Yiddish term for the gentile woman, is for the Jewish man the highly eroticized image of cultural difference. A forbidden fruit, the *shiksa* becomes an object of consumption analogous to the unkosher foods that tempt the Jew to disobey the rules that identify his body as Jewish and hence neither a "man" nor fully "American." The *shiksa* reminds the Jew of his exclusion from the rewards of the masculine myth, challenging him to erase the opposition of Jew and goy in sexual congress and to reverse the implied hierarchy in that opposition by penetrating gentile America. So construed, the idea of the *shiksa* dictates Portnoy's unmitigated objectification of the women who fill the role for him, as is evident in his belittling nicknames for them: the Monkey, the Pumpkin, the Pilgrim.

Roth's extravagant comedy in the scenes with Portnoy's *shiksas* may temporarily obscure the misogyny in Alex's view of these women, especially since the reader is never permitted a perspective outside Portnoy's voice. Yet Roth evinces ambivalence toward his protagonist. Portnoy's persistently whining self-aggrandizement allows us distance on a man so wrapped up in his own performances. Indeed, Roth punishes Portnoy; confronted with a *shiksa* in the flesh rather than fantasy, for example, he finds his "circumcised little dong . . . simply shriveled up with veneration" (162). The *shiksa* reenacts the Jew's emasculation rather than curing his impotence. So it is that, as self-aware as Portnoy seems, he never escapes the masculinist construction of his identity, never reckons with the ethical implications of his objectification of others, and, possibly, never makes any progress, as the doctor's punch line, "Now vee may perhaps to begin" (309), suggests. Rather, he is still making the same complaints in the closing pages: "The things that other men do – and get away with! . . . It makes me want to *scream*, the ridiculous disproportion of the guilt! May I?" (308–09). Even in the privacy of the doctor's office, he must ask permission, like the nice Jewish boy he inescapably is.

Deconstructing the binary gender system

When Roth returns to the question of gender in *The Breast* (1972),[14] he leaves aside the Jewish context for masculinity in order to inquire into deeply held assumptions about the body's function in the construction of a gender identity. If *The Breast* may have looked to readers largely like a gesture of pornographic provocation – a man turns into a female breast and then describes his sensory experience in detail! – they might be surprised by the degree to which the novella anticipates the serious inquiry into the ideological matrix of gender construction that occurred at the end of the twentieth century. When the Kafkaesque parable of *The Breast* transforms David Kepesh into a six-foot mammary gland, Roth reveals the body as central to the existential question of selfhood. His focus on the body challenges fundamental oppositions that structure our thinking about the self: masculine vs. feminine, human vs. nonhuman, subject vs. object. Roth leads the reader to see that such binary thinking is essentialist in interpreting the body, whose lineaments are normally transparent – or at any rate unquestioned – under the conventional terms of gendered subjectivity.

When Kepesh metamorphoses into a human breast, the normal categories of selfhood are dismantled – he proves that the self is not irreducible. Roth exposes our assumption that the body is an object and consciousness is the seat of subjectivity, with the corollary that mental experience as distinct from the physical constitutes identity. We are accustomed to think that our consciousness is other than the vessel which contains it. When that vessel becomes unrecognizable, the membrane between consciousness and the body is torn. Once Kepesh declares "I am a breast" (13) he is awash in contradictions. His "I" – the sign of human subjectivity – has become an object, a dismembered body part without a claim on human agency. If "I" am a breast, then "I" am no longer a man, neither "manly" nor "human."

Kepesh is unequipped to grapple with his now inchoate selfhood. The language available to describe his condition cannot capture his liminality with respect to such categories as masculinity and femininity. In this sense, *The Breast* is an outlandish joke about the myth of masculinity, which is founded upon the simplistic binary of male and female. Trapped inside an apparently alien housing, Kepesh still insists that he is a "male" consciousness within a "female" body. Roth's choice of a *breast* as the body part into which Kepesh is transformed draws starkly upon the iconography of gender categories. The breast is a body part indelibly marked as female. The fetishized object of the erotic male gaze, it is also the maternal object of infant gratification whose loss inserts a child into the symbolic order in which sexual difference is one of the many differences comprising the world of human meaning. Both meanings attaching to the breast would locate Kepesh firmly within the realm of the feminine, were it not that all his intellectual and sense perceptions are filtered through a selfhood that stubbornly continues to feel "masculine." He longs, for example, to insert his highly sensitive nipple – his transformed penis – into his nurse's orifices, but when a male rather than female nurse tends him, he feels an illogical disgust at the "homosexual act" (45). The metamorphosis embodies Kepesh's castration anxiety, because he can only think within the opposition of male to female. According to the Freudian model, therefore, his hysterical symptoms are inscribed upon his body as he realizes the fantasy that masculinism deems most monstrous for a man: to be turned into a woman. Blind and inert, he is reduced to being the object of others' looking, wholly dependent on others to minister to him. Like the visual image of his body, his helplessness apparently places him in the ideologically defined position of woman.

Yet clearly Kepesh occupies neither the male nor female position. In *The Breast*, Roth deconstructs the myth of male/female bipolarity upon which masculinism depends, but in doing so, he demonstrates the degree to which we, and perhaps he as well, are hard pressed to move beyond this construction of gender and sexuality. Kepesh does not fundamentally rethink the categories defining who he is; he continues to wish to return to the uncomplicated *man*hood he still experiences as defining his identity. In discussing with his doctor whether he should go public with his condition, he recognizes that, no matter how he urges observers to look beyond his absurd body, "I'll still be a joke" (88) – and this persuades him to remain in seclusion. Michael Kimmel reports a survey in which, asked their greatest fear, women named rape and murder while men named being laughed at; Kepesh's fears, reasserting the binary system, continue to define his selfhood in the terms of the masculinist myth.[15]

The gendered subject: essence or performance

From the late 1980s to the end of the twentieth century, Roth's fiction has explored a central ontological problem of the period: is selfhood an essence, an autonomous construction, or an artifact of conditions beyond the self? *The Counterlife* (1986),[16] for example, openly challenges essentialism and determinism by adopting a performative paradigm of identity, hinging on the titular notion of the *counterlife*. Dismissing the pretence of a coherent "I," the plot shifts startlingly so as to follow logically upon the shifting identities that characters perform as they enact alternative, or counter, lives. Roth engages the postmodern possibilities for indeterminate, linguistically constructed selfhood – a game that he later plays in both *Deception* (1990) and *Operation Shylock* (1993)[17] – and he finds it especially appealing that one might have some agency in inventing selves in place of the (absent) irreducible self.

If the logic of essentialism informs the bipolarities of the masculine myth, then indeterminacy would seem to promise an escape from the binary system of gender. Yet Roth does not break the ideological bonds of masculinism and seems to arrive at an essentialist paradigm rather than a performative one.

However verbally acrobatic the performance of his characters' subjectivity, for example, they remain limited to either/or choices – nice Jew/Jewboy, diasporic manhood/militant Israeli manhood. Subsequently, the agonized comedy of *Sabbath's Theater* (1995)[18] explicitly takes up the question of essentialism and the performance of identities in the terms of the masculinist myth. When Zuckerman asserts in *The Counterlife* that "I am a theater and nothing more than a theater" (321), Roth establishes the guiding metaphor for Mickey Sabbath. Sabbath is the puppeteer of the "Indecent Theater of Manhattan" (12) whose professional performances rely upon ventriloquism. His theater is "indecent" precisely to the degree that in displacing women's voices, literally and figuratively, he enacts the myth of "male dominance and potency" Roth described in *My Life as a Man*. Sabbath's two wives function as his puppets, instruments for both his stage performances and his sexual mastery. Roth brilliantly demonstrates that Sabbath *performs* his masculinity when Sabbath tells of a 1956 street performance in which he invites a young woman to talk, mesmerized, to his middle finger while the other hand slowly unbuttons her blouse. The finger Sabbath uses as a puppet is an obvious metaphor for his penis. Sabbath is the Jewboy incarnate; when he brags that "I carry my puppet between my legs" (314), he clearly conflates his puppet shows with his exercise of phallic power. His indiscriminate and immoderate desires, his objectification of women, his flippant tyrannies and uncensored expressions, all serve to make Sabbath appear as Roth's most ruthless, unapologetic epitome of the hydraulic model of masculinity. Yet it is precisely in Sabbath's excesses that Roth offers a profound critique of both masculinism and the freely chosen performance of identity as he confronts the realities of the material body.

Writing about the constitution of lesbian subjectivity, Judith Butler makes a crucial point about an individual's need to repeat consistently the performance of gender: "the 'I' is a site of repetition, that is, . . . the 'I' only achieves the semblance of identity through a certain repetition of itself . . . [T]he repetition, and the failure to repeat, produce a string of performances that constitute and *contest* the coherence of that 'I.'"[19] If repetition is the key to one's conviction of a coherent subjectivity then the inability to repeat a performance of the "I" destabilizes selfhood, stripping away the illusion that there exists some prior or essential "I." Roth runs Sabbath up against this conundrum. Haunted by the disappearance of his wife Nikki and the deaths of his mother, his brother, and finally, his lover Drenka, Sabbath faces indisputable evidence that the body cannot sustain performances of the "I." Physical diminishment banishes the possibility of an essential selfhood, however construed. Sabbath's inability to repeat a coherent identity is signified by the arthritis that requires him to give up his career as a puppeteer. The crippling of his fingers, which performed his masculine potency in his youth, is a clear allusion to the impending impotence of age. In Zuckerman's terms, if he is no longer a theater, he is no longer an autonomous self, and certainly not a *man*.

Sabbath's failures – his discovery that he can no longer "run a '29 penis on ruthless mistrust, cunning negativity, and world-denouncing energy" (219) – enable Roth to question Sabbath's masculinist ideology at its root. Roth implies that the impermanence of the body is an immutable fact in the construction of identity, and insofar as identity is a gendered, temporal artifact, it must exist in relation to the sexual functions and signifiers that mark out gender. Roth does not suggest that there is an essential "I," but that the "I" must reckon with the flesh – an "essence" that paradoxically is defined by its mutability. Sabbath has created a self through mastery of his body and he can no longer repeat his physical performances; if he is to define a selfhood at all, he must, like Kepesh in *The Breast*, draw upon the materiality of the body as well as longer-term ideological constructs. That this is not an easy lesson for Sabbath conveys the degree to which ideology blinds us. Roth sends him on a quest that Sabbath stubbornly perceives as the search for erotic gratification – the confirmation of his masculine power – but that confronts him instead with death and impotence. The Freudian doctrine that frames this novel is not the Oedipal story, nor the story of instinctual renunciation, but the story the older Freud devised in *Beyond the Pleasure Principle* (1920)[20] about the tension between the erotic and death drives. In bracketing the novel within Drenka's story, that is, Roth presses Sabbath to face an essentialism of the body even as he persistently ignores the fact of decay.

Drenka has a surprising precursor in *The Counterlife*'s Maria, lover of the writer Nathan Zuckerman, who marks a turning point in Roth's representations of women. Whereas Libby Herz in *Letting Go* and Lucy Nelson in *When She Was Good* are damaged and made monstrous by the ideologies that construct their femininity in conformity with virtuous domesticity, whereas Amy Bellette in *The Ghost Writer* exists in the text largely as either the unknowable Other or an object for Zuckerman's fantasy, and whereas Wendy in *The Counterlife* itself is strictly an old-fashioned fantasy object for Henry Zuckerman, Maria makes a start on being a subject in her own right. Though she is but one of Nathan's "fictive propositions" (*Counterlife*, 319), Maria resists the role to which he has consigned her, preferring to disappear from the novel – to "die" – rather than remain the object of Nathan's language. While Roth's male figures persist in staking their freedom on performing masculinity autonomously, it is the woman who is in some sense freest. Ambiguously enough, Maria's relative freedom can be read to support either the masculinist suspicion of woman's elusive power or the feminist vision of woman as a subject in herself – a sure index to the degree of flux in the ideologies underlying Roth's representations.

So, too, is Drenka's characterization a testament to Roth's resistance to category. She may appear at first as a victim of misogyny, not just Sabbath's but the writer's as well, because she seems to embody male fantasy. A maternal figure at whose breasts Sabbath suckles, she is also sexually adventurous, feels most powerful when she carries a man's semen after intercourse, and, in her inability to grasp English idiom, seems incapable of the rational discourse attributed to the masculine. Indeed, when in a visit to her gravesite the grief-stricken Sabbath cries "I am Drenka!" and the narrator follows with "Something horrible is happening to Sabbath" (*Sabbath's Theater*, 78), the "horrible" at first seems to be his feminization. Yet Drenka is not the woman-as-object she may appear. Sabbath may be her teacher in their taboo-breaking sexual affair, but Drenka is the principal teacher because she forces him to see the dying body, the decay of the "wet sauce" of intercourse into the bodily fluids that stain her hospital bed as cancer turns her flesh into "carrion" (424). Roth does not make Drenka solely the bodily object the images of disease portend, however, instead conveying her vitality and position as an active subject in her speaking voice after the body is lost to her. If a female character's possession of a voice is one sign that a text is not objectifying her, then Drenka, like Maria, escapes misogynistic representation.

Strictly speaking, Sabbath may not be transformed into a feminized object, but he is still objectified as a *body*. Drenka teaches him his condition as an object in time, his future in waste and impotence, irrespective of his gendering. In this sense, Roth deconstructs the opposition between the essence and performance of subjectivity. Sabbath may initially assert the outrageous freedom of performative identity with considerable success, but Roth drives him to acknowledge that he can install through repetition neither phallic power nor the stable identity that hinges upon it. Roth disrupts the myth of male inviolability if not its hold upon the male imagination. When Sabbath visits the cemetery not to masturbate but to urinate over Drenka's grave, he can no longer delude himself that his penis is the phallus of sexual and cultural potency; instead it is a dripping "spout without menace or significance of any kind" (445). In *Sabbath's Theater* the self is performative for Roth only within the limits set by the physiologies of desire and the timebound essences of the flesh. Roth suggests not that Sabbath – or any man – fails to measure up to the myth of masculinity, but that the myth itself is just that, an insupportable fiction.

The Dying Animal (2001)[21] picks up where *Sabbath's Theater* lets off, offering both epilogue and elegy to the story of the mortal body that inhibits the performance of the masculine myth. The epigraph that Roth quotes from Edna O'Brien captures the novel's hard truths: "The body contains the life story just as much as the brain." David Kepesh returns, no longer a breast but still yearning for one. In *The Breast* and especially in Kepesh's background story in *The Professor of Desire* (1977),[22] he was torn between gratification and renunciation. In his old age in *The Dying Animal*, however, he unashamedly assumes the mantle of the Jewboy – not with the violent impetuosity of Mickey Sabbath, but with the utter narcissism of the self who knows only what he desires and knows women only as the objects who might satisfy those desires. Sabbath can be despicable, but his humor and passion enlist a reader's sympathy; Kepesh, coolly calculating his erotic economy, challenges a reader to give him any quarter. That seems to be Roth's aim, however. Some readers simply cannot get beyond disgust at the elderly Kepesh's self-serving, untoward obsession with sex, but this portrait is required by Roth's brutally honest exploration of male sexuality confronted by desires that will not die even in the face of disease and decay.

Kepesh's hard-nosed masculinism appears in his undisguised objectification of women. He fetishizes the "gorgeous breasts" of the "fertile female" Consuela Castillo, and he goes so far as to arrogate the function of thought to himself: "I was Consuela's awareness of herself" (*The Dying Animal*, 28, 38). The myth also appears when he conceives the sexual dance in terms of dominance; he is excited by the "perpetual *imbalance*" of power relations as they are played out sexually (20). But Kepesh's masculinity undergoes threat from the aging body – since "the organ most conspicuous throughout [his] life is doomed to dwindle into insignificance" (34) – and from Consuela's challenges to his authority as a subject. When, after he forces her to an act of fellatio, she snaps her teeth at him, she not only alludes to castration, an act that is explicable according to the masculine dynamic of force, but, by not biting him, indicates the power she has as a subject *not* to act if she so chooses. Years later, diagnosed with breast cancer and preparing for a mastectomy, Consuela visits Kepesh because she knows he loved her body. She thereby turns his objectification of her into something very different. Understanding what Kepesh learned in *The Breast*, that the self is at once not-body and inextricable from it, she sees that this love is also for *her*, echoing her tenderness for her own body. Roth inverts Kepesh's defiant anti-feminism when Consuela asks him to photograph her while she performs a striptease, in an apparently classic act of objectification: the woman as specular object under the technologically mediated gaze of the male subject. But Roth offers a critique of this analysis, since Consuela performs the act for her own pleasure and not to instigate Kepesh's. She assumes the position of the object in order to record her own subjectivity as constructed in relation to her body. Appearances to the contrary, she gains possession of the gaze.

The narrative viewpoint is crucial in *The Dying Animal* because male objectification of women depends on the capacity for a detached perspective. Kepesh is narrating his own story to an anonymous interlocutor; squeezed into the framework of his unregenerate masculinist point of view, the story emerges as a history of late twentieth-century American sexuality, keyed to memorable moments in Kepesh's life. He charts the rules of the 1950s, when men expected to impose their will on their wives; the "Pill that gave parity to the woman" in the 1960s (54); the shift toward feminist politics that turns Kepesh's son into a man terrified of being judged selfish or "manly." But this represents Kepesh's version of history, supporting his self-construction in the terms of power and pleasure. Consuela, however, exemplifies someone who escapes Kepesh's point of view and troubles his history by disabling his detachment.

Aptly, Roth sets the novel just after the millennial New Year, when people anticipated an apocalypse and, as Kepesh points out, celebrated "the disaster of the end [that] will now never arrive" (145). Kepesh in effect articulates a sanguine point of view with respect to his identity. Roth suggests the degree to which such a view is delusory, however, demolishing the masculinist ideology that supports it. For in the prospect of his own physical disintegration and in his revulsion at Consuela's impending dismemberment, Kepesh gains an inkling of apocalypse, of the end of history in the bodily failing that is everyone's "dying animal," and even of his own abandonment of the model of masculinity to which he has clung. His ambivalence – and perhaps Roth's as well – is captured in the final line of the novel. When, as in *Portnoy's Complaint*, the silent interlocutor finally speaks on the last page, he or she warns Kepesh not to go to the terrified Consuela, who has just called for succor, "Because if you go, you're finished" (156). Kepesh does not answer, nor does the speaker explain. To go is to reject Kepesh's point of view, which has been devoted to the detachment necessary to self-gratification and even selfhood; to go is to accept his own death, with Consuela's – to be indeed finished. But that Roth leaves the reader unsatisfied, in the dark as to what Kepesh will choose, is to remind us of just how difficult it is to act outside the myths that sustain us.

That enduring difficulty seems to animate Roth's imagination as he returns almost obsessively to the circus of being a man as a main attraction in his work. At times he achieves the detachment that Kepesh loses and Portnoy lacks, rising above the pull of the masculine myth to expose its cruelties and illogic; elsewhere, he exhibits tenderness for its avatars, like Sabbath, whose fervor in pursuit of the masculinist ideal almost, startlingly, redeems it.

That Roth can premise his fiction upon apparently contradictory notions – even in the same book – as when he convincingly offers both essentialist and performative notions of selfhood, may in the end bespeak incoherence. But first, his capacity to rove among so many vivid, if competing, versions of what men can be indicates a willingness to engage fictive possibilities and flexibility in the face of unstable social norms, whose shifting valences and definitions he has presciently represented in a series of memorable male figures.

NOTES

1 Philip Roth, *My Life as a Man* (New York: Farrar, Straus and Giroux, 1974; New York: Vintage, 1993), p. 118.
2 "Philip Roth," documentary for French television series *Writers of the Century* (1997).
3 Arthur Brittan, *Masculinity and Power* (Oxford: Blackwell, 1989), pp. 4, 16, 11, 47.
4 Michael S. Kimmel, "Masculinity as Homophobia: Fear, Shame, and Silence in the Construction of Gender Identity," in *Toward a New Psychology of Gender*, eds. Mary M. Gergen and Sara N. Davis (New York: Routledge, 1997), p. 237.
5 Philip Roth, *Goodbye, Columbus and Five Short Stories* (Boston: Houghton Mifflin, 1959; New York: Bantam, 1963).
6 Philip Roth, *Portnoy's Complaint* (1969; New York: Fawcett Crest, 1985).
7 Philip Roth, "In Response to Those Who Have Asked Me: 'How Did You Come to Write That Book, Anyway?'" in Philip Roth, *Reading Myself and Others* (1975; New York: Farrar, Straus and Giroux, 1985), p. 35.
8 Sander Gilman, "Damaged Men: Thoughts on Kafka's Body," in *Constructing Masculinity*, eds. Maurice Berger, Brian Wallis, and Simon Watson (New York: Routledge, 1995), pp. 177, 176.
9 Sander Gilman, *The Jew's Body* (New York: Routledge, 1991), pp. 119, 62–76.
10 Philip Roth, *Letting Go* (New York: Random House, 1962); and *When She Was Good* (New York: Random House, 1967).
11 Sigmund Freud, *Civilization and Its Discontents*, trans. James Strachey (New York: Norton, 1961).
12 J. Laplanche and J.-B. Pontalis, *The Language of Psycho-analysis*, trans. Donald Nicholson-Smith (New York: Norton, 1973), p. 314.
13 See David Biale, *Eros and the Jews: From Biblical Israel to Contemporary America* (Berkeley: University of California Press, 1997), p. 56.
14 Philip Roth, *The Breast* (1972; New York: Vintage, 1994).
15 Kimmel, "Masculinity as Homophobia," p. 235, citing V. Noble, "A Helping Hand from the Guys," in *Women Respond to the Men's Movement*, ed. K. L. Hagan (San Francisco: HarperCollins, 1992), pp. 105–06.
16 Philip Roth, *The Counterlife* (1986; New York: Penguin, 1989).
17 Philip Roth, *Deception* (New York: Simon and Schuster, 1990); and *Operation Shylock: A Confession* (New York: Simon and Schuster, 1993).

18 Philip Roth, *Sabbath's Theater* (New York: Houghton Mifflin, 1995).

19 Judith Butler, "Imitation and Gender Insubordination," in *The Judith Butler Reader*, ed. Sarah Salih (Malden, MA: Blackwell, 2004), p. 125, emphasis added.

20 Sigmund Freud, *Beyond the Pleasure Principle*, trans. James Strachey (New York: Liveright, 1970).

21 Philip Roth, *The Dying Animal* (New York: Houghton Mifflin, 2001).

22 Philip Roth, *The Professor of Desire* (New York: Farrar, Straus and Giroux, 1977).

9

TIMOTHY PARRISH

Roth and ethnic identity

An American who happens to be a Jew

Addressing an audience in Israel, Philip Roth once defined himself as an American writer who happens to write about Jews. With this simple statement Roth perfectly captures the complicated blending of cultural identities that marks his work. The irony one may perceive from noticing that one of Roth's most quoted statements about his cultural identity as a writer occurs before an Israeli audience should not prevent one from recognizing that it is impossible to talk about Roth's Americanness without also addressing his Jewishness. Perhaps more powerfully than any other writer, Roth exemplifies a cultural pattern endemic to post-World War II American writing: the more ethnic his work seems, the more American it becomes. Thus, Roth has always insisted that he is primarily an American writer, yet his work cannot be fully understood without addressing how Roth engages a sense of Jewish history that cannot be understood to be equivalent with his perspective as an American writer. From this perspective, Roth's work has been part of a large turning point by which contemporary American writers have been reinventing diverse literary and cultural heritages through fictive reconstructions of ethnic pasts. Many contemporary African-American, Native-American, Hispanic-American, and Asian-American writers look to, or invent, pre-American pasts in order to define their present American identities. Roth's work has as its premise the knowledge that his historical situation as an American is known to him through the eyes of being a Jew and the descendant of Jews. More explicitly, but no less crucially than Toni Morrison or Leslie Marmon Silko, Roth's work asserts not only that his American identity is a consequence of his ethnic identity but also that his ethnic identity is a consequence of his American identity. Better than any other American writer of the past fifty years, Philip Roth portrays the inevitable possibilities allowed and the restrictions imposed by a diverse multicultural American society.

Roth's characters usually hazard theories about the meaning of their own identities and then subject these theories to intense criticism, or risk, through the experience they enact. As often as not, Roth's characters find themselves revising their theories when they try to live them, which means – and this is why Roth is not a conventional ethnic writer – that no identity, ethnic or otherwise, is stable. Where writers such as Morrison or Silko describe a specifically American experience inflected through their particular ethnic history, Roth never lets the reader forget that the ethnic group history he tells, even if "true" in some historical sense, is also invented, just as his fictional characters Philip Roth, Nathan Zuckerman, or Alexander Portnoy are invented.

As Roth himself has often noted, his orientation toward questions of cultural identity formation derives from the work of Ralph Ellison. Like Roth, Ellison was often accused by readers within his ethnic group to have betrayed the singular experience of his ethnic experience in order to ingratiate himself with the white (gentile) American mainstream majority. Roth specifically identifies his plight with Ellison's in "Writing About Jews" when he argues that "Just as there are Jews who feel that my books do nothing for the Jewish cause, so there are Negroes, I am told, who feel that Mr. Ellison's work had done little for the Negro cause."[1] In his 1960 essay "Writing American Fiction," Roth expresses his admiration for Ellison's willingness to risk creating a fictional self politically engaged with his world. Here Roth speaks of his desire to create subjects not simply at odds with society, as classic American heroes from Melville's Ishmael to Bellow's Eugene Henderson generally are, but who would take responsibility for the communal predicament, as Ellison's invisible man does. Roth and Ellison's method of taking responsibility is not to highlight how they champion the uniqueness or singularity of the ethnic group they represent (though they could be read that way), but to insist that their "Americanness," rather than their personal ethnic history, is the key to their freedom as individuals to express themselves. This recognition is the key to Ellison's protagonist's final gesture to the reader in *Invisible Man*. Although "Writing American Fiction" shows how Roth at the beginning of his career understood Ellison as a touchstone for understanding self, identity, and art with respect to the larger community, his work has been a nearly fifty-year struggle with the question of how effectively one person's story can truly be said to represent a particular group. Thus, while Roth began his career hoping to write fiction that takes responsibility for a communal predicament, he also had to confront accusations that his work selfishly instigated communal predicaments.

Roth's first book, *Goodbye Columbus* (1959), won the National Book Award, but even before that honor Roth had already achieved notoriety among many Jewish readers upset by Roth's account of how urban American Jews were becoming assimilated into mainstream American society. After *The New Yorker* published "Defender of the Faith" in 1959, some Jewish readers protested that Roth was more dangerous to Jews than any organized anti-Semitic group. As Roth relates in his essay, "Writing About Jews," one rabbi was so incensed by the story that he asked the Anti-Defamation League, "What is being done to silence this man? Medieval Jews would have known what to do with him" (*Reading Myself and Others*, 216). Opposed to these parochial readers were prominent Jews in the American literary establishment (Saul Bellow, Leslie Fiedler, Alfred Kazin, and Irving Howe) writing reviews and essays identifying Roth as a powerful new voice in American literature. In part, they meant to defend Roth from the accusations of readers whose sense of literature had not been refined by a healthy dose of Modernism. They also gave to Roth's work an early stamp of seriousness that it likely would not have received were he not writing about Jews. Roth himself seemed uncomfortable that he could excite so much critical attention from this fact and his next two works, *Letting Go* and *When She Was Good*, in different ways veered considerably from the cultural milieu of *Goodbye, Columbus* and the early stories.

Roth's return to an aggressively "Jewish" subject matter with *Portnoy's Complaint* again touched off a critical firestorm among his Jewish audience. Here Roth seemed intent to take on his antagonists' assumptions directly and turn them inside out as his protagonist projects to the most outrageous degree every conceivable stereotype of American Jews. The violent critical reaction to *Portnoy* exacerbated the uneasiness – or the betrayal – that Jewish readers had already felt with Roth's previous work. Irving Howe's reaction was the most virulent. Howe retracted his good opinion of Roth's early work and in effect canonized Roth as the Jewish writer whose chief contribution to Jewish-American literature was as a transgressor against the Jewish community. Arguing that Roth wrote out of a "thin personal culture," Howe's point was that Roth's fiction had strayed from the rich heritage of Jewish immigrant culture that Howe admired and from which Howe thought *Goodbye Columbus* (1959) emerged.[2] To Howe, *Portnoy's Complaint* celebrated a rootless, transitory, assimilated American culture over a backwards, provincial immigrant tradition. In fact, what Roth did with *Portnoy* was to update the immigrant sensibility that Howe championed by showing its inevitable transformation through the immigrants' descendants' interaction with American culture.

In "Writing American Fiction" Roth had already emphasized how his Jewish characters differed from the tradition that Howe protects. Contrasting his work with that of the "timeless" Jews that Bernard Malamud represents, Roth's work imagines Jews specific to their situations as Americans. Ironically, this also means that Roth has rejected many of the elements of identity that have historically made one "Jewish." Of Roth's characters Aharon Appelfeld writes: "They are the descendants of the Eastern European Jewish tribe who in the beginning of the century were threatened by evil forces, both from within and without, that dispersed them to the four corners of the world. Some came to America."[3] Tersely eloquent, the sentence "Some came to America" acknowledges that Roth writes about Jews from within an American sensibility. Appelfeld maintains that Roth is unquestionably "a Jewish writer," even if "Roth's Jews are Jews without Judaism." Thus, "Roth's works have no Talmud, no Jewish philosophy, no mysticism, no religion."[4] Roth's primary focus is not European Jews, Israeli Jews, or even immigrant American Jews. Rather, he writes about the descendants of those immigrants who have found in America something they never imagined in Europe: the opportunity to define how they perceive or do not perceive themselves to be Jews. He also writes as an American Jew aware that two epochal events in Jewish history occurred during his lifetime: the Holocaust and the founding of Israel as a nation state and eventually a world power.

Thus, if Roth's Jews are "American" in the way that they conceive the fluidity of their cultural identity, they are also "American" in their insistence that without a prior ethnic cultural identity with which to invent themselves they would have no identity at all. Roth's novels can be read as a search to locate some essential or authentic Jewish self and as an attempt to discover, or create, a self that need not be bound by any social or cultural constraints. In negotiating this tension between the historically situated and the freely imagined, Roth habitually defends his depictions of Jews by claiming the artistic right to aesthetic integrity. For Roth, *the self is fiction*; hence, he understands narrative form and personal identity to be in reciprocal relation. At the conclusion of *The Counterlife* (1986), Roth's alter ego, Nathan Zuckerman, decides that if there is such a thing as "an irreducible self, it is rather small, and may even be the root of all impersonation – the natural being may be the skill itself, the innate capacity to impersonate."[5] Roth's heroes delight in the provisional, contingent status of their of self-making and role-playing. It is not enough to say, though, that Roth works out of the familiar American imperative to invent the self, since he would not find self-invention interesting if it were not done in the context of other selves. That is, Roth looks to examine how one's identity impinges on those of others and does so within a context of pluralistic, or multicultural, American identity making.

Roth writes not so much to define himself either as a Jew or as an American but to locate the point at which one's self and the history that makes one's self possible intersect. Without a sense of his own Jewishness, Roth would have no obvious context out of which to write. In *The Facts* Roth portrays how his own recognition that he is, inescapably, a Jew came to be what we might call the centrifugal point of his work. Here he recollects the night he was publicly "branded" – the word is Roth's – a Jew in a way that even Roth could not deny. This branding occurred at the 1962 Symposium at Yeshiva University devoted to "The Crisis of Conscience in Minority Writers of Fiction." Wary of attending an event that was likely to be hostile toward him, Roth considered it his "duty to respond to the pronounced Jewish interest my book continued to evoke."[6] Invoking Kafka, Roth characterizes the experience as "the trial." The moderator and the audience who question him are his unforgiving judges. "Mr. Roth," the moderator intones, "would you write the same stories you've written if you were living in Nazi Germany?" (*The Facts*, 127). (Nathan Zuckerman would be posed this question in *The Ghost Writer*.) Eventually, Roth is "grilled" until his "combative instinct" abandons him. By the end of the evening he is staring into "the faces of my jury" and confronting "the final verdict against me, as harsh a judgment as I hope to hear in this or any other world." Roth leaves Yeshiva with a vow he will be unable to keep: "I'll never write about Jews again," he tells his friends and himself (129). Now branded a Jew, Roth from this point on would write his most compelling fiction about the permutations of Jewish-American identity (130).

Were Roth's career arrested at *Portnoy's Complaint*, Howe's charges might have stood as the defining word on Roth. Instead, since *Portnoy*, Roth, has expanded his treatment of Jewish-American identity so that it engages a broad array of critical contexts and historical dilemmas concerning Jewish identity, albeit filtered through a prosperous American's eyes. As Donald Kartiganer and Michael Rothberg discuss elsewhere in this volume, Roth's presentation of Jewish identity became more complex once the Holocaust became a dominant theme of his work. With *The Ghost Writer* (1979), as well as in the interconnected sequence of novels that followed this one, Roth explicitly moves beyond the more restricted concerns of Jewish-American identity to explore his authorial relationship to the Holocaust – a history that he had escaped, yet which had also somehow touched him.

What begins in *The Ghost Writer* as Nathan Zuckerman's literary pilgrimage to visit an American-Jewish master, E. I. Lonoff, in the Vermont woods, ends in *The Prague Orgy* (1985) as a pilgrimage to Eastern Europe to recover the missing manuscripts of a Jewish writer slain during the Holocaust. In the later novel, he literally trades places with the Eastern European writer, Sisovsky, who convinces Zuckerman to recover the manuscripts. Yet, by the end of the novella when Zuckerman returns to America without the lost manuscripts, he recognizes that he cannot truly trade places with either European writer – the contemporary one, Sisovsky, or the one killed in the Holocaust. Zuckerman, like Roth, can only embrace the fate that made him an American writer. When Zuckerman's father, on his deathbed, calls his son a "bastard" and Zuckerman's brother accuses Nathan of betraying the family through his art, Zuckerman confronts as deeply as possible the kinds of affiliations that a shared ethnic heritage demands. *Zuckerman Bound* progresses to reveal Zuckerman's increasing sophistication concerning his identity as a Jewish writer.

Zuckerman's subject, American Jews, requires that he confront the Holocaust; yet, even the fact of the Holocaust cannot prevent Zuckerman from being the artist he aspires to be and thus shaping his understanding of history to suit his aesthetic purposes. At times Roth's challenging account of the Holocaust seems secondary to his willingness to use the Holocaust as the staging ground for Nathan Zuckerman's questions about how free he is to define his art as he pleases. When, in *The Ghost Writer*, Anne Frank becomes not just a historical figure but an invented character brought to life in the mind of an imaginary novelist, Roth eloquently portrays how the memory of the Holocaust may diminish one's ability to portray the Holocaust's meaning. However, the meaning of the Holocaust cannot remain static and consequently must be subject to revision. Zuckerman's account of Anne Frank's history after the Holocaust suggests how malleable even the most stubborn facts of history can be.

An authentic postmodern American Jew

Against charges that his fiction has compromised an essential Jewish identity, Roth has repeatedly and flagrantly violated Jewish cultural taboos in order to assert his primacy as an artist – a power that he also associates with the freedom to invent himself as an American. For Roth, the act of writing and the act of inventing an identity are intertwined. Roth's elaborate formal strategies are not deployed only to deconstruct his works as fictions separate from life or even to engage in contemporary philosophical debates concerning the nature of the self. Rather, his formal experimentation is intimately bound up in the cultural issues he depicts. Roth's characters assume "authentic" identities only to find that experience causes them to revise what they once took for granted. Instead of championing an essential Jewish identity against an oppressive, monolithic American society, his novels examine how American culture enables his characters to transform radically their sense of themselves as Jews. Although nearly all of Roth's protagonists confront the consequences of having a strong sense of ethnic identity, Roth's subject is not, finally, Jewishness per se. Nonetheless, as a writer committed to a sense of his own chosen American identity, he also asserts his power to reinvent the meaning of that historical fate in order to claim authorship of the process by which he came to be the Jew that he now portrays himself to be. As Roth explains in *The Facts*, the relation between his so-called real self and the self that exists in fact stems from the shared assumption that both are inventions: "It isn't that you subordinate your ideas to the force of facts in autobiography but that you construct a sequence of stories to bind up the facts with a persuasive *hypothesis* that unravels your history's meaning" (8). A self is invented through narrative form; conversely, narrative forms create possibilities for different self-inventions. Thus, Roth's fiction perpetually betrays the compelling but ultimately futile desire of achieving an authentic identity of any kind.

Roth's most complex treatment of this theme occurs in his Israel novels, *The Counterlife* and *Operation Shylock* (1993). Initially, one might think that these books are meant to prove Irving Howe wrong – to show that Roth's books are as essentially Jewish as Moses' are. However, Israel, the essential Jewish homeland, attracts Roth not as a final destination but as a setting for asking what it means to be an American who is also a Jew. In *The Counterlife*, Nathan's brother, Henry, hopes that Israel will resolve the identity crisis he suffers as an American-Jewish man. He trades his comfortable assimilated existence as a dentist in New Jersey for a life in a hazardous kibbutz in Israel. When Nathan journeys to Israel to hear his brother's story, he learns, predictably, that living in Israel has made Henry free at last because he has discovered, finally, his essential Jewish self. Henry's epiphany occurs when he hears Israeli children chanting their lessons. Henry describes to Nathan how he discovered that, "at the root of my life, at the very *root* of it, I *was* them" (*Counterlife*, 60). That he could not understand a word of the Hebrew language the children were chanting is irrelevant, since, "I am not *just* a Jew, I'm not *also* a Jew – *I'm a Jew as deep as those Jews*" (61). Initially, one may note that Henry's desire to be "a Jew as deep as those Jews" may betray a feeling of American cultural inadequacy – a sense that, in America, his Jewishness is deracinated and hence inauthentic. Henry's speech betrays a deep dissatisfaction with the materialistic, acquisitive life often thought of as the embodiment of the American dream. Henry's condemnation of American life is reflected in the self-revulsion he feels as a consequence of risking his life in order to continue his affair with his office assistant. Speaking of those "hellenized – hedonized – egomaniaized" American Jews – "galut

Jews, bereft of any sort of context in which to actually be Jewish," Henry is critiquing himself and, possibly, Roth (111). He sees his betrayal of family and self as emblematic of "liberal" and "pluralistic" America. Earlier, we saw that Roth defined being Jewish as being part of a historical situation, one that for him could not be separated from a history of being American. For Henry, however, American identity and Jewish identity are incompatible. This means that he cannot be a Jew in Newark, New Jersey, surrounded by Jews though he was, because, according to Henry, these people have surrendered their claim to being Jewish. To be authentically Jewish, then, Henry must be surrounded by authentic Jews. Returning to Israel, therefore, becomes the means by which Henry can re-enter the eternal Jewish family free of the self-conflict that his hyphenated American identity causes him.

Roth ingeniously structures *The Counterlife* so that Henry's self-discovery is not final. In one section of the novel Henry is dead; in another Zuckerman dies and Henry, no longer an American-Israeli immigrant, performs the eulogy. The effect is to contextualize any character's claims to an authentic identity as contingent and therefore not final. One is born into an inescapable history, but one may also define for oneself what that history means and thus one's relation to that history. In *Operation Shylock* Roth gives Henry's identity conflict to a character named Philip Roth. In this novel it is Philip Roth who must journey to Israel to claim not just the meaning of his Jewish identity but his entire oeuvre up to that point in his career. Roth's antagonist is himself, or a double of himself: another character named Philip Roth who has usurped the "true" Roth's identity. This "other" Roth has turned up in Israel, claiming the fame and notoriety of the true Roth, and advocating the controversial position that Israel the country should be disbanded as a failed historical experiment and the Jews should return to Europe as soon as possible. Pipik's (Roth's name for his double) philosophy of "diasporism" celebrates "the Jew for whom *authenticity* as a Jew means living in the Diaspora" – a position, ironically, that mirrors Roth's frequent justification of himself as an American a writer whose subject is Jews.[7] Roth may also be using Pipik to criticize Israel's military might and to suggest that Israel treats Palestinians not unlike how Nazi Germany once treated Jews. Certainly, he allows Arab characters within the novel to voice such concerns. As in *The Counterlife*, no one point of view, however passionately held and historically justifiable, trumps any other point of view. As in *The Ghost Writer*, the agony of a people's history becomes the staging ground for self-examination by Roth's artist-hero. Thus, Pipik's arguments threaten the identity of Israel as a country and the identity of Roth as an author. The playful suggestion is that to threaten one is to threaten the other, as if one is somehow a version of the other. Roth leaves the reader free to make the inference that this connection between Israel and himself implies: just as Israel has come to dominate the Middle East, so has Roth come to dominate post-World War II American literature.

However, the novel cannot finally insist that Israel or Philip Roth represent the endpoint of thousands of years of Jewish history. Roth generally thinks of his characters – even one with his name – as impersonators rather than realistic entities. He told Hermione Lee, "Nathan Zuckerman is an act. It's all the art of impersonation, isn't it? That's the fundamental novelistic gift" (*Reading Myself and Others*, 143). In this context, Pipik seems less like an "other" to Roth than a version of Roth as plausible as any Roth himself has authenticated – an interpretation that is confirmed by the ease with which Roth impersonates Pipik impersonating him. Moreover, the character Philip Roth, though presented as if he were authentically Philip Roth, must also be seen as an impersonation. That the real author Philip Roth must necessarily remain in control of both Pipik and the character, Philip Roth, in order for his novel to work is a premise that the reader may easily forget, even though remembering it is crucial to understanding how Roth's novel works. Although the novel's structure demands that Roth travel to Israel to enact the drama of reclaiming his authentic Jewish-American identity, *Operation Shylock* never actually refutes Pipik's position. Indeed, Pipik becomes the medium by which Roth, who begins the work in a state of near suicidal depression, recovers his sense of himself as a Jewish-American author. This renewed Roth, who would after *Shylock* write a series of well received novels, does not believe his Jewishness needs to be authenticated by any force other than his own personal history. In this context, Roth's Jewishness does not depend on a privileged relationship with Israel, even if the fictional Roth also pretends to be a spy for Israel. Pretending to be a spy for Israel is likely Roth's cover for a spy-game whose central subject and object is himself.

In that same interview with Lee, Roth speaks of "the difficulties of telling a Jewish story – How should it be told? In what tone? To whom should it be told? To what end?" (*Reading Myself and others*, 166). In *Operation Shylock* Roth answers these questions by having what is arguably the novel's key scene take place not in Israel but in a Jewish food store on Amsterdam Avenue in New York where he meets with an Israeli spy, Smilesberger. Thus, Roth reinforces the point that his Israel novel takes its fullest meaning only in an American context. Recalling a similar deli he frequented as a boy where his family purchased "silky slices of precious lox, shining fat little chubs, chunks of pale, meaty carp and paprikaed sable, all double wrapped in heavy wax paper," Roth describes with Proustian richness fragrances that take his memory back to a time he himself did not experience – "back to the shtetl to the medieval ghetto and the nutrients of those who lived frugally and could not afford to dine a la mode, the diet of sailors and common folk, for whom the flavor of the ancient preservatives was life" (*Operation Shylock*, 378–79). As an account of how everyday details are transformed into personal and cultural mythology, this passage is a beautiful evocation of a continuous, ever evolving Jewish history fixed to a specific place within America. Yet, as Roth observes, by 1993 "the ordinary fare of the Jewish masses had become an exotic stimulant for Upper West Siders two and three generations removed from the great immigration" (379). For Roth, the American Jew, one's Jewish homeland may not be Israel or Europe, but a New York restaurant where Yiddish is still spoken. This provisional home is redolent with the smells of Galicia, but gives off none of its torments. Among those Upper West Siders are, presumably, non-Jews who have no authentic connection to the "bitter fragrance." The aroma of a Jewish past – sharp and full of difference remembered and preserved – now permeates a present that includes, in this case, diners who come from different pasts, ones who may or may not visit Israel as many of these Jews do. Together the multicultural diners take in an ambient smell that has, in America, become savory, without bitterness.

From this perspective, one could argue that the deli is less an image of Jewish assimilation than a reflection on the process of how the assimilation of the Jews in America has assimilated non-Jews too. The experience of the deli perhaps communicates to those non-Jews who also recognize this deli as a home a nostalgia that has become their own though it emerges out of somebody else's past. Here, where cultural memory is consumed with lox and bagels, Roth is at last in his element. Indeed, the joke that Roth gives to Smilesberger to tell defines this element perfectly. It also suggests how malleable identity is even when situated within what seems to be a carefully defined historical context. Smilesberger's ethnic joke concerns a Chinese waiter working in a Yiddish deli. A customer comes into the deli and is startled to find that his waiter is a Yiddish-speaking Chinese immigrant. Later, when paying for his meal, the customer raves to the owner of the deli about not only the terrific meal but also the Chinese waiter who speaks perfect Yiddish. "*Shah*, shhh," the owner replies with the joke's punch line, "not so loud – he thinks he's learning English" (385).

The joke is not an instance of assimilation as it is usually understood, where the new immigrant is expected to conform to an already existing and basically static conception of national identity. The point of the joke is not that Yiddish has been assimilated into American culture, but that Yiddish has become a medium through which one becomes American. The lesson of the joke is appropriate for an author who imagines Israel to be in its essence the invention of and repository for American Jews. In suggesting that Yiddish is no longer the tongue by which great writers such as I. L. Peretz or I. B. Singer are nourished but has instead developed into but another *American* possibility, Roth's "Chinese waiter joke" undermines the logic that there is such a thing as an "authentic" ethnic identity not implicated within a broader system of identity acquisition. The joke conveys two interrelated ideas: first, that immigrants are never fully absorbed into a prior, stable national norm; second, that prior immigrants help to establish and therefore change the context in which later or future immigrants will know themselves as Americans. The Chinese waiter achieves his identity as an American through an ethnic identity that is not "truly" his. Likewise, this "American" restaurant, redolent with the odors of food that Jews have eaten for centuries, is home to Jews who speak only American English, or, in some cases, Americans who have no Jews for ancestors. You visit this place when in the mood – maybe to pick up a snippet of Yiddish, to breathe air that carries the aroma of your ancestors, to soak up the atmosphere as if it were your very own.

The Jew that remains

Operation Shylock can be read as Roth's ultimate statement on his own identity, and complicated career, as a Jewish-American writer. However, Roth's career did not end with *Shylock*, and his writing since has brought him closer to the position that Irving Howe criticized him for when *Portnoy* was published. In *American Pastoral* (1997), *The Human Stain* (2000), and *The Plot Against America* (2004), Roth explores the costs of sacrificing one's ethnic identity for the pursuit of American success. Where Roth in *Operation Shylock* imagined a self that could in a sense triumph over history, in these later works history more often determines the self's possibilities. Through Nathan Zuckerman's identification with Swede Levov, "the blue-eyed blonde born into our *tribe*," Roth explores the possibility of writing what amounts to a kind of tribal narrative (emphasis mine). In Roth's earlier Zuckerman books, Zuckerman battled against the limitations imposed upon the individual by tribal demands. In *American Pastoral* Zuckerman as narrator identifies with an assimilated Jew whose assimilation into mainstream American culture is portrayed as a tragic fall rather than a comic success. Swede, "the blue-eyed blonde born into our tribe" is cursed by an "unconscious oneness with America."[8] "Where," Zuckerman asks at one point of Swede, "was the Jew in him?" and the answer seems to be that the Jew in Swede has been destroyed by the empty promises of American life (*American Pastoral*, 20). As such, he is a version of what Henry Zuckerman feared becoming in *The*

Counterlife and thus fled to Israel to escape. Moving away from the individualistic perspective of his previous fiction, Roth's *American Pastoral* documents, through Swede, an entire generation of Jewish-Americans destroyed – as Jews – by their mainstream American success. In writing an elegy for the sort of Jewish identity that his novels have generally undermined, Roth's *American Pastoral* critiques his own previous assumptions about the self and its relation to Jewish identity.

American Pastoral marks a departure for Roth because it questions the American ideal of cultural assimilation. According to Zuckerman, Swede Levov is to inhabit the "American Pastoral" by being an American rather than a Jew who lives in America. Instead of idyllic bliss, Swede experiences "the counterpastoral," what Zuckerman calls the "American berserk" and which he personifies as the social unrest of the sixties (86). Here, Roth broadens the novel's context so that the Jewish family story is contained within yet also suggests a national American drama. Thus, the story of how the descendants of immigrant Jews achieve the American Dream but become divided from each other is mirrored by the story of how the United States itself tragically divided during the 1960s. The two stories intersect when Merry, Swede's daughter, bombs the local post office to protest the United States' war against Vietnam. Merry's rage, though seemingly political, is also cultural. Her fury is directed not only at the US government but the idealized American success that her father represents. To Merry, Swede's assimilation embodies the mixture of American exceptionalism and cultural imperialism that justified the war against Vietnam.

Not only is Swede an example of an American Dream that promises greater success for each new generation, but also as the owner of glove factories in Newark and Puerto Rico his success derives from exploiting non-white, non-mainstream Americans – African-Americans and Puerto Ricans. When Merry becomes a revolutionary and detonates a bomb that kills or injures "innocent" bystanders, she collapses national history into her own family history. By conflating Merry's revolt against her father with the social unrest of the sixties that included race riots in the major American cities (Swede's glove factory in Newark is the target of one riot), Roth suggests that the unrest of the sixties was caused not by American foreign policy but by racial inequities exacerbated by the American belief in cultural transformation as an inherent social good. The novel ultimately mourns what was lost when Jews, among other Americans, suffered their unique cultural identity to be sacrificed in order to become assimilated: the American Dream becomes the American Berserk. Zuckerman offers Swede's story as a lament for the time during and after World War II when Swede, Zuckerman, and Philip Roth were simply boys who knew themselves only as American Jews among other

American Jews. This point is underscored at the end of the novel through Zuckerman's portrayal of Swede's father's skepticism concerning the wisdom of his Jewish son marrying a *shiksa*, a Catholic girl and former Miss American contestant. In retrospect, the father is the Cassandra-like prophet whose true prophecy went unheeded. His son's "mixed" marriage inevitably results in family tragedy.

The American Berserk of the past fifty years is also the context out of which *The Human Stain*'s Coleman Silk, arguably Roth's most remarkable protagonist, emerges. Coleman is an African-American who until his death successfully passes for white – passes, specifically, as a Jewish intellectual. In a way he is an intellectual version of Swede Levov – except secretly black. At first glance, Coleman seems a return to Roth's earlier heroes – he will let no one but himself define who or what he will be. Rather than suffer the prejudices of being "black," he heroically decides to transcend others' prejudice by becoming his own man. Coleman is also a version of Ellison's invisible man – one whose "true" identity is invisible to everyone except himself. Zuckerman tells Coleman's story as a version of his own autobiography. Like Zuckerman, Coleman must separate himself from his family's expectation of how he should live his life. Like Zuckerman, he must withstand accusations of cultural self-hatred. On a certain level, Coleman's story is a success. He achieves his ambition of becoming a successful academic. Although he resigns in disgrace over a misunderstanding about whether he had accidentally denigrated two students with a racial slur (he did not), he is allowed to die happy, in control of his destiny.

Yet, Roth ingeniously frames the novel so that Coleman's view of himself as the heroic individual is not necessarily the one the reader endorses. Zuckerman only learns of Coleman's story through his African-American sister, Ernestine, and Zuckerman identifies as much with her point of view she does Coleman's. Telling Coleman's story from the perspective provided by her own family history, Ernestine reclaims him as an African-American whose passing remains peculiarly African-American. At novel's end, Zuckerman is to join Ernestine at the Silks' Sunday family gathering as a version of Coleman. Zuckerman is not passing as African-American, however, but accepting through Coleman's failed example his own identity as one of a group: a Jewish-American who owes his identity not only to his marvelous capacity for self-invention but to the history of Jews before him who made his story possible.

Roth's next novel, *The Plot Against America*, draws on the memory of the Holocaust in order to examine his own sensibilities as a Jewish writer.[9] An elaborate historical fantasy and fictional autobiography, Roth reimagines his childhood from the premise that Charles Lindbergh, not Franklin Delano

Roosevelt, was elected President in 1940. By this account, the United States became an ally not of England, France, and Russia but the Axis powers of Japan, Italy and, most importantly, Nazi Germany. With Germany as an ally, the lives of American Jews are at risk to be sacrificed to history in the same way six million European Jews were. Roth has said that for him the appeal of the book was not to imagine America as a place where pogroms could happen, but to imagine how his parents might have responded to such a situation. *The Plot Against America* is a fitting place to end a discussion of Roth as an ethnic writer because it suggests that the best way to understand Roth's orientation as a Jewish-American writer is, finally, as a Jewish son. The novel's power resides in Roth's moving portrait of his parents as a refuge from all fear. Although Roth's brother, Sandy, flirts with participating in Lindbergh's plan and his aunt actually becomes a type of aide to Lindbergh, Roth's childlike worship of his parents as Jewish heroes is powerful and not to be questioned. Consequently, the fear that Roth identifies on the first page of the novel and that so compellingly pervades the novel comes from outside the family. Roth's family – the nuclear Jewish family – is a sanctuary against the oppressive and very real fears generated from without by the hostile, potentially murderous gentile American culture. Reading Roth's oeuvre through *Plot*, one can understand what terrible personal risks were taken by Nathan Zuckerman or Philip Roth when they challenged their family order.

Roth ends his moving memoir to his father, *Patrimony*, with a harrowing dream in which he is a child "standing on a pier in a shadowy group of unescorted children who may or may not have been waiting to be evacuated."[10] The fear of being orphaned – being evacuated from your parents and thus your history – is at the heart of *The Plot Against America*. Likewise, this same fear may also be, for Roth, what encourages ethnic Americans to remain in the safety of their own ethnic history, regardless of how hostile or friendly mainstream American culture truly is. In *Patrimony* Roth intuits that the empty ship that approaches the children on the dock is a manifestation of his dead father and that his father would remain with him "sitting in judgment of whatever I do" (238). In *Plot* Roth affirms this vision by bringing his father back to life as the undying conscience of the Jewish son. A Jewish-American writer, who began his career by writing fiction that offended many readers whose prime of life would have coincided with the time period depicted in most recent novels, is ending his career by offering his work as the living memory of the Jews who created him and the history that has enabled him to write their story. As even *Plot* acknowledges, America is the only possible stage Roth can imagine for acting out his – and their – dramas.

NOTES

1 Philip Roth, *Reading Myself and Others: A New Expanded Edition* (New York: Penguin, 1985), pp. 222–23.
2 Irving Howe, "Philip Roth Reconsidered," in *Philip Roth*, ed. Harold Bloom (New York: Chelsea House, 1986), p. 82.
3 Aharon Appelfeld, "The Artist as a Jewish Writer," in *Reading Philip Roth*, eds. Asher Z. Milbauer and Donald G. Watson (New York: St. Martin's Press, 1988), p. 14.
4 *Ibid.*, p. 14.
5 Philip Roth, *The Counterlife* (New York: Farrar, Straus and Giroux,1986), p. 320.
6 Philip Roth, *The Facts: A Novelist's Autobiography* (New York: Farrar, Straus and Giroux, 1988), p. 125.
7 Philip Roth, *Operation Shylock: A Confession* (New York: Simon and Schuster, 1993), p. 170.
8 Philip Roth, *American Pastoral* (Boston: Houghton Mifflin, 1997), p. 20.
9 Philip Roth, *The Plot Against America* (Boston: Houghton Mifflin, 2004).
10 Philip Roth, *Patrimony: A True Story* (New York: Simon and Schuster, 1991), p. 234.

IO

MARK SHECHNER

Roth's American Trilogy

Judging from the fiction alone, Philip Roth experienced a spiritual meltdown during the second half of the 1990s. We'll leave it to the biographers to tell us why. And yet, paradoxically, he responded with a creative burst. From 1995 to 2001 he published five novels, each one more depressive than the last, and the first, *Sabbath's Theater* (1995), was an extended suicide note by its central character, Mickey Sabbath. It was followed in quick succession by *American Pastoral* (1997), *I Married a Communist* (1998), *The Human Stain* (2000), and *The Dying Animal* (2001). If we need an analogy to this collaboration of low spirits and high energy, this clamorous bleakness, we could turn to the blues, a music of great vitality whose lyrics commonly bemoan everything that is despairing in human existence. The only Roth novel of the past ten years (I write this in late 2005) to feel as if it came from something like personal equilibrium was *The Plot Against America* (2004), and that was about a Nazi takeover of America. This essay takes up the three central novels of this period, *American Pastoral*, *I Married a Communist*, and *The Human Stain*, those acid dissertations on the heart of American darkness that are commonly called the "American problem" novels and have been much celebrated for Roth's turn toward social issues with what appears to be a conservative agenda. Maybe so, though I tend to see these books as "Roth Problem Novels," telling us more about the man than they do about the nation. This essay could well be titled "Blues in the Night," but the title of a well-known Sigmund Freud essay seems to be more apposite: "Mourning and Melancholia."

Merry the fanatic: *American Pastoral*

American Pastoral is Roth's return to the scene of his 1959 novella, *Goodbye Columbus*: Newark, New Jersey and its ring of affluent suburbs. In the earlier book, the promised land was Short Hills; in the later it is a mythic exurban retreat called Old Rimrock. Neil Klugman has bulked out into Seymour

"Swede" Levov, one-time star athlete for Weequahic High School, while Brenda Patimkin has *shiksa*'d up into Dawn Dwyer, the former Miss New Jersey of 1949. Unlike Neil, Swede gets the girl and makes a life. Forsaking his fielder's glove for Newark Maid Gloves, the family business, he moves out to Old Rimrock and fulfills the dream of his immigrant grandparents: a piece of land, a business of his own, and – in a departure from grandpa's script – a *shiksa*. It sounds like a setup for a fall, and all roads out of Old Rimrock lead downhill. With the world as his oyster and a life that fits him like a glove, Levov gets sucked into the maelstrom when his daughter Merry (Meredith) signs on with the anti-Vietnam War movement, becomes a Weathermen groupie in New York, and bombs the Old Rimrock post office, killing a local man who just stopped by to pay his bills. She becomes a fugitive for five years, while the Levovs descend into the foulest circles of hell that Roth can dream up for the unreflective: tormented self-reflection. Their lives are shattered by questions. How did this Jewish athlete and this Irish knockout produce this urban terrorist, this teenage guerilla? And after Newark is laid waste by riots in 1967, how has the post-immigrant trajectory of upward mobility come to this?

The novel opens with Nathan Zuckerman's forty-fifth high school reunion and his thoughts are on his childhood hero worship of one of the greatest athletes Newark ever produced: the Swede, the neighborhood talisman, who might well have signed with the New York Giants after the war were it not for pressure to go into the family glove business. Marrying Miss New Jersey, he settled down to become a businessman, a paterfamilias, and a Jewish pioneer in those neighborhoods that used to be called "exclusive." At the reunion Zuckerman meets up with Swede's younger brother, Jerry, a former classmate and now a Florida surgeon, and learns that the Swede's life had been hell, after his sixteen-year-old daughter became a terrorist in the late 1960s. With that story buzzing around in his mind, Zuckerman, finding himself in the arms of Joy Helpern while dancing to the strains of Johnny Mercer's "A Dream," slips into a reverie and daydreams Swede Levov's life, "not his life as a god or a demigod in whose triumphs one could exult as a boy but his life as another assailable man . . ."[1]

So, *American Pastoral* is a book of bad dreams, but what, as Drs. Freud and Spielvogel would ask, is their latent content? While we can't get at the infantile or the repressed, we can confidently single out the fixed ideas that keep rumbling to the surface: fatherhood and Newark. The sixties Cultural Revolution is merely backstory, Zeitgeist, a bridge to get from insurrection in the street to mutiny in the family room. Roth is otherwise preoccupied: he is vexed mainly by fatherhood, which he has experienced only as calamity. He does try to imagine it otherwise: to conjure up the tenderness that can be aroused in fathers by daughters, and some of the book's most heart-tugging sequences involve Swede Levov's recollected moments of bonding with Merry in her childhood. The final coda, with its Molly Bloom-like soliloquy racing through Swede Levov's shattered mind, recalls his walks across the field with Merry as they identify flowers together and she points out, "See, Dad, how there's a n-notch at the tip of the petal?" (*American Pastoral*, 419). Sure, that delicacy is set up against the book's other indelicacies, but it also takes us to the father's heart in Levov and shows us what can be broken.

Then there is Newark. As the Jews once lamented Jerusalem, Roth laments Newark. Only here it is not the residential paradise of *The Plot Against America* but industrial Newark, smoke-belching, beer-brewing, freight-handling Newark. Newark Maid is a stand-in for industrial North Jersey from Jersey City to Bayonne, that concentration of foundries and factories and shipping docks and mills that once gave employment and nourishment to the city. The long sequences about the Newark of Swede Levov's childhood are virtually biblical passages. Not just the Weequahic section, that Mesopotamia of Roth's civilization, but the Italian neighborhood, Down Neck, where immigrant families from Naples did piecework in tenement workshops.

> The old Italian grandfather or the father did the cutting on the kitchen table, with the French rule, the shears, and the spud knife he'd brought from Italy. The grandmother or the mother did the sewing, and the daughters did the laying off – ironing the glove – in the old-fashioned way, with irons heated up in a box set atop the kitchen's potbellied stove. (221)

This isn't Marx's alienated labor or Merry Levov's exploited proletariat; these are people sewing together their very own lives. And after the riots, the flight of the Jews and the Italians, of business, of the middle-class, what is left makes mere industrial alienation look like the Italian Riviera.

> On the east side of the street, the dark old factories – Civil War factories, foundries, brassworks, heavy-industrial plants blackened, from the chimneys pumping smoke for a hundred years – were windowless now, the sunlight sealed out with brick and mortar, their exits and entrances plugged with cinderblock . . . It was Newark that was entombed there, a city that was not going to stir again. The pyramids of Newark: as huge and dark and hideously impermeable as a great dynasty's burial edifice has every historical right to be. (219)

Roth laments the fall of Newark as though it were the Third Temple itself fallen to infidels, sending out yet another Jewish diaspora to – to where? To Old Rimrock.

This devastation is charged to the 1960s, a decade that set children against parents and black against white. It was the decade of burning cities, political assassinations, the Vietnam War, of Off the Pigs and Strawberry Fields Forever. Though it helps us understand Newark, which did go up in flames during the Martin Luther King riots of 1967, it is nevertheless a smokescreen for the story that Roth was not, in 1997, prepared to tell. That would be a story of personal domestic turbulence and collapse, and at the moment Roth needed the sixties for a prop.

American Pastoral is a bit of a sermonizing tract, and so there seem to be two Merries: the daughter and the bomber, and while the first is recognizably human and an agonizing rebuke to her family, the second is right out of central casting: some casting director's amalgam of Kathy Boudin, Cathlyn Wilkerson, Bernardine Dohrn, et al. You can observe Roth laboring mightily to anoint Merry with a distinctive profile: a stutter, a 4-H club membership, and an Audrey Hepburn scrapbook. She even undergoes a phase of extreme Catholic devotion, moving up from adoration of the soubrette to worship of the Madonna. But as a revolutionist, she is off the shelf. Possibly Merry's failure to become convincing is the point: you join The Movement and you cast off your bourgeois individuality to become a soldier for your favorite fundamentalism: Maoist, Taoist, Leninist, Islamist, Jainist, Hasidic. The complex, layered self is useless, once you've cast your fate with Fidel and Che and the monotonous chants of ideological armor. As a sixteen-year-old revolutionist in the making, while still living at home, the surly Merry Levov is all teenage bluster and sub-articulate resentment. She denigrates President Johnson as an imperialist dog and compares him with Hitler.

Nothing much happens in *American Pastoral*, except that Merry reappears after her five-year exile as a Jain, veiled and penitential and so worshipful of life that she refuses to kill even the bacteria on her body. The book otherwise has no plot, just encounters that set the Swede on the path to learning "the worst lesson that life can teach – that it makes no sense" (81). Roth's *port-parole* here, as elsewhere, Nathan Zuckerman, who daydreams the entire story, informs us that getting things wrong is what life is all about,

> so ill-equipped are we all to envision one another's interior workings and invisible aims . . . The fact remains that getting people right is not what living is all about anyway. It's getting them wrong that is living, getting them wrong and wrong and wrong and then, on careful reconsideration, getting them wrong again. That's how we know we're alive: we're wrong. (35)

Maybe that alone explains Merry Levov, who runs through teenage infatuations and grows into an all-American cultist for whom terrorism is twentieth-century Americanism. What are we are supposed to understand about this cloudburst of travail? What does Roth want us to know? Not only about Merry Levov and her multiple conversions away from the safety and security of Old Rimrock, but about the middle-class litany of shoulder to the wheel and slow and steady wins the race? Has Merry Levov seen through an elaborate ruse to the radical core of things – capitalist exploitation, white domination, American hegemony? Or has she herself been taken in by the monotonous platitudes of romantic revolutionism?

In the latter years of the 1960s, when white middle-class revolutionaries did go around blowing things up, sometimes themselves, those questions were worried to death. But the question is why Roth chose to dust off that history when he did and write a book that would seem to be, on the face of it, a late response, as if a delayed fuse had suddenly gone off in him.

One can't discount Roth's smarting over old attacks and deciding to put the sixties behind him once and for all. Wounds may fester for ages, and lashing out, as Roth had done so vehemently in *The Anatomy Lesson*, had failed of its purpose – if its purpose was to ease the pain – and had, if anything, reinforced Roth's image as a literary saboteur. Finally the moment had come for saying, "I, too, recall the sixties as an abomination, and I am no longer, if I ever was, a Jewish Panther, let alone the Laureate of the New Class. Enough of this *mishegas*: the world in revolt, the city in flames, the ten commandments overthrown, and orally fixated Alex Portnoy, that Che Guevara of cunnilingus, calling the shots. Time to get back down to basics: hard work, long hours, thrift, family values, and supporting the United Jewish Appeal." Could it be?

The Roth canvas is always vertical, in portrait mode, not horizontal, in landscape. *American Pastoral* is a family drama, played out on a stage no larger than North Jersey, and we don't need to know much about Merry as the incarnation of Kathy Boudin et al. but as the daughter of Swede and Dawn and granddaughter of Lou. And we hardly need to look beyond the history of Roth's own career to see the essential drama here. Did not Flaubert say, "Madame Bovary, *c'est moi?*" Could Roth not echo, "Merry Levov, *c'est moi?*" The book suddenly comes into focus as another act in the theater of rebellion and atonement that has been Roth's personal theater ever since he first found himself singled out as a literary terrorist. This drama would have been sharpened for Roth by the death of his father in 1987, which would have occasioned one last look at the entire business of how middle-class families with decent values produce resentful offspring like himself.

Finally, though, *American Pastoral* is about fanaticism, Jewish fanaticism, making it consistent with almost everything Roth has written since the story "Eli, the Fanatic." The mystery of Merry Levov's revolutionism is hardly mysterious at all once we have spent time with Lou Levov, the glove manufacturer, and met also the brother Jerry, grown up from being an awkward boy to a heart surgeon who seems always in a rage of resentment. Merry a genetic anomaly? A mystical self-creation? A dupe of Frankfurt School dialectics, in violent revolt against "repressive tolerance"? A victim of her father's blandness, her mother's blindness, her family's stolid and unreflective bourgeois comfort out there in toney Old Rimrock? If the book shows us anything, it is that Merry's politics and her obstinacy are bred in the bone. The arrow of fanaticism runs straight from grandfather to grand-daughter, skipping only Swede and singling him out as the anomaly. Listen to Lou Levov, the intemperate man with the skull of a brawler, carry on when President Nixon appears on television during the Watergate hearings. " 'That skunk!,' the Swede's father said bitterly. 'That miserable fascist dog!' and out of him, with terrifying force, poured a tirade of abuse, vitriol about the president of the United States that absent the stuttering that never failed to impart to her abhorrence the exterminating adamance of a machine gun, Merry herself couldn't have topped in her heyday" (299).

Merry Levov comes from somewhere after all. Not from Old Rimrock but from Newark, from Poland, from revolutionary Russia, from the Ashkenazi Diaspora, from Masada itself. Swede doesn't understand it, but Roth understands it well indeed. Given the combustible emotions of her family and grandpa's blast furnace of a heart, one wonders where Swede came from. Maybe the baseball bleached it out of him, having to learn patience and balance in waiting for the hard slider. Incendiary? Jain? American Bakunin? Look farther back than that. Merry Levov is an Essene at heart, and it is to Essene asceticism and zealotry that she returns. She isn't such an aberration after all. She is her father's own Jewish unconscious; she is the return of the repressed.

Every fiber of my being: *I Married a Communist*

To pour out a tale of woe to the aging, rusticating Nathan Zuckerman in the Connecticut wilderness, comes Murray Ringold, who was once Zuckerman's English teacher at Newark's Weequahic High School and is now, at age ninety, a pilgrim to the Berkshire hideaway where Nathan has retreated to strip back to essentials and decontaminate himself of striving. Ringold is infected with the past, especially with the 1950s, a decade in which his kid brother Ira played a supporting role. The star-crossed marriage this time is that between Ira Ringold, a.k.a. Iron Rinn, and Eve Frame, née Chavah Fromkin, and the long dying fall of the relationship takes place between 1948 and 1952, between Henry Wallace's failed campaign for president under the banner of the Progressive Party and the rise of Senator Joseph McCarthy.

At the start, Ira Ringold, a Jewish laborer from Newark, New Jersey, a zinc miner with a heroic physique and a hot temper, is a media celebrity, starring on the radio program *The Free and The Brave*, where, under the name of Iron Rinn, he impersonates Abraham Lincoln and other icons of national adoration. By 1948, Ringold/Rinn, having taken up the persona of Lincoln in union hall fund-raisers, is famous and married to a silent-film actress whose career has been in limbo since films began to talk.

Murray remembers his brother as a footsoldier of the revolution and a righteous pontificator. "Ira swallowed the dialectical justification for Stalin's every villainy. Ira backed Browder when Browder was their American messiah, and when Moscow pulled the plug and expelled Browder, and overnight Browder was a class collaborator and a social imperialist, Ira bought it all – backed Foster and the Foster line that America was on the road to fascism."[2]

Ira Ringold had picked up his doctrinaire habits from an army buddy named Johnny O'Day, who combined revolutionary asceticism with muscle and Marx. Ira is the most unreflective of all Roth's unreflective characters – Swede Levov is Proust in comparison. He had come of age during the Popular Front, when the Moscow party line was that Communism was twentieth-century Americanism, wholly consistent with the democratic sentiments of Tom Paine and Lincoln. Ira's liberationist's handbook is a prison house of language, and when once, during a dinner party, he berates the black maid about the Negro community's failure to support Henry Wallace, the reader prays for his fall to come swiftly. When Ira finally does go down, undermined by his own delusions, his infidelities, and by *I Married a Communist*, the book his wife has had ghost-written for the occasion, he is tragic in the Shakespearean mold: self-betrayed by a blind and obstinate will. Like Othello, he seems hopelessly stupid, which becomes a problem as the book goes on, because you can't extend sympathy, the reader's version of credit, to someone who is so doggedly clueless.

Ira's womanizing is no more reflective, and this being a Roth novel after all, infidelity comes with the marriage vows. The first lover is a flutist from London and a friend of Eve's daughter Sylphid named Pamela Solomon, who has a perky sense of adventure and a youthful urge to cast off English decorum for American licentiousness. It doesn't take much for her to vamp Ira or sensibly to call it off after a few months. Shortly thereafter, arthritic Ira is seduced by his Estonian masseuse, the gold-toothed Helgi Pärn, who is some years his senior. When as part of her massage she administers a blow job, Ira discovers yet another wonder of existence that had gone unmentioned by Johnny O'Day, probably because Marx failed to mention it in *The 18th Brumaire of Louis Bonaparte*.

Eve Frame is not cut out for Browder or Foster or Eros run amok. "A spiritual woman with décolletage," she has a distaste "for the Jew who was insufficiently disguised" (*I Married a Communist*, 55). Murray recalls her to Nathan with a cruel and unsparing intelligence.

> She could go along parallel to life for a long time. Not *in* life – parallel to life. She could be quite convincing in that ultra civilized, ladylike role she'd chosen. The soft voice. The precise locution . . . She knew all the moves, the benign smile, the dramatic reserve, all the delicate gestures. But then she'd veer off that parallel course of hers, the thing that looked so much like life, and there'd be an episode that could leave you spinning. (53)

Like Ira, Eve is masked and inaccessible, but if his mask is the square-jawed face of the earnest proletarian, the Yankee Stakhanovite, acting out a role in the WPA mural of his life, hers is that of the lady, the sea captain's daughter. Eve Frame despises the Chava Fromkin in herself, the Jewish-American princess from Brooklyn. She had gone to Hollywood not only to seek her fortune but to undergo that ultimate nose job – the total history replacement. There she married a fellow actor, a silent film star with a pedigree named Carlton Pennington, a member of the polo set who just happened to have more passion for boys than he did for her. So here they are, Ira and Eve, the raw and the cooked, the bohunk Yankee Joodle and the diva *shayne madel*, bound together at first by a desperate sensuality, then by perplexity and deception, and finally by the logic of the feud: to destroy the other.

Ira is Roth's stick to beat the old Stalinist Left, while Eve Frame is his stick to beat his ex-wife. But what a difference! Though Roth encountered Stalinism in Prague, American Stalinism is only a reflex of a history that Roth knows as a reader of the liberal anti-Communist journals of his time, like *Partisan Review*. The fifties may have been a nightmare but on the page it is canned history. Marriage, however, lives on in the marrow, which is why when nitty meets gritty in *I Married a Communist*, it isn't the Red scare that erupts like swamp gas: not *Red Channels*, not HUAC, but Sylphid, who emerges as Iago. Or, rather, as Goneril and Regan rolled into one, in a *King Lear* without a Cordelia.

Sylphid Pennington is a zaftig and ruthless young woman who refuses to leave the maternal nest so long as by staying she can make her mother wretched. She calls Ira "the Beast" and accuses her mother of having destroyed her childhood by leaving Pennington, who, despite parading his boys through the house, was a good father! There is no more chilling scene in the book than the one that finds Ira going to Sylphid's room only to find mother and daughter in bed together, "Eve on her back screaming and crying, and Sylphid in her pajamas sitting astride her, also screaming, also crying, her strong harpist's hands pinning Eve's shoulders to the bed." Sylphid screams, "Can't you stand up to *anyone*? Won't you once stand up for your own daughter against him? Won't you be a mother, *ever? Ever?*" (174–75).

If the ex-wife is fair game, especially after Claire Bloom had struck first with her book about Roth, *Leaving a Doll's House*, is the daughter a fair target as well? It is bootless to ask this of Roth, for whom turning aside wrath is a crime worse than McCarthyism. Privacy? What privacy? In tabloid America, where all is material, closed doors are open invitations, and what is the envious novelist to do but press on with the illicit pleasures of exposure and revenge, with all the bile he can muster. In the end, Eve herself is undone as her book is exposed in *The Nation* as having been ghost-written and Eve herself is revealed to be a Jewish girl from Brownsville, not the sea captain's daughter from New Bedford.

There is comedy here to be sure. Consider Eve Frame's "as told to" denunciation of Ira, *I Married a Communist*, ghost-written by her friends Bryden and Katrina Van Tassel Grant. "How can I possibly consider it my moral and patriotic duty to inform on a man I loved as much as I loved Iron Rinn?" she asks. Eve declares that "as an American actress" she has the "solemn responsibility" to "expose the extent of the Communist grip on the broadcasting industry" and thus must expose "a man I loved more than any man I have ever known" (244). He was my man, but he done America wrong. Its actual author, Katrina Van Tassel Grant herself, a society matron and hostess of her own radio program, is also a novelist of historical bodice rippers, including *Eloise and Abelard*. "His hands clasped about her waist, drawing her to him, and she felt the powerful muscles of his legs. Her head fell back. Her mouth parted to receive his kiss. One day he would suffer castration as a brutal and vengeful punishment for this passion for Eloise, but for now he was far from mutilated." It gets zanier. She cries out, "Now teach me, please. Teach me, Pierre! Explain to me your dialectical analysis of the mystery of God and the Trinity" (134). Is this a right-wing prose style?

All this furious striving and star-crossed destiny does not lead to revelation, either for the characters or for the reader. The novel is resolved in a vision of Nathan Zuckerman himself, up in rural Connecticut on a starry night, lying in his deck, looking up at the stars, content to be depleted of his own stories. Contemplating the stars and their great hydrogen flares, he imagines a place where there is no betrayal. "There is no idealism. There are no falsehoods. There is neither conscience nor its absence. There are no mothers and daughters, no fathers and stepfathers. There are no actors. There is no class struggle" (322). And what are we left with at the end of any Roth novel anyway but the gorgeous prose, the feverish notes? And the rancor. Stars or no stars, that tincture of rancor is the fuel that has always driven Roth's writing. *I Married a Communist* is all prose and rancor, blended in a fine, clear vitriol, every phrase measured by the milliliter, by the drop, by the atom. Writing well *is* the best revenge.

Still, it is a headache of a novel. It is among the noisiest of Roth's books, and the uninterrupted rant grows quickly monotonous. The plot disappears, dragged under by the concrete shoes of fulmination. The waves of indignation that sweep through the novel eventually become the novel. Johnny O'Day fulminates at Ira Ringold; Ira fulminates at anyone in earshot; Sylphid fulminates at her mother; her mother fulminates at Ira; Murray Ringold fulminates for six nights at Nathan in the latter's Connecticut retreat, and Nathan passes it on to us, raw, unedited, a steamroller of woe.

I Married a Communist may not be Roth's most readable book, but it is among the most quotable, on the subjects of lying, betrayal, revenge, recrimination, power, the daily theater, language, pretense, on talk itself. A wilderness of miscalculations, it is a forest of epigrams. Nathan Zuckerman thus thinks of his life as a long speech that he has heard since memory began: "how to think, how not to think; how to behave, how not to behave; whom to loath and whom to admire; what to embrace and when to escape; what is rapturous, what is murderous, what is laudable, what is shallow, what is sinister, what is shit, and how to remain pure in soul" (222). It is the cacophony of these voices, bearing down not only on Nathan Zuckerman but on us also that is the book's tonic note, and whatever is appealing in it can't be disentangled from what is infuriating.

The protagonists die: Eve in a drunken stupor in a Manhattan hotel room; Ira of heart failure in Zinc Town. Murray Ringold's wife is murdered on the streets of Newark, where they are the last white couple on a black street, and Murray himself does not long outlast his disburdening to Nathan Zuckerman. Only Zuckerman remains, cocooned in his clapboard monastery in the Connecticut countryside. Roth offers no consolations here, least of all the consolation of human attachment. And is that not also a fanaticism, the fanaticism of retreat, decontamination, self-absolution, and self-reliance? "What are you warding off?," Murray asks him as he leaves. "What the hell happened?" (320). Roth is not yet finished with fanatics, only fanatics with dreams, with blueprints for self-improvement or changing the world. A fanaticism of disillusionment is still a live option, and it is precisely that fanaticism of *tohu bohu* that runs as a dark thread from *Sabbath's Theater* to *The Human Stain*, the books of Philip Roth's blues in the night.

Race, class, and gender: *The Human Stain*

In *The Human Stain*, Roth's martyr to himself is a classics professor and university dean, Coleman Silk, a ponderous pedant who teaches Greek literature at Athena College, somewhere in the rolling Puritan hills of New England. To all appearances he is a *mentsch*: a dean, a husband, a paterfamilias, and a figure of distinction in academic dullsville. His achievements at Athena consist of having weeded out academic deadwood on the way to becoming deadwood himself. Of his publications or intellectual convictions we haven't a clue. He's Mr. Chips. He also lives something of a half-life, harboring a secret from not only his colleagues and students but also from his family. Silk is a black man – whatever that can possibly mean of someone so fair-skinned – who has spent his adult life passing for Jewish. (And what was Silk in the Old Country? Silberzweig, he tells his family.) *The Human Stain* is a moral romance, the *Scarlet Letter* of race, class, and gender, and all we can do is take a deep breath and see what Roth can make with his modern Dimmesdale.

What Roth does is blow his man to bits for the sin of passing. In taking roll in class one day Silk asks about two students who have never shown up, "Does anyone know these people? Do they exist or are they spooks?"[3] "Spook" is one of the magic words that everybody knows except a man who has grown so remote from his roots that he has forgotten the taboos. Silk writes and stars in his own Greek tragedy, and the furies that hound him from the college are all rolled into one Professor Delphine Roux, a self-exalted feminist, a French poststructuralist, and a distracted woman who writes personals ads to the *New York Review of Books* and accidentally e-mails them to her colleagues. (Talk about Freud's "psychopathology of everyday life"! Couldn't Spielvogel get an article out of her?) Silk is denounced as a racist and is obliged to retire. The crisis kills his wife Iris, and in his vexation he turns to the local novelist, Nathan Zuckerman, in the hopes of getting his story told. So, the man gets his first scarlet letter: a red "R" for Racist.

The reclusive Zuckerman, now *hors de combat* from life, impotent from prostate surgery, and living his monastic life, has lately become an ear on life for those who track him down with their tales of woe and betrayal. A rustic Anne Landers, Zuckerman takes a liking to his stricken informant, with whom he shares a fondness for the music of the 1940s and even dances one lonely night in his cottage in the Berkshire countryside. Zuckerman becomes the Greek chorus to Silk's downfall. Rejuvenated by Viagra, Silk has taken up with a woman half his age, a janitor at the college and a part-time farm hand, Faunia Farley, who has her own blues, having suffered abuse both as a child and as an adult and having lost her children in a fire while she was outside giving a blow job. It takes no time for Delphine Roux to unleash a venomous memo: "Everyone knows you're sexually exploiting an abused, illiterate woman half your age" (*The Human Stain*, 38). Second scarlet letter: "E" for Exploiter. Nor does it take long for Faunia Farley's ex-husband, Les, a crazed Vietnam vet and a helicopter door gunner, to vow to kill the Jew who is dating his ex. His third letter, "J" for Jew. This is Hawthorne country, where every community has a volunteer accusation department the way others have their volunteer fire departments.

In the background is the daily Bill and Monica extravaganza. Indignation has become to the nation's emotional life what day trading is to its economic life. It is the summer of 1998, the summer of impeachment, and America is on "an enormous piety binge, a purity binge" (2). The President has been getting head from a chubby Jewish intern and the bill has come due. Get blown and get blown away. It this Greek or is it biblical?

Roth plays it Greek: hubris and nemesis. Coleman Silk is depicted as a man driven by his ghosts. His life reads like a CV, a roundup of highlights that come in categories: son, boxer, lover. He has a Ph.D. in classics and reads Greek and Latin, sure, but what does he think about with his gigawatt power plant of a brain? Sex. And resentment. What we see is a man devoted mainly to denying, reversing, projecting, sublimating, blaming, erupting, and general amnesia. He is a Rothist; he's got issues.

Roth modeled Silk in part on former *New York Times* book editor Anatole Broyard, who also made a life of passing and of keeping his parents at a distance. Critic Henry Louis Gates wrote of him,

So, here is a man who passed for white because he wanted to be a writer and he did not want to be a Negro writer. It is a crass disjunction, but it is not his crassness or his disjunction. His perception was perfectly correct. He *would* have had to be a Negro writer, which was something he did not want to be. In his terms, he did not want to write about black love, black passion, black suffering, black joy; he wanted to write about love and passion and suffering and joy. We give lip service to the idea of the writer who happens to be black, but had anyone, in the postwar era, ever seen such a thing?[4]

But there are differences as well. Broyard was intensely bookish all his life, while we are not sure about Silk. In reviews for *The Times* and in his late books, *Intoxicated by My Illness* and *Kafka Was the Rage*, Broyard wrote with pungency and wit about those things in his own life that he could openly acknowledge. Coleman Silk doesn't write; he only complains and appears to know his own life only through the fogs of indignation and grief, the fog of self-intoxication, the fog of self-loathing, the fog of self-misunderstanding, the fog of occluded desire, the fog of self-forgetfulness. Lacking the benefit of Roth's own splendid radar and Broyard's bookishness, Coleman Silk comes across as a pasteboard prof., clever enough to teach literature but not interesting enough to be literature.

What is *The Human Stain* all about? That isn't easy to say, but Roth does have Greek tragedy in mind. Coleman Silk himself, that Achilles of Athena College, is as accountable for his own catastrophe as Ira Ringold is for his. It would not have been lost on Roth that in uttering the word "spooks" when he did, Silk meant just what everyone thought he meant. If ever there was a classic Freudian slip, there it is. Why? Silk was dying to be found out, and if he had to smash his life to do it, at his age, with the children gone and alienated, his wife indifferent to him if not outright hostile, his sexual potency in the deep freeze, his colleagues whispering in corners, his lies grown rank and horrible in his own ears, and having become the Deadwood Dick of his college, wasn't it time to step out of the shadows and kill off the old life? The book makes scant sense unless Coleman's Silk's self-demolition is undertaken with gusto. The game is up at the moment when his lawyer gives him the perfectly sensible advice to stay away from Faunia Farley, and Silk responds, "I never again want to hear that self-admiring voice of yours or see your smug fucking lily-white face" (81). Lily white? And so after leaving the lawyer's office, Silk decides to take a last look at Athena College, thinking to himself, "One last look at Athena, and then let the disgrace be complete" (85).

That's part of it, the *Schadenfreude*: the strategic slip of the tongue in a time of weakness. But Silk also wants to be restored to the last vital time, when he was most himself, Silky Silk, the smart, tough cookie from East Orange, New Jersey and the star pupil in Doc Chizner's boxing class at the Newark Boys Club, who went 11–0 as an amateur before his father made him stop. He had sweet moves: he could slip a punch and he could bang. It was the high time of his life, and he took on the toughest of Newark and beat them. It was the last honest time as well, when he could strike blows and dance away; everything since has been masquerade and manners. The dishonesty quickly becomes routine; the illness is in the blood, and he obeys the rule laid down by Doc Chizner: "If nothing comes up, you don't bring it up" (98). At first, picking up women, passing for white, and making his own destiny is a snap. Until, that is, he takes his deception right into marriage with Iris Gittelman and has to go home to tell his mother that he will never see her again and she may not see her grandchildren, unless she agrees to sit silently at the zoo or the train station while he parades by with them. His brother phones him afterwards and orders him to never show his "lily-white face around that house again" (145).

What goes on, then, between Coleman Silk and everyone else follows the inexorable logic of self-loathing. He wants to come roaring out of his corner and deliver combinations – head, body, head. He wants to be Silky Silk again, the Sugar Ray Robinson he might have been. His legs are gone and his reflexes are shot, but what the hell? What goes on between himself and Faunia Farley is primal enough. Viagra has restored him to life as a man, and nothing will stand in the way of his comeback.

Is Roth too eager to turn passing to tragedy – to recreate that old stereotype, the "tragic mulatto"? From what we know, Broyard carried off his masquerade, though his background wasn't exactly secret to those who knew him in his Village days. Nevertheless, he kept his children in the dark and it was not until after his death in 1990 that they learned their father's secret. Could Coleman Silk, starting out in the 1940s, have become a professor of Classics in an academia that was still adjusting to the novelty of Jews? No, not in the kingdom of the one-drop rule, which was as firm in the North as anything Jim Crow had devised in the South. The word "passing" still implies illegitimacy and deviousness, even selling out, while "living out one's dreams" implies courage and adventure. That Roth plays Coleman Silk's choice as tragedy is hardly out of bounds. Coleman Silk is confronted by a choice known to most of us: how to be liberated from the last liberation?

What of Faunia Farley, the janitor-sybarite who becomes Coleman Silk's lover, teacher, and femme fatale, as the two are run off the road and killed by Faunia's ex? What she is doing there is being the anti-Delphine Roux, that race, class, and gender cop who brings Coleman low because, ostensibly, he isn't stirred by either her looks or theories. Faunia Farly is conspicuous for *not* having a privileged 16th *arrondisement* childhood, for *not* having attended every lycée known to Paris, and for *not* graduating from Yale with a dissertation on "Self-Denial in Georges Bataille." She's the natural, and we've encountered her before: in Drenka Balich of *Sabbath's Theater* and Helgi Pärn of *I Married a Communist*. She's got the glands of her class. After the wrath of hurricane Delphine, Faunia Farley is the healing, lubricious earth mother, though being half Coleman Silk's age she is more the earth daughter. She is also a shanty town Sybil, whose illiteracy conceals a hard-bitten wisdom. She may swab out toilets and talk to crows, but she is full of messages that strike one as odd fusions of trailer park dejection and *King Lear* metaphysics. "We leave a stain, we leave a trail, we leave our imprint.

Impurity, cruelty, abuse, error, excrement, semen – there's no other way to be here" (242). So, she is here to sing the theme song, deliver the valedictory, and to speak for Roth, now that Zuckerman has been reduced to basically listening.

Paradoxically, *The Human Stain* does turn into something Professor Roux would understand: a race, class, and gender novel. Roth has touched on sex and class often enough and he has his own traumatic views on love and sex outside of one's class. *My Life as a Man*, the book about Roth's own marriage into the heartland working class, is the locus classicus of all such imaginings. If you take that plunge, he has shown us before, be prepared to die for your sins.

Though much praised in reviews, *The Human Stain* strikes me as the most ponderous of these three novels. As a social novel it strays too far outside the perimeter of Roth's understanding: Newark, Jews, and himself. While Roth is nominally present in Zuckerman, there isn't enough of him in Silk to bring the character fully to life. Yes, there is the familiar fierce self-laceration and the love of 1940s big-band music. But the book is set in an abstract New England with abstract characters in an abstract college. I mean, Delphine Roux as a 24-year-old department chair! Gimme a break! And it is garrulous. Looking for plot, for characters, the reader has to machete his/her way through forests of beseeching and denunciation in voices that sound uncommonly alike. They're all Nathan Zuckerman's puppets after all, and he is the Pavarotti of indignation. Coleman Silk rages; Delphine Roux rages; Les Farley rages, and America rages over the president's hubris. There is a line between making indignation your subject and making it your muse, so that reprimanding and pontificating are all your characters can do. Roth can occasionally make it work. His sendup of Delphine Roux's "all encompassing chic" and "Ecole Normale sophistication" will warm the heart of anyone who has spent five minutes in the academy. But he hasn't a clue about Les Farley, who is Brand-X Vietnam Vet, all shattered nerves and tripwire rage, or Faunia, who is generic underclass, complete with childhood molestation and goatish appetites: the overscale eroticism that is a Roth trademark.

The prior two novels tell us something about Jews: Jewish history in America, Jewish fanaticism, the Jewish revolutionism of the 1930s, the seething, mutinous, demanding heart that cries and whispers "I want I want" in every book. *The Human Stain* is one of those detours into AAA guide-book America, like the early novel *When She Was Good*, set on a sound stage called Liberty Center. Athena College is the new Liberty Center, a Rothian dreamscape where bad things happen because Philip Roth has bad dreams.

NOTES

1 Philip Roth, *American Pastoral* (Boston: Houghton Mifflin, 2004), p. 89.
2 Philip Roth, *I Married a Communist* (Boston: Houghton Mifflin, 1998), p. 181.
3 Philip Roth, *The Human Stain* (Boston: Houghton Mifflin, 2000), p. 6.
4 See Henry Louis Gates, "The Passing of Anatole Broyard," in *Thirteen Ways of Looking at a Black Man* (New York: Random House, 1997), pp. 180–214.

HANA WIRTH-NESHER

Roth's autobiographical writings

> "You remember Lou Holtz? He used to say, 'Vas you dere, Chollie?'"
> "Is that who said that? I've often wondered. I always say it to Claire but I
> never knew who the comedian was. He's before my time, Lou Holtz. Vas you
> dere, Chollie?"[1]

This exchange between the ailing Herman Roth and his son Philip in the
account of his father's last days in *Patrimony* can serve as a signature of
Roth's autobiographies as literary, historical, and ethical works. First, no
matter how skeptical we may be about the truth of any autobiography, we
rely on the author's account of his or her own life because we would always
have to reply in the negative should the author ask his readers, "Vas you dere,
Chollie?" Although we have learned to read autobiographies for emotional
or psychological insights glimpsed through partial memory, evasion, and
desire, we continue to search for truths unlike the ones we expect to uncover
in fiction because we could never be "there," inside someone else's life. That
is the great appeal of this literary genre – the transitory glimpse into the life of
another. It is a clever move on Roth's part to splice this quip into his memoir,
a disarming technique that he will employ in his other autobiographical
writings, to anticipate and defuse our skepticism.

This apparently ordinary conversation between a father and son who both
know that the father is facing imminent death and that no amount of sympathy can bridge the gap between the dying and the spectator – "vas you
dere?" – locates Philip Roth not only artistically, as a comic, unsentimental,
yet touching writer, but also historically, as a generation removed from Lou
Holtz and borscht-belt humor. A stand-up comic who also had his own radio
show, Lou Holtz was "before my time," in Herman Roth's era of vaudeville
and dialect comedians like S. J. Perelman, Molly Goldberg, Marx Brothers,
and Mickey Katz. Even for Herman, native-born son of immigrants, mimicry
of Yiddish-accented English signals distance from his parents' world and his
own successful Americanization. For Roth, the language of his New Jersey
childhood is without accent, part of the general language of America. For his
notorious character Alexander Portnoy, as for Roth, the quest for freedom
takes the form of wanting to detach his life from the world of Jewish comedy.
"Spring me from this role I play as the smothered son in the Jewish joke!"[2]

Nostalgic parody of the Yiddish inflected one-liner is a sure sign of having arrived as an American.

However, Roth's fictional and nonfictional works demonstrate that to be a Jewish-American two generations removed from immigration is both to embrace America and to acknowledge the claims made on a New Jersey Jew in the name of a transnational Jewish people whose history in Europe has been traumatic. In Cynthia Ozick's *The Shawl*, Holocaust survivor Rosa Lublin accosts an American Jew in a Florida hotel lobby with, "Where were you when we was there?"[3] The accusation in "Vas you dere, Chollie?" rings a more somber tone in Roth's other works, from "Eli, the Fanatic" to *The Ghost Writer*, playing on the name Charlie in its postwar expression as stand-in for American (Checkpoint Charlie marking the infamous border crossing into Berlin's American zone). Roth has admitted that "there," namely Europe, played a key role in his formative years, "The disparity between this tragic dimension of Jewish life in Europe and the actualities of our daily lives as Jews in New Jersey was something that I had to puzzle over myself, and indeed, it was in the vast discrepancy between the two Jewish conditions that I found the terrain for my first stories and later for *Portnoy's Complaint*."[4] And, I would argue, also for his autobiographies.

Although many, if not all of Philip Roth's works, could be considered to be autobiographical, three stand out: *The Facts: A Novelist's Autobiography* (1988), *Patrimony: A True Story* (1990), and *The Plot Against America* (2004). The first two are self-professed autobiographies – of Roth the writer in *The Facts* and of Roth the son in *Patrimony*, while the third is a work of fiction that, in offering an alternative imagined history of America, brings European Jewry's "there" to America's shores. What has marked Roth's career since the publication of *Portnoy's Complaint* is an aura of scandal as Jewish-American readers have insisted on reading his satires as autobiographical works that betray his community by exposing Jewish warts to gentile eyes. The attacks on him have been vociferous: he has been accused of unfocused hostility and self-hatred, of provoking anti-Semitism and jeopardizing the Jew's hard-won and tenuous security in the United States. In his repeated self-defenses, Roth has portrayed himself as a victim of incompetent readers, philistines impervious to irony and artistry. In short, as far as Roth is concerned, his readers have often lacked the sophistication to distinguish fiction from autobiography, art from history. With implicit analogues to Joyce, Roth has depicted himself as an artist-rebel, unfettered by social restraints and collective anxieties. To this end, Roth wrote *The Facts: A Novelist's Autobiography*.[5]

Autobiography is often motivated by a desire to set the record straight, to tell the "facts." Corrective retelling depends on how much information about the life is already available to readers before the autobiographer assumes the authority that comes with being the subject of the story. And this, in turn, will depend on the extent to which the autobiographer presents his life as representative of a collective identity or as a unique person who has been misrepresented. These are not mutually exclusive, and Roth is not the first to write more than one version of his life. When Frederick Douglass sets the record straight in *Narrative of the Life of Frederick Douglass*, he does so as a representative slave who may be individually unknown to his white readers but whose collective life, he maintains, has been distorted and misconstrued. When he publishes his second autobiography, it is to set the record straight about the personal details of his *individual* experience, after he has already attained public recognition and fame. Setting the record straight by exposing "the facts" assumes even more complex twists when public figures are artists whose fictions have been the source of their readers' constructions of their "real" lives. Having drawn on their lives for the fictions, novelists nevertheless insist on the autonomy of art, and when the public persists in "misreading" the art and the life, the author may eventually succumb to the temptation to relate the "truth." How do we read the autobiographies of writers who have been preoccupied with storytelling and the creation of fictional worlds, and later shift into a genre that presumably unmasks the author in order to disarm the reader, those who write *A Novelist's Autobiography*?

The coyness of his title, coming from an author who has been playing a fast game of hide-and-seek with his readers, does not reassure. Exhibiting what Lejeune calls "the autobiographical pact," namely, the identical name for author, narrator, and character, *The Facts* certainly qualifies as an autobiography, yet given the self-conscious play of life and art in Roth's novels, we might ask to what extent he is testing the limits of the genre. Moreover, given the unease of Jews when it comes to asserting and celebrating the "I" narrator as opposed to the communal "we," how is Roth's intersecting of fiction and reality an anti-autobiographical strategy? The Philip Roth "I" narrator emerges as an arena for dialogue between the author and his readers, an act of community as much as it is an assertion of self.

Roth recalls that when he left home for college, "My interest was in my personal freedom." *The Facts* chronicles this journey, starting with the credo of his childhood – "*Hear, O Israel, the family is God, the family is One.*"[6] "In our lore," he writes, "the Jewish family was an inviolate haven against every form of menace, from personal isolation to gentile hostility." His father, he maintains, became the original model for his identity, which he lists in the following order: American, Jew, citizen, man, writer. Each successive chapter recounts attempts at assimilation into American life. The opening sentence of the first chapter underscores the centrality of his *American* identity:

"the greatest menace while I was growing up came from abroad, from the Germans and the Japanese, our enemies because we were American." But in the same paragraph, he qualifies his Americanness with a reminder of his minority status: "At home, the biggest threat came from the Americans who opposed or resisted us – or condescended to us or rigorously excluded us – because we were Jews" (*The Facts*, 20). In that first paragraph, the keynote for a good portion of the autobiography appears: "Though I knew that we were tolerated and accepted as well – in publicized individual cases, even especially esteemed – and though I never doubted that this country was mine (and New Jersey and Newark as well), I was not unaware of the power to intimidate that emanated from the highest and lowest reaches of gentile America" (20). Taking his cue from the framed copy of the Declaration of Independence that hung above the telephone table in the hallway of his parents' home, Roth recounts his own quest for independence from family and collective identity of any sort: "I was determined to be an absolutely independent, self-sufficient man" (160). It is a statement of intention, not achievement. But it is an intention that conforms to the model of self-reliant American hero, from Natty Bumppo and Emerson to Huck Finn, Jake Barnes, Humphrey Bogart, and the Lone Ranger, and that denies the Jewish imperative for communal life.

Entitled "Safe at Home," the first chapter contrasts a homogenous Jewish world, a childhood arena as all-American as baseball, with an occasionally inhospitable gentile world, from the corporate boardrooms of his father's insurance company, where promotion beyond a certain point was unthinkable for a Jew, to the lumpen kids at the Jersey shore hollering "Kikes! Dirty Jews!" (23). Being Jewish, he recalls, was like "having two arms and two legs. It would have seemed strange *not* to be Jewish – stranger still, to hear someone announce that he wished he weren't a Jew, or that he intended not to be in the future" (31). The following chapter, "Joe College," is a rite of passage into American academe with Jewish quotas, campuses like Princeton that simply didn't "take Jews," and fraternities divided along religious and ethnic lines. By far the most dramatic boundary crossing from "Safe at Home" to the perils of gentile America takes place in mid-book, the chapter satirically entitled "Girl of My Dreams," when he meets his muse and nemesis, turned wife. She is more than the exotic Aryan gentile woman, the *shiksa*/temptress who promises uninhibited sexuality and the surest sign of making it in WASP America; she is also a victim of that world who craves the nurturing and security from which Philip seeks to escape. This incompatibility of their backgrounds was for Roth the decisive evidence that he was free from the pressures of convention. As he put it, "I was not only a man, I was a free man" (87). Thus, in his marriage to the gentile woman from an abusive family, he turns his seeming un-American Jewish background into an asset. "The stories I told of my protected childhood might have been Othello's tales about the men with heads beneath their shoulders" (92).

With Shakespeare as key to understanding his early years, it becomes clear that Roth is chronicling the portrait of the artist alongside his tale of Americanization. With hindsight, he realizes that she initiated him into the world of Sherwood Anderson and Theodore Dreiser, into the "menacing realism of benighted American life that so far I had only read of in novels." His own role was drawn from literature as well: "I cast myself as the parfit Jewish knight dispatched to save one of their own from the worst of the gentile dragons" (94). After itemizing her vices and naming her "my worst enemy ever," he concludes with, "Reader, I married her," an ironic reference to Brontë that casts Josie as the madwoman in the attic, and Roth as both a long-suffering Rochester and a moralistic Jane (112).

This idealization of Jewish family life rapidly gives way to fierce intra-communal strife in the fourth section, when Roth the artist is attacked by American-Jewish readers for what they detect as anti-Semitism in his satirical fictions. At a Yeshiva University symposium, the moderator asks him: "Mr. Roth, would you write the same stories you've written if you were living in Nazi Germany?" one of many occasions on which he is asked to measure his life "here" against a counterlife "there." After thirty minutes of grilling by the audience, he could see that he was "not just opposed but hated" (127). This "bruising public exchange" marked a turning point in his writing career. The fierce repudiation of his work by many Jewish readers would be transformed into a major theme in his writing – the role of Jewish self-definition and allegiance in the dialogue between art and society, aesthetics and morality, the facts and their literary representation. The artist finds his true subject as a result of the wound inflicted on him by his own community, conveyed in the chapter entitled "All in the Family," an allusion both to the commandment in the prologue about the sanctity of the family in Jewish life and to America's popular television series, where representative blue-collar Archie Bunker derides every minority in his society. Moreover, having been accused of ignoring Jewish experience in Europe, Roth will bring that world into his writings over and over again.

"Now Vee May Perhaps to Begin," the title of the final section, calls into question the veracity of this autobiography, first, because it is a reference from one of his own fictions, the famous last line of *Portnoy's Complaint*, the novel judged as obscene autobiography by his Jewish readers who feared it would damage their community's acceptance among "Americans." Second, because the voice of the Viennese psychoanalyst signals storytelling as therapy, whose goal is the reconstruction of a coherent narrative, not the innocent retrieval of facts. Moreover, "to Begin" here refers not only to the beginning of the talk cure, but also to the new start in the author's life, having extricated himself from wife and family. Roth's finale echoes the Modernist artist's credo from *Portrait of the Artist*, as Stephen Daedalus declares his freedom from the nets that restrain him, and the traditional Emersonian model of the independent loner – "I was determined to be an absolutely independent self-sufficient man."

The autobiography doesn't end with this pronouncement. In a metafictional frame, Roth submits his manuscript to his most critical reader, his invented alter ego Nathan Zuckerman, who strongly disapproves of *The Facts* in the appended letter. Reminding him of the Philip Roth persona that the author has discarded in the writing of his autobiography, Zuckerman accuses him of idealizing his family past in order to curry belated favor with an audience that has convicted him of treason. "Your Jewish readers are finally going to glean from this what they've wanted to hear from you for three decades . . . that instead of writing only about Jews at one another's throats, you have discovered gentile anti-Semitism, and you are exposing *that* for a change" (166). He advises Roth to "give up on giving them, thirty years too late, the speech of the good boy at the synagogue." "I'm not a fool," writes Zuckerman, "and I don't believe you" (168).

Zuckerman's attack on Roth effectively anticipates and neutralizes criticism by inscribing the skeptical reader into the text. The novelist in this *Novelist's Autobiography* is all too aware of the partial self that is always reconstructed in autobiography. Zuckerman's tongue-lashing is an acknowledgment that the autobiography may satisfy the needs of the writer, but it is not a reliable chronicle of "the facts." By creating an adversarial relationship between his writing self and social self, he allows the reader to witness his wrestling with his own shadow, that same Jewish community that has, by its criticism and accusations, shaped the self that is, in turn, the very subject of the autobiography.

His two invented readers of the autobiography deduce two entirely different Philip Roths. "Only an American," says his imaginary British gentile wife (unlike his Jewish wife Claire Bloom) "could see the fate of his freedom as the recurring theme of his life" (189). Zuckerman, on the other hand, reads *The Facts* as a tale of the victimized Jew who needs his persecution, indeed savors the wounds inflicted on him by his abusive Jewish public. That he makes his Jewishness the determining factor in his parents' and his own life is Roth's shaping principle in the book – "To me, being a Jew had to do with a real historical predicament into which you were born" (126). The metafictional dimension, therefore, is not merely obligatory pyrotechnics for a postmodern narrative. It is an admission that the autobiographical genre poses problems for the Jewish writer. Multiculturalism has produced a contemporary American self that no longer believes in an essential American experience, but is equally skeptical about ethnic or racial identity as a safe haven. Identity politics is deterministic about each American's point of departure but stubbornly idealistic about the freedom to maneuver between categories and to sustain multiple identities. The splintered self that enters into dialogue with its autobiographer, then, is a new form of American, while the insistence on community and "historical predicament" as the core of this self-making is a Jewish version of this genre.

Certainly the desire for freedom and the recognition that there are limits on that freedom is a psychic story shared across cultures. In Roth's literary world, America is the sign of freedom and Jewish civilization the sign of limits, exemplified in *The Facts*. Published three years later, his memoir *Patrimony* offers a sharp contrast by underscoring two other kinds of limits: hindsight and mortality. During the time that Philip self-consciously fathers Herman, whose health deteriorates from a brain tumor, he himself undergoes an emergency quintuple bypass. Written after his father's death and his own heart surgery, *Patrimony* contemplates the aging body (a theme to which he returns in *Dying Animal*, the title borrowed from Yeats's metaphor of the body's betrayal), Jewish male lineage, and manhood. An elegy for Herman Roth, as individual and as representative of his father's generation, *Patrimony* circles around survival and manhood. Recalling the boxing matches that his father had taken him to when he was boy, Roth "tried to get his mind as far from death as I could by telling him about a book that I'd just finished reading . . . *The Jewish Boxers' Hall of Fame*." Herman notes that "these kids" fought "two battles. They fought because they were fighters, and they fought because they were Jews. They'd put two guys in the ring, an Italian and a Jew, an Irishman and a Jew, and they fought like they meant it, they fought to hurt" (*Patrimony*, 203). Roth depicts his father's dying as a battle – "He's fought such a long, long . . . distinguished battle" – and as another job that has to be faced, "Dying is work and he was a worker" (123).

His father's and his own mortality, that inescapable limit to their manhood, shadows this autobiography. Just as his aging body constrains his manhood, his hindsight constrains his artistry. Like all autobiographies, *Patrimony* is also shaped by hindsight, the knowledge that limits freedom of the imagination. Because the autobiographer knows the outcome of events, he cannot recapture that most fundamental experience in the story of a life, uncertainty. The lived life is marked by openness, by the freedom that is the other side of angst. The written life is marked by closure, by the knowledge of the future beyond the event recorded, by the limits of certainty. Although autobiographers can and do reconstruct their past anxieties, recorded experience can never be severed from hindsight. Every decision that Herman and his family face during his illness is colored by retrospection. The subtitle *A True Story*, then, refers to what happened as Roth remembers it, but it cannot refer to the truth of how it felt when it happened, to the emotional truth which is always dependent on uncertainty of outcome (a point that Roth will later make in *The Plot Against America*). The gap between being there and writing there is another way to understand Herman's reminiscence about Lou Holtz – "Vos you dere, Chollie?"

In light of the ineffectual Jewish father in *Portnoy's Complaint, Patrimony* is a memoir that also sets the record straight in its emphasis on Herman Roth's manhood. Philip's patrimony centers on three objects: tefillin, a shaving mug, and excrement. Philip is surprised to learn that his father did not consider passing his tefillin on to his sons or grandsons. "I could have imagined him," writes Roth, "instead of parting with his tefillin, rediscovering in the mere contemplation of them something of their ancient fetishistic power. But my imagining this old man meditatively fondling his long-neglected tefillin was so much sentimental kitsch. How my father actually disposed of the tefillin reveals an imagination altogether bolder and more mysterious" (96). Instead of giving them to a synagogue, he left them in a paper bag in the locker room of the YMHA (Young Men's Hebrew Association) where he went for his regular swim. Registering some disappointment that his father did not bequeath them to him – "I wouldn't have prayed with them, but I might well have cherished them, especially after this death," Roth understands the logic of leaving them at the YMHA, "where Jewish men stood unashamedly naked before one another," and therefore, "he could lay his tefillin to rest without worry . . . where they would not be profaned or desecrated." Furthermore, the men's locker room at the YMHA "was closer to the core of Judaism he lived by than the rabbi's study at the synagogue." Roth locates his father's Judaism in that generation's fraternity, in Jewish male camaraderie where "they shvitzed, they stank . . . told their dirty jokes . . . made their deals . . . where they remained Jews" (96).

Insofar as Hebrew script on tefillin encapsulates Jewish patrimony, what remains as Roth's share in this tradition is only the acknowledgment of its loss. Yet he does inherit paternal script – his grandfather's shaving mug "inscribed in faded gold Gothic lettering" with "S. Roth 1912" (27) – the surname of the male line, and the initial S. for "Sender" transliterated into the Roman alphabet, into the English that remained alien to its owner. "The mug was our family heirloom as far as I knew" (27). Roth's memories of his paternal grandfather is that "he smoked all day long, spoke only Yiddish, and wasn't much given to fondling the American children" (27). When Philip

attends to his father's needs in his last days, he is acutely aware of his actions
rehearsing those of Herman when he nursed his father Sender after his stroke,
"Twice a day he lit cigarettes and stuck them in his father's mouth for him
and in the evening he sat beside the bed and read to him from the Yiddish
paper." That shaving mug on his father's sink, passed down to him in brown
wrapping paper bearing the dedication, "From a Father to a Son" (118), signifies Philip's patrimony as the daily act of shaving, one that often replaced
the daily act of laying tefillin for Jewish immigrants bent on assimilating.
Sender, Herman, and Philip, generation after generation, put on their American manhood by removing their European facial hair, and thereby their
resemblance to the bearded Jewish male.

Whereas the shaving mug is a sign of control over the body, trimming its
excrescence so that it conforms to a prevailing social norm, the excrement
that Roth cleans up after his father is a sign of loss of control, of the corporeal
vanquishing the will. This too is depicted as Herman's valiant battle,

> I felt awful about his heroic, hapless struggle to cleanse himself before I had
> got up to the bathroom and about the shame of it, the disgrace he felt himself
> to be, and yet now that it was over and he was so deep in sleep, I thought I
> couldn't have asked anything more for myself before he died – this, too, was
> right and as it should be. (175)

Once the job is done, Roth concludes, "There was my patrimony: not the
money, not the tefillin, not the shaving mug, but the shit" (176). Insofar
as Herman's shit provides an opportunity for his son to care for his father
("Philip is like a mother to me" [181]), the patrimony is the commandment
to care for his father as his father had done before him, except that by
likening Philip to a mother, Herman has acknowledged filiation but denied
him paternity. Roth reports that Herman begged him not to divulge his
disgrace to Claire, a fact that he subsequently divulges not only to her, but
also to each of the readers of this memoir. Although in many ways *Patrimony*
is the attempt to rewrite the father in a more positive light, it is also an
exercise of power over the father who had always wielded authority over
him. Excreted by the father's body, his patrimony is neither historic, nor
religious, nor textual – it is the act of caring irrespective of the cause: "So
that was the patrimony. Not because cleaning it up was symbolic of anything
else but because it wasn't, because it was nothing less or nothing more than
the lived reality that it was" (176).

To elevate his father's indignities, Roth borrows images associated with
European Jewry: "survivorship, survivorhood, and survivalism" (125).
According to Roth, the most sympathetic ear during his filial ordeal was
that of a Polish refugee whose father had been killed by the Germans. "The

Europe in him is his survivorship," he observes, "These are people who will never give up" (125). Characteristically, Roth attempts to close the gap between the parallel lines of European and American Jewry, in this case by conflating the historical sense of the word "survivor" with its general sense of resilience and determination to live. In Roth's memoir, Herman's battle with disease and his devotion to memory (communal and familial) resonate with Holocaust survival and with the Jewish people's imperative to remember. Having internalized the Jewish obligation to remember, Roth invokes it during tender moments of bathing his father after he has soiled himself: *"You must not forget anything"* (177). His patrimony, therefore, is not the tefillin which enjoins the male Jew to remember the covenant between God and the children of Israel, but rather "the shit," which enjoins the male Jew to remember his personal, biological, and bodily father.

When faced with the choice of burying Herman in a business suit or a traditional shroud, Roth chooses the shroud. Six weeks after his death, Philip wakes up from a dream in which his father, in a hooded white shroud, reproaches him, "I should have been dressed in a suit. You did the wrong thing." Initially, Roth reprimands himself in the borscht-belt humor of a Lou Holtz, "I had dressed him for eternity in the wrong clothes" (237). But in the morning he recognizes that the dream was an indictment of his memoir *Patrimony* where he exposes his father to the world. "The dream was telling me," reflects Roth, that "at least in my dreams, I would live perennially as his little son, with the conscience of a little son, just as he would remain there not only as my father but as *the* father, sitting in judgment on whatever I do. You must not forget anything" (238).

If *The Facts* is the making of the artist and *Patrimony* is the making of the son, *The Plot Against America* is the making of the Jew. Having admitted that "the disparity between this tragic dimension of Jewish life in Europe and the actualities of our daily lives as Jews in New Jersey" became the "terrain" for his work, and responding to the global rise of anti-Semitism in recent years, Roth brings a version of that tragic European Jewish life to the shores of the United States in *The Plot Against America,* so that the American-Jewish experience rejoins a version of Jewish history whose distinguishing feature is persecution as a minority. "The idea that Roth would portray American culture as a kind of anti-Semitic conspiracy," writes Timothy Parrish, "contradicts Roth's familiar and frequent defense of his right to think of himself as American first and Jewish second."[7] In *Patrimony*, Roth sets the record straight regarding discriminatory practices at Metropolitan Life Insurance in order to prove that the allegations about unfair treatment of his father set forth in the first chapter of *The Facts* and contested by the company, were based on historical documents and not his father's paranoia. Although

Herman is proud of the detailed letter that his son sends to the company, he asks him not to send another one, leading Roth to conclude that what made his father nervous was not what he had written about Jews, but "what I had now written about Gentiles . . . and to Gentiles that had been his bosses" (*Patrimony*, 188).

In *The Plot Against America* as family history, Herman Roth's dignity and manhood are restored, as are his mother Bessie's resourcefulness and kindness, due to their heroic response to the challenges posed by anti-Semitism in the United States.

In an interview with Jeffrey Brown, Roth dates the inception of the book to a single line in a book by historian Arthur Schlesinger stating that some Republicans in 1940 had considered nominating Charles Lindbergh for President. "My eyes landed on that sentence, and in the margin I wrote, 'what if they had?' "[8] Roth found himself contemplating what effect it would have had on America if Lindbergh and not Roosevelt had been elected in 1940 in two respects: Lindbergh was an isolationist, and America would have gone to war; given his anti-Semitic remarks, Lindbergh would have been a genuine threat to Jews. The "plot" in the title, therefore, refers to the story spun out of his imagination, to the enduring anti-Semitic accusation of how Jews plot against their host societies, and to the Fascist plot against America that is grounded in history but given a fictional twist in his autobiographical novel. *The Plot Against America* underscores the force of collective identity and destiny that Jewish authors, even American ones bent on personal freedom and creativity, are also inevitably bound by. If his New Jersey childhood pales beside the great subject of his generation, the Holocaust, and if Newark seems marginal, even trivial, when seen in the shadow of the cataclysmic events of his time for his people, what can the Jewish-American author do?

Roth had already experimented with alternative histories in earlier works: Kafka living out his life as Hebrew school teacher in New Jersey in "I Always Wanted You to Admire my Fasting; or Looking at Kafka" (1973) and Anne Frank surviving the war and immigrating to America in the fantasy of his writer alter ego Zuckerman in *The Ghost Writer*. *The Plot Against America* differs from the others in that the alternative history impacts directly on his personal family autobiography.

What if his childhood had not been marked by the security that American Jews felt under Roosevelt, but instead had been a period of the same vulnerability, fear, discrimination, exclusions, and persecution (albeit in a limited sense) that Jews were facing in Fascist Europe in the years that led to the Final Solution? What emerges is a somber, persuasive, and sometimes chilling dystopia, fictional counter evidence of "It can't happen here," the title of Sinclair Lewis's 1935 dystopia of America turned Fascist, based on the Louisiana populist demagogue, Huey Long. Roth's transnational work takes on anti-Semitism, the Nazi movement in America, and the entangling of foreign policy – fierce isolationism and a non-aggression pact with the Third Reich – and domestic policy exemplified in legislation such as the "Just Folks" program that relocates Jews in the American gentile heartland presumably to Americanize them, but effectively to diminish their political power through population dispersal.

Roth nostalgically describes a prelapsarian Newark imperiled by Lindbergh's presidency: "Israel didn't exist, six million European Jews hadn't yet ceased to exist, and the local relevance of distant Palestine . . . was a mystery to me." Recalling the occasional bearded and hatted stranger who would come to the door asking "in broken English for a contribution toward the establishment of a Jewish homeland in Palestine," Roth observed that "the poor old man . . . seemed unable to get it through his head that we'd already had a homeland for three generations."[9]

The power of *The Plot Against America* lies in the incremental, credible, and sinister steps that lead to the systematic targeting of America's Jews. An Office of American Absorption is established for the benign goal of accelerating Americanization for outsiders, mainly Jews. In compliance with the "Just Folks" project, Philip's older brother Sandy is selected to live with a family of Kentucky farmers where he can acquire bigger biceps, a taste for ham and sausage, and a regional accent, "caint for can't," "rimember for remember," and "agin for again" (*The Plot Against America*, 92–93). In other words, to become Just Folks, unlike Newark Jews. This is followed by a "Good Neighbor Project" – the deportation of entire Jewish families to the gentile hinterlands resulting in the dismantling of the Jewish community by importing gentiles to reside in predominantly Jewish neighborhoods in order to "enrich" everyone's "Americanness." The Italian-American Cucuzzas move into the apartment one floor down from the Roths, in the apartment vacated by Philip's schoolmate Sheldon. During the implementation of Lindbergh's policies, Philip's father Herman maintains his optimism, although he is badly shaken during a family trip to Washington when he is denied a hotel room and publicly accused of being a "loudmouth Jew" (65).

What is achieved in a fictional autobiography that cannot be achieved by historical writing? Although we concede that the rights of the imagination are not the same as the rights of history, and that artists have poetic license to exercise their imagination, we are nevertheless troubled when we feel that artists have gone so far in their imaginings that their work poses some ethical dilemma. Perhaps we should approach the subject by reminding ourselves that both history and fiction aim for truth of a certain kind. History aims to determine what happened, to ascertain the facts, and then to write a story that is the result of interpreting and evaluating those facts. Fiction aims to give us the truth of lived experience, the truth of emotional and psychological affect, rather than a cool appraisal of past events. In other words, what is lost in "history" is uncertainty, whether it is personal history in autobiography or group history. For the participants in any historical period, everything could have turned out differently. In Roth's own words, expressed through his narrator in *The Plot Against America*, "as Lindbergh's election couldn't have made clearer to me, the unfolding of the unforeseen was everything. Turned wrong way round, the relentless unforeseen was what we schoolchildren studied in 'History,' harmless history, where everything unexpected in its own time is chronicled on the page as inevitable. *The terror of the unforeseen is what the science of history hides*" (114).

To put it another way, a Lindbergh presidency is imaginary, but the anti-Semitism of the real historical Lindbergh was not, nor was the movement toward his nomination within the Republican party. And he wasn't alone. Philip Roth adds a long postscript to the novel with historical documentation to persuade us of the plausibility not only of a Lindbergh presidency, but also of the forces that would have been set in motion had this occurred. Just a few lines from Henry Ford's *Dearborn Independent* would be enough to make his case: "German-Jewish bankers caused the war," wrote Ford about World War I in a newspaper with a circulation of 300,000 that was forced upon all Ford dealers, and that printed *The Protocols of the Elders of Zion* in serial form (378). In a 1923 interview, Adolf Hitler stated, "We look to Heinrich Ford as the leader of the growing fascist movement in America" (379). According to Ford in 1940, the numerous meetings between Lindbergh and himself focused on one issue: "When Charles comes out here, we only talk about the Jews" (379).

If restoring the terror of the unforeseen is one of Roth's goals in his recent novel, why chronicle the imagined fears of his family between 1940–42 in the year 2005? First, there is the temptation to create parallels. Lindbergh was an isolationist who blamed the Jews for wanting to involve America in a war for their own sectarian interests. Lest readers reach any conclusions about parallels with the war in Iraq, Roth cautions them against taking "this book as a roman à clef to the present moment in America." Second, the re-emergence of global anti-Semitism. According to Thomas Friedman, some Iraqis took to calling American troops Jews, Israelis, and Americans interchangeably as manifestations of Satan. Roth has confirmed that he chose the Lindbergh character because he wanted "America's Jews to feel the pressure of a genuine anti-Semitic threat."[10] Finally, with Kristallnacht in New Jersey, Roth's parents are transformed from the comic, parodic figures of the bourgeois suffocating Jewish family, into figures of integrity, resilience, and dignity. As Ruth Wisse has observed: "Without the anti-Semitism, they were simply the Jewish bourgeoisie, avatars of the reviled middle class; magnify the background of fascism, and they step forth as moral heroes."[11]

If the mark of Jewishness in *The Plot Against America* is its emphasis on communal rather than individual identity achieved by importing Jewish collective trauma to Philip Roth's family, then the mark of Americanness in this novel is its happy end. With the disappearance of Lindbergh's aircraft and the re-election of Roosevelt in 1942, order is restored, and America returns to itself. But the very notion of an interlude in history that does not continue to influence subsequent events is the greatest illusion of all. "If there had been a Lindbergh presidency," writes J. M. Coetzee, "our lives would be different today, and probably worse."[12] In short, the finale of *The Plot Against America* affirms Roth's conviction that "it can't happen here" and raises the question as to whether it is, finally, an exercise in paranoia.

Philip Roth's autobiographical writings share an insistence on granting the artist his subject, which in his case translates into granting the legitimacy of the life of the Jewish-American male, defending it against charges of triviality or marginality when measured against the tumultuous Jewish history of this century. Ironically, this American life is often portrayed as shadow-boxing with its counterlife in Europe, as subverting a collective identity on which it is also dependent. In fact, the only collective identity to emerge in his memoirs is that of the artist who must paradoxically always assert his singularity. Roth depicts the facts, his patrimony, and historical plots as singular inventions, yet he can never sever himself from the communal, whether it takes the form of his critical Jewish readers, his demanding Jewish fathers, or the ghosts of his European Jewish brethren. Roth's autobiographies are exercises in asserting his freedom as an artist within the constraints of being a Jew, constraints that lead him, in *Patrimony*, to the universal constraints of the aging and dying body, and to the individual mind forever limited to its individual point of view. "Vas you dere, Chollie?" is another way of saying that fiction writers pretend they were, autobiographers insist they were, and Philip Roth refuses to take sides.

NOTES

1 Philip Roth, *Patrimony: A True Story* (New York: Simon and Schuster, 1991), p. 221.
2 Philip Roth, *Portnoy's Complaint* (New York: Bantam, 1970), p. 124.
3 Cynthia Ozick, *The Shawl* (New York: Vintage, 1990), p. 51.
4 *Conversations with Philip Roth*, ed. George J. Searles (Jackson: University Press of Mississippi, 1992), p. 128.

5 My discussion of *The Facts* is a somewhat revised version of the essay "Facing the Fictions: Henry Roth's and Philip Roth's Meta-Memoirs," *Prooftexts: A Journal of Jewish Literary History*, 18.3 (September 1998): 259–75.
6 Philip Roth, *The Facts: A Novelist's Autobiography* (New York: Penguin, 1988), p. 14.
7 Timothy L. Parrish, "Review of *The Plot Against America*," *Philip Roth Studies*, 1.1 (2005): 93–101.
8 Jeffery Brown, "The Plot Again," www.pbs.org?newshour/bb/entertainment/july-dec04/philiproth_ 10-27.html
9 Philip Roth, *The Plot Against America* (London: Jonathan Cape, 2004), p. 3.
10 Philip Roth, "The Story Behind *The Plot Against America*," *New York Times Book Review*, September 19, 2004: 10.
11 Ruth Wisse, "In Nazi Newark," *Commentary*, 118.5 (December 2004): 65–70.
12 J. M Coetzee, "What Philip Knew," *The New York Review of Books* 51.18 (November 18, 2004): 4–6.

GUIDE TO FURTHER READING

Primary works

Novels and longer fiction

American Pastoral. Boston: Houghton Mifflin, 1997.
The Anatomy Lesson. New York: Farrar, Straus and Giroux, 1983.
The Breast. New York: Holt, Rinehart and Winston, 1972. (Revised edition published in *A Philip Roth Reader*, 1980.)
The Counterlife. New York: Farrar, Straus and Giroux, 1986.
Deception: A Novel. New York: Simon and Schuster, 1990.
The Dying Animal. Boston: Houghton Mifflin, 2001.
Everyman. Boston: Houghton Mifflin, 2006.
Goodbye, Columbus and Five Short Stories. Boston: Houghton Mifflin, 1959.
The Ghost Writer. New York: Farrar, Straus and Giroux, 1979.
The Great American Novel. New York: Holt, Rinehart and Winston, 1973.
The Human Stain. Boston: Houghton Mifflin, 2000.
I Married a Communist. Boston: Houghton Mifflin, 1998.
Letting Go. New York: Random House, 1962.
My Life as a Man. New York: Holt, Rinehart and Winston, 1974.
Operation Shylock: A Confession. New York: Simon and Schuster, 1993.
Our Gang (Starring Tricky and His Friends). New York: Random House, 1971.
The Plot Against America. Boston: Houghton Mifflin, 2004.
Portnoy's Complaint. New York: Random House, 1969.
The Prague Orgy. New York: Vintage, 1996. (First published in *Zuckerman Bound*, 1985.)
The Professor of Desire. New York: Farrar, Straus and Giroux, 1977.
Sabbath's Theater. Boston: Houghton Mifflin, 1995.
When She Was Good. New York: Random House, 1967.
Zuckerman Unbound. New York: Farrar, Straus and Giroux, 1981.
Zuckerman Bound: A Trilogy and Epilogue. New York: Farrar, Straus and Giroux, 1985.

Memoirs and autobiographical essays

The Facts: A Novelist's Autobiography. New York: Farrar, Straus and Giroux, 1988.

Patrimony: A True Story. New York: Simon and Schuster, 1991.
A Philip Roth Reader. New York: Farrar, Straus and Giroux, 1980.

Essays and interviews with Philip Roth

Conversations with Philip Roth. Ed. George J. Searles. Jackson: University Press of Mississippi, 1992.
Reading Myself and Others. New York: Farrar, Straus and Giroux, 1975. Rev. ed. New York: Vintage, 2001. (Includes interviews with Roth as well as essays by him.)
Shop Talk: A Writer and His Colleagues and Their Work. Boston: Houghton Mifflin, 2001.

Secondary works

Collections of essays

Bloom, Harold, ed. *Philip Roth.* New York: Chelsea House, 1986. Rev. ed. 2003.
Philip Roth's Portnoy's Complaint. New York: Chelsea House, 2004.
Milbauer, Asher Z. and Donald G. Watson, eds. *Reading Philip Roth.* New York: St. Martin's Press, 1988.
Pinsker, Sanford, ed. *Critical Essays on Philip Roth.* Boston: G. K. Hall, 1982.

Books

Cooper, Alan. *Philip Roth and the Jews.* Albany: State University of New York Press, 1996.
Halio, Jay L. *Philip Roth Revisited.* New York: Twayne, 1992.
Lee, Herminone. *Philip Roth.* New York: Methuen, 1982.
McDaniel, John N. *The Fiction of Philip Roth.* Haddonfield, NJ: Haddonfield House, 1974.
Pinsker, Sanford. *The Comedy That "Hoits": An Essay on the Fiction of Philip Roth.* Columbia: University of Missouri Press, 1975.
Posnock, Ross. *Philip Roth's Rude Truth: The Art of Immaturity.* Princeton: Princeton University Press, 2006.
Rodgers, Bernard F., Jr. *Philip Roth.* Boston: Twayne, 1978.
Shechner, Mark. *Up Society's Ass, Copper: Rereading Philip Roth.* Madison: University of Wisconsin Press, 2003.
Shostak, Debra. *Philip Roth – Countertexts, Counterlives.* Columbia: University of South Carolina Press, 2004.

Chapters in books

Berger, Alan L. "Holocaust Responses iii: Symbolic Judaism." *Crisis and Covenant: The Holocaust in American Jewish Fiction.* Albany: State University of New York Press, 1985. 151–85.
Berman, Jeffrey. "Philip Roth's Psychoanalysts." *The Talking Cure: Literary Representations of Psychoanalysts.* New York: New York University Press, 1985. 239–69.

Cooper, Alan. "The Jewish Sit-Down Comedy of Philip Roth." *Jewish Wry: Essays on Jewish Humor.* Ed. Sarah Blacher Cohen. Bloomington: Indiana University Press, 1987. 158–77.

Ezrahi, Sidra DeKoven. "The Grapes of Roth: 'Diasporism' Between Portnoy and Shylock." *Literary Strategies: Jewish Texts and Contexts.* Ed. Ezra Mendelsohn. New York: Oxford University Press, 1996. 148–58.

Goodheart, Eugene. " 'Postmodern' Meditations on the Self: The Work of Philip Roth and Don DeLillo." *Desire and Its Discontents.* New York: Columbia University Press, 1991. 157–72.

Guttman, Allen. "Philip Roth and the Rabbis." *The Jewish Writer in America: Assimilation and the Crisis of Identity.* New York: Oxford University Press, 1973. 64–76.

Kazin, Alfred. "The Earthly City of Jews." *Bright Book of Life.* Boston: Little, Brown and Co., 1973. 144–49.

Krupnick, Mark. "Jewish Jacobites: Henry James's Presence in the Fiction of Philip Roth and Cynthia Ozick." *Tradition, Voices, and Dreams: The American Novel Since the 1960s.* Ed. Melvin J. Friedman and Ben Siegel. Newark: University of Delaware Press, 1995. 89–107.

Parrish, Tim. "Philip Roth: The Jew That Got Away." *Walking Blues: Making Americans from Emerson to Elvis.* Amherst: University of Massachusetts Press, 2001. 141–80.

Shechner, Mark. "Dear Mr. Einstein: Jewish Comedy and the Contradictions of Culture." *Jewish Wry: Essays on Jewish Humor.* Ed. Sarah Blacher Cohen. Bloomington: Indiana University Press, 1987. 141–57.

Wisse, Ruth R. "Requiem in Several Voices." *The Schlemiel as Modern Hero.* Chicago: University of Chicago Press, 1971. 118–23.

"Writing Beyond Alienation: Saul Bellow, Cynthia Ozick, and Philip Roth." *The Modern Jewish Canon: A Journey through Language and Culture.* New York: Free Press, 2000. 295–322.

Articles

Aarons, Victoria. "Is It 'Good-for-the-Jews or No-Good-for-the-Jews'?: Philip Roth's Registry of Jewish Consciousness." *Shofar,* 19.1 (2000): 7–18.

Alexander, Edward. "Philip Roth at Century's End." *New England Review,* 20.2 (1999): 183–90.

Blues, Thomas. "Is There Life after Baseball: Philip Roth's *The Great American Novel.*" *American Studies,* 22.1 (1981): 71–80.

Cohen, Sarah Blacher. "Philip Roth's Would-Be Patriarchs and Their *Shiksas* and Shrews." *Studies in American Jewish Literature,* 1.1 (1975): 16–22.

Furman, Andrew. "The Ineluctable Holocaust in the Fiction of Philip Roth." *Studies in American Jewish Literature,* 12 (1993): 109–212.

"A New 'Other' Emerges in American Jewish Literature: Philip Roth's Israel Fiction." *Contemporary Literature,* 36.4 (1995): 633–53.

Girgus, Sam B. "Between Goodbye, Columbus and Portnoy: Becoming a Man and Writer in Roth's Feminist 'Family Romance.' " *Studies in American Jewish Literature,* 8.2 (1989): 143–53.

Howe, Irving. "Philip Roth Reconsidered." *Commentary,* 54.6 (1972): 69–77.

Kauvar, Elaine M. "This Doubly Reflected Communication: Philip Roth's 'Auto-biographies.'" *Contemporary Literature*, 36.3 (1995): 412–46.
Lyons, Bonnie. "'Jews on the Brain' in 'Wrathful Philippics.'" *Studies in American Jewish Literature*, 8.2 (1989): 186–95.
Malin, Irving. "Looking at Roth's Kafka; or Some Hints about Comedy." *Studies in Short Fiction*, 14 (1977): 273–75.
O'Donnell, Patrick. "The Disappearing Text: Philip Roth's *The Ghost Writer*." *Contemporary Literature*, 24.3 (1983): 365–78.
Parrish, Timothy L. "Ralph Ellison: *The Invisible Man* in Philip Roth's *The Human Stain*." *Contemporary Literature*, 45.3 (2004): 421–59.
"*The Plot Against America*." *Philip Roth Studies*, 1.1 (2005): 93–101.
Pinsker, Sanford. "The Facts, the 'Unvarnished Truth,' and the Fictions of Philip Roth." *Studies in American Jewish Literature*, 11.1 (1992): 108–17.
Podhoretz, Norman. "The Adventures of Philip Roth." *Commentary*, 106.4 (1998): 25–36.
Rodgers, Bernard F., Jr. "*The Great American Novel* and 'The Great American Joke.'" *Critique*, 16.2 (1974): 12–29.
Royal, Derek Parker. "Postmodern Jewish Identity in Philip Roth's *The Counterlife*." *Modern Fiction Studies*, 48.2 (2002): 422–43.
Rubin-Dorsky, Jeffrey. "Honor Thy Father." *Raritan*, 11.4 (1992): 137–45.
"Philip Roth and American Jewish Identity: The Question of Authenticity." *American Literary History*, 13.1 (2001): 79–107.
Shechner, Mark. "Zuckerman's Travels." *American Literary History*, 1.1 (1989): 219–30.
Shostak, Debra. "Roth/Counter Roth: Postmodernism, the Masculine Subject, and *Sabbath's Theater*." *Arizona Quarterly*, 54.3 (1998): 119–42.
Siegel, Ben. "The Myths of Summer: Philip Roth's *The Great American Novel*." *Contemporary Literature*, 17 (1976): 171–90.
Solotaroff, Theodore "Philip Roth and the Jewish Moralists." *Chicago Review*, 13 (1959): 87–99.
Solotaroff, Theodore. "The Journey of Philip Roth." *Atlantic Monthly*, 223.4 (April 1969): 64–72.
Walden, Daniel. "Goodbye Columbus, Hello Portnoy and Beyond: The Ordeal of Philip Roth." *Studies in American Jewish Literature*, 3.2 (1977–78): 3–13.
"The Odyssey of a Writer: Rethinking Philip Roth." *Studies in American Jewish Literature*, 8.2 (1989): 133–36.
Wirth-Nesher, Hana. "The Artist Tales of Philip Roth." *Prooftexts*, 3.3 (1983): 263–72.
"Resisting Allegory; or, Reading 'Eli, the Fanatic' in Tel Aviv." *Prooftexts*, 21.1 (2001): 103–12.
Wisse, Ruth R. "Philip Roth Then and Now." *Commentary*, 72.3 (1981): 56–60.
For a comprehensive Roth bibliography, see http://orgs.tamu-commerce.edu/rothsoc/society

INDEX

CAMBRIDGE COMPANIONS TO LITERATURE

CAMBRIDGE COMPANIONS TO CULTURE

*The Cambridge Companion to Modern
German Culture*
edited by Eva Kolinsky and Wilfried van der
Will

*The Cambridge Companion to Modern
Russian Culture*
edited by Nicholas Rzhevsky

*The Cambridge Companion to Modern
Spanish Culture*
edited by David T. Gies

*The Cambridge Companion to Modern
Italian Culture*
edited by Zygmunt G. Baranski and Rebecca
J. West

*The Cambridge Companion to Modern
French Culture*
edited by Nicholas Hewitt

*The Cambridge Companion to Modern Latin
American Culture*
edited by John King

*The Cambridge Companion to Modern Irish
Culture*
edited by Joe Cleary and
Claire Connolly

*The Cambridge Companion to Modern
American Culture*
edited by Christopher Bigsby

6797